'It's one of our greatest fears—that [...] Robin, in his honest, meticulous w[...] plunge into our own murky depths [...] don't repeat them. A breakthrough book, full of surprises, honest, vulnerable and real.'

— **Steve Biddulph**, AM, author, *10 Things Girls Need Most, Raising Girls, Raising Boys, The Complete Secrets of Happy Children,* and *The New Manhood*

'As parents we either unconsciously parent exactly as we were parented or we consciously try to do the exact opposite. Either way our parenting is trapped by how we were parented, I can think of no more important and liberating work for parents to do than to take this Inner Child healing Journey with Robin Grille as their guide.'

— **Pam Leo**, author, *Connection Parenting*

'What an insightful book. We couldn't put it down!'

— **Dominique Ben** and **Mim Dart**, directors, MummyCon

'This book is gold! Robin's practical approach will leave you, and those you love, feeling like a fresh summer breeze has come through your life.'

— **Roger Harman**, CEO, Corporate Heart International

'As a former relationship counsellor, I have found inner child work to be one of the most profound approaches to clients' wellbeing I know. As a mother, I found Inner Child Journeys made sense of the confusion, shame and helplessness that could sometimes rob me of the joy and wonder of parenthood. As a daughter, it helped me to understand and forgive my own parents for the neediness of their own Inner Child. There are very few books I would assert are essential reading for parents. This is one of them.'

— **Elly Taylor**, Perinatal relationship expert, author and founder, *Becoming Us,* becomingusfamily.com

Inner child

Journeys

How Our children
Grow US UP

Published by Vox Cordis Press
PO Box 388, Avalon Beach, New South Wales, Australia 2107

Ordering information:
www.robingrille.com

ISBN 978-0-6486535-0-9

Library of Congress Control Number: 2019910634

Mind-Body Therapies
Self-healing
Inner Child
Parenting

A catalogue record for this book is available from the National Library of Australia

Illustrations © 2019 Jon Cooper
joncooperillustration.com

First Edition

Permissions

The author gratefully acknowledges the permissions granted to reproduce the copyright material in this book. While every effort has been made to contact the copyright holders and obtain permission for the use of copyright material, some owners of copyright could not be reached. The author apologises for omissions and would be grateful if notified of any corrections that should be incorporated in future reprints or editions of this book.

Inner child

Journeys

How our children

grow us up

Robin Grille

To the Universal Child:

May your path Home be gentle and clear.

'I believe that what we become depends on what our fathers [elders] teach us at odd moments, when they aren't trying to teach us.'
— Umberto Eco, *Foucault's Pendulum*

Toutes les grandes personnes ont d'abord été des enfants. (Mais peu d'entre elles s'en souviennent.) [All grown-ups were children first (but few remember it).]
— Antoine de Saint-Exupéry, *The Little Prince*

contents

APPENDICES

Tables

Foreword

Ray Castellino, DC, RCST*

Robin Grille came into my life in September 2016 in Findhorn, Scotland. He and I had the privilege of speaking at the same conference. This offered us the opportunity to get to know each other while hanging out in the cool evening Findhorn air. I knew immediately that, with Robin, I have a brother-in-kind. Robin is the real deal! He's as authentic as they come. He's passionate, personable, wonderfully skilled and exquisitely articulate.

Today, as I'm writing this, I'm also experiencing my 74th birthday. I'm in my third read of Robin's new book, *Inner Child Journeys*.

This book is more than another parenting book by another expert. This is Robin personally and eloquently guiding us through an introspective process in order to know ourselves better, heal old wounds and expand our ability to intuit and to give and receive love. Robin's wisdom is this: if we do indeed come to know the depths of ourselves, we are empowered to create deeper connections with others. As parents, grandparents, professional caregivers and teachers, we increase our capacity to support the flourishing of our children.

In the 1970s, for five years, I was a single dad raising my young son. I was fortunate to have excellent counseling and a group of like-minded parents to help me become the kind of father that could truly learn from his son. When I first began reading Robin's *Inner Child Journeys*, I thought about how much I could have used this book back then! Robin, where were you in the early 1970s? This is not to diminish the value of this book today; and how it has helped me as a grandfather in my relationships with my adult children, grandson and life partner.

You see, this is not a book to just read; it is an interactive process. It is a stimulant for deep reflection, loaded with illustrative stories and helpful exercises. More than reading, you find yourself stirred to the most visceral feelings, while at

---

* Ray is a chiropractic physician and craniosacral therapist. He founded Castellino Prenatal and Birth Training for health professionals and co-founded and co-directs, Building and Enhancing Bonding and Attachment (BEBA), CastellinoTraining.com.

the same time savoring the many insights, the bursting 'aha's.' Robin guides us through wisely designed exercises that support us to integrate the most challenging imprints from our distant past and to find a way forward, relieved and renewed.

As you enter these pages you will find yourself led by an expert and articulate thinker, philosopher, professional therapist, writer, husband, father—a deeply feeling human being. Robin does not leave himself out of the writing. He includes himself in intimate, contemplative and uplifting ways. Many of the examples that he offers are from his own life and his own struggles. His candid self-disclosure creates an alchemy that helps alleviate my own harsh inner critic. My sense of aloneness and isolation dissipates as I move into the realization that our most core experiences are actually shared.

Through Robin's transparency, I feel him there with me as I journey through the exercises. I'm not alone on the journey. Furthermore, Robin shows us how to share our inner journeys with our loved ones and friends, and with like-minded folks who can gather in supportive groups.

A consistent theme throughout Robin's work is, that by coming to appreciate how we came into this life and grew up, we grow in our compassion for ourselves and each other, especially our loved ones and our children. There is no question that my children are, and have been, among my greatest teachers. Children are programmed to bring us great joy; but at the same time they are capable of provoking the darker depths of our being. By design, our children will often touch us in those regions of our consciousness that we least want to look at.

My kids have done their jobs well; our interactions have often forced me to have to look into myself. So many times, especially when I was a single dad with my firstborn, I would be triggered into anger. I had clung to the idealistic belief that I would never ever find myself treating my own children as I had been treated as a child. I never wanted to rage, especially not at them. Yet, there I was, as a parent, wrestling with the forces of raw, early childhood rage that had remained inside me from before I could talk. What to do with all this anger?

I remember such a day when my son was barely four years old. I felt totally unable to reach him, to connect with him. Although I was knee-deep in helplessness and frustration, I remember looking at him and feeling that somehow, in some miraculous way, we were going to get through this. Somehow I had a flash that my son was doing an amazing job of communicating how he was feeling. He and I were raging at the same time, together. I realized that we both knew how the other was feeling. What my son had brought back to me, in an instant, was the distinct memory of what it felt like to be a little boy, out of control with unspeakable anger. It was at that moment that I learned that my young son and I could be on the same side of the fence—with each other rather than in destructive opposition to each other. Instead of trying to get him to 'behave' and connect with me, I saw then what he was communicating through his behavior and the raw energy of his emotion. I got it!

As soon as this 'ah-ha' hit me, I was calm. It was as if I had been given a new set of eyes, a new way to listen, and a new way to feel and be with my son. This was a parenting game-changer for me; to understand my child from the inside, through the senses of my own Inner Child. This new perspective transformed me as a parent. The guidance Robin gives us lines us up for many such inspired realizations, and the deeper connections with our children that these new perceptions bring.

Robin lucidly shares neuro-scientific research that sheds light on why the emotions and sensations of childhood, from the dawn of life onward, can so readily be triggered to resurface. In the most accessible terms, he introduces us to the neurobiological underpinnings of human empathy, explaining how we affect each other so profoundly; why we humans seem so irrevocably intertwined. We are wired to have our own internal template for what others are experiencing and feeling. The feelings of helplessness and rage that my son had triggered in me, for instance, were a window into myself—showing me when and how I had once felt exactly as he was feeling—we were deeply connected to one another.

With *Inner Child Journeys,* Robin has helped me better understand myself and my children at the same time, assisting me to become more conscious, mindful and present with myself and with my loved ones. This introspective method provides a vessel in which we can differentiate feelings that arise from our past from feelings that make sense in the present context, to recognize when we have been triggered and to distinguish our projections from our children's real needs. These gains in self-awareness enable us to choose more wisely how to respond to our children.

I found Robin's anecdotes particularly inspiring. The stories feel close to home; the challenges they depict involving family or classroom dynamics have a poignantly familiar ring. We are brought home to the most universal agonies and triumphs of human growth and transformation. These real-life tales do what a didactic explanation cannot: they make the rich and complex psychological concepts come alive, in crispy clarity and full color. Swinging back and forth between anecdotes and exercises, Robin creates a rhythm between them; the anecdotes give me inspiration while the exercises give me the opportunity to pause, look inward and feel. I experienced this rhythm in the narrative like a pendulum; moving me through my own inner world in a slow and gradual integrative cadence. Robin's pace is gentle, always prioritizing our emotional safety so we don't have to take in our own childhood story in big unmanageable chunks. We are reminded to pause, take our time and to modulate our passage through the Journey.

So far, I've been mostly speaking as a parent and grandparent, but I have also found Robin's *Inner Child Journeys* equally useful as a professional who works with families, adults and trains other professionals. Whether we are physicians, nurses, psychologists, body-oriented somatic therapists or teachers, so much of our training emphasizes the primacy of an empathic rapport with our clients: the people we are treating, counseling or instructing. Robin advocates for the need to cultivate self-knowledge, before we can properly understand others. Only when we can tap into our own historical joys and sufferings can we achieve our fullest potential for compassion, intuition and the ability to support and guide others.

I remember being a music teacher in the late 1960s and early '70s, in an upper-middle-class white, suburban seventh and eighth grade junior high school, with students in the range of 12 and 13 years. I was young and very idealistic. I had the hope of contributing to the transformation of what was then a very demanding, teacher-centred junior high school, into a truly student-centred educational system. Beside me, there were a few other colleagues—the art teacher and the Spanish teacher—who valued student-centred learning. This was in a school that still in 1970 administered occasional corporal punishment. The wood-crafted paddle on the wall in the principal's office hung as a reminder for students to 'behave' and 'obey' rather than seek authentic connection.

I would have so loved to have a copy of *Inner Child Journeys* in those days. My like-minded colleagues and I knew and appreciated each other, but we needed more guidance on how we might be able to truly support one another. I am deeply moved by Robin's description of an Australian high school where the faculty are committed to understanding their own Inner Child processes, and where the teachers are encouraged to explore their own psychological roots of the challenges and impasses they face daily with their students. I am so heartened by the synergy and mutual support and cooperation that story presents between the teachers, as well as between the teachers and students. Even more heartening is the fact that this type of guidance is more available today for teachers around the world.

Robin's *Inner Child Journeys* is full of wonderful, enlightening wisdom that I remain excited to share with my family, loved ones, my clients, colleagues and students.

I firmly believe that the more of us who take Robin's invitation into our own Inner Child Journeys, the better parents, grandparents and professionals we collectively become.

I want to see this book in the hands of all the people I am fortunate to work with: clients, families and students of all ages and walks of life. *Inner Child Journeys* is a must-read for all of us, parents, grandparents, teachers and health professionals.

Thank you Robin for giving us such strong, well constructed and passionate guidance to journey into the emotionally rich, wisdom-filled realms of our Inner Child.

Respectfully,
Ray Castellino
Ojai, California
July 11, 2019

PART A: Introducing the Journey

Preparing for a Journey

A Special Welcome—to You

Greetings!

If you have come as far as this page, it's probably because you're interested—just enough—in finding out more about your own Inner Child and the Inner Child that lives within the people you care about. To begin with, you probably want to find out what an Inner Child is, why the Inner Child matters—and how this part of who we are affects our lives, our work and our relationships. You most likely want to know how this realm of our consciousness affects the way we parent and educate our children. Most of all, you probably want to learn how, by becoming more aware of this phenomenon, you can use it to enhance your life, to bring healing to yourself and your relationships, and to become a better parent and teacher for the children in your care.

If that sounds like you, I welcome you to this book. I've been looking forward to sharing the ideas in these pages with you. This book has been taking shape in my mind over many years, informed by my work as a psychologist, my own personal Inner Child Journeys, my experiences of fatherhood and the influence of many teachers and writers whom I admire. It is a manual that guides you through inward journeys for personal healing and growth, closer relationships and powerful new insights as a parent or teacher. You can also use this manual to help other adults, if they are willing, to get to know their own Inner Child better. Inner Child Journeying is the best way I know to better understand our children and become more effective and loving guides for them. I particularly love how Inner Child Journeying generates more vibrant and intimate relationships with the people who mean the most to us. As a shared ritual, Inner Child Journeying is a wonderful method for deepening relationships in groups. And lastly, I am excited about sharing how Inner Child Journeying can enhance our creativity and bring us a greater capacity for joy and pleasure.

Do you ever find yourself re-experiencing feelings you have not felt since you were a youth, a child, even a baby? Do you find yourself craving the same things that you longed for as a child? These are just some of the ways your Inner Child speaks to you. Would you like to understand more about how these visitations influence your life-choices? Your relationships? Your parenting style and what you pass on to your children? What if the more you get to know your Inner Child, the more fully you live your life? What gifts might your Inner Child have in store for you, and might some of these gifts be as yet unknown to you? This book invites you to get closer to the Child who lives within you. The Inner Child has more to offer us than most people can imagine. But it takes no small amount of courage to connect with the tender, vulnerable heart of this Child. Most of us feel a little awkward, to say the least, when we touch upon this secluded part of ourselves. So it's only fair that I begin by sharing my own story, my beginnings. And the Child that I still am, from time to time.

The more I contemplate my early years, the more clearly I see how the yen for my vocation, and ultimately the seeds of this book, were sewn in pivotal passages of my childhood. My story contains clues as to why I've needed to write this book, why Inner Child Journeying matters to me, and why I have invited you to join me and share this most human and universal rite.

But before I say more about myself and how I came to write this book, take a moment to think about how you'd best like to read it. From start to finish? Back to front? Taking chapters randomly, as they capture your interest? Skipping straight to the instructions for the Inner Child Journey in Part B and then returning to read this Part at the end? Whatever your preferred approach, that's absolutely fine. Your Inner Child will appreciate having a say, and will help you derive more enjoyment from your reading. Above all, I hope you relish your travels through this book at least as much as the benefits you'll get from using it as a resource.

CHAPTER 1

Beginnings

To begin with, I would like to share some stories that make me *me*—and about how I came to write this book.

Montevideo, Uruguay, City of My Birth

When they came, the streets would go silent. Even the birds would stop singing.

I must have been no more than 3 or 4 years old, clutching my mother's leg so tightly, peering out from behind her. At first you couldn't tell their direction; all you'd hear was the growing thunder of *Candombe*.

But you could *feel* they were coming your way, inexorably, getting louder. Without warning, a vague and distant thudding would begin, growing more insistent as they approached. The *baracatú-baracatú-baracatú-chas-chas!* built to deafening; bouncing off the terrace walls on both sides of the street.

Possessed, I became frozen—overcome by a noise too big and powerful for my small body to contain. Entranced by the ancient *llamada*, call of ancestral West Africa re-worked for the Montevidean barrios. *Candombe* shakes you to the marrow. Afraid as I was, I could not avert my gaze when the drummers marched past.

My bones rang to the beat; the *doom-doom* of calloused hand on leather hide cast an irresistible spell. I was bewitched.

After school I would come home and bang out my best rhythmic approximations on our melamine kitchen table. Which of course would drive my mother crazy.

And I have not been able to stop. The memory of this sound and rhythm, primal anthem of my childhood, lives in every fibre of my body—still rises within me, demanding re-expression.

What power; the early imprints of our lives. Our bodies remember; we relive ancient feelings, archived in flesh. I'm still irresistibly drawn to the sound of hand-drums, like the child to the piper. In my 20s I finally answered this call. I learned to play the congas; an Afro-Cuban style that I adapted to jazz.

In my new Anglo world, this was the closest I could find to the sounds I had missed since I was ten. Though today I cannot properly reproduce *Candombe*, the urge to beat a drum and recreate my childhood trances has never left me. When I thump out a rhythm with my bare hands, that immense awe I first felt on cobbled streets returns to me—though my images from boyhood are now fleeting and elusive. Few things have helped to silence my furtive mind better than a hit on the congas. My Inner Child carried this gift across the Pacific Ocean. What a mystery, this Inner Child. How deeply and abidingly the Child remains within us, shaping our destinies.

I was just shy of 10 years old when my family left Uruguay, as if running from a burning building. Uruguay had been swept up, along with its much larger neighbours, as a proxy battleground for the Cold War of the 1960s and '70s. It was the bull-pit where the world's two Big Empires traded blows. Our little football nation was now itself a football; kicked between hostile giants. For me it was like being woken from a happy dream by a loud, crashing noise.

Almost overnight, fear descended everywhere like a clammy blanket of fog. Young activists, some still in high school, began to be targeted. Streets rang with shouts, the thud of exploding tear-gas canisters and the occasional gunshot. Families and neighbourhoods were rent apart along partisan lines. My own family succumbed to this contagion. Opinions were spat out hotly—hand-grenades at the dinner table. Battlelines were drawn across the generations. Screams and slamming doors inside, jamming with the sounds of rage that tore through the street.

My father's tirades grew more intense, more urgent and more violent by the day, sending shock waves through our home. His shouting pounded my eardrums; a discordant, arrhythmic contrast to the wild harmony of *Candombe*. I became terrified of my dad and could not have hoped to comprehend what was driving his madness— that is, not until much later in my life. All I knew is that everything that had made sense and felt safe to me until that point, had gone up in smoke. Security shattered, paradise lost.

The world seemed to fracture when my family began to abandon our home in a series of staggered migrations. My sister, cousins, uncle, aunt and grandparents all stayed behind, making the Pacific crossing later, in dribs and drabs. It took several years for all of us to be together again, in the comparative blandness and innocence of 1970s Australia.

Today, when I open a newspaper, I read the world news first, still seeing the world through a migrant's eyes. Childhood taught me to never take my eyes off what comes from afar. I'm convinced that what happens a long way away will reach us soon enough, no matter where we are. There is no 'somewhere else', there is no 'over there'.

For my Romanian-Jewish parents, this exodus was not their first. They had been pitched from the firepan of World War and persecution, into the fires of Nicolae Ceaușescu's suffocating communism. In 1948, with my father in the throes of a life-threatening illness, they made their first getaway, clinging to each other and the few clothes they'd managed to salvage. My father would rather die where he could speak freely, than live on in fear and humiliation.

My father was a democracy-chaser; always ready to leave at a moment's notice if tyranny reared its head. What I heard many times over as a child is that the same was true for so many of my ancestors. The migrant's frame of reference is not easily erased. *Always be ready to pack your bags. Keep two passports—at least. And don't idealise the world around you; things can turn for the worse, unexpectedly.* Like an ominous footnote in my Inner Child's diary, this vigilant sense of non-belonging has never left me.

Despite never feeling truly secure anywhere, however, my perpetual disquiet is not for naught. On balance, it has also given me the gift of non-complacency, and a visceral rejection of petty tribalism. I will not identify with any culture, dogma or creed. Humanity is far more important to me than any team colours or temporaneous belief system.

This early preoccupation with geopolitics and global citizenship was eventually to become a major driving force behind my first book, *Parenting for a Peaceful World*. Though I instinctively distrust formalised religion, I religiously trust the principles of democracy. Only recently has it dawned on me how much these twin sentiments—obsessions that drive so much of my writing—reflect my father's influence. Despite his red-hot temper and my boyish fear, I must have heard his message. But the legacy of my familial and ancestral dislocation; a pervasive loneliness and existential anxiety, has not been easy to bear.

What a strange place Australia seemed at first. How peculiar its people. What whacky fauna—and most of all, what bizarre sports! And how very odd was the landscape that greeted me as a blinking new arrival. But not until half a century later did I finally begin to grieve the loss of the place we'd once called *home*. The sorrow of leaving our land forever would have been too unbearable to feel all at once, at 10 years of age. But the heartstrings remain attached and intact. Today, the sound of *Rioplatense* Spanish still rocks my soul. It turns my head when by chance I hear it in a crowd, on the street. The speakers immediately feel like family to me. They bring back the presence of elders that made my universe feel safe and cosy as a child, before everything fell to pieces.

As we settled into our new Australian life, my brother Alan, five years my senior, became my mentor; he helped shape many of my interests. He introduced me to a fabulous world of esotericism, meditation and all things transcendent. Instead of reading Superman comics, I delved into an intoxicating mix of Lobsang Rampa and Edgar Cayce. He taught me how to play bar-chords on the guitar, and oversaw my musical initiation with Crosby, Stills, Nash & Young, Orville Stoeber, Wishbone Ash and The Moody Blues. My mind was blown open, my imagination stretched out wide. I loved my conversations with Alan, and when we played guitar and sang together I thought we were the two coolest guys in the world. Considered a gifted young man; a formidable artist with a 'genius' IQ, Alan was also a deeply troubled soul.

I can't remember if he was 15 or 16 when I came home one day to find him gone; held in a psychiatric hospital, accused of adolescent schizophrenia. The world can seem so confusing and overpowering to a child. I had no words for my bewilderment. No one would tell me what would happen to my brother. When the world tells you something is deeply wrong with your hero, you are stunned— propelled into a mental wilderness without a map. In those days, adults did not bother to explain things to children; we just tagged along behind, bobbing with the current.

I somehow decided that, given half a chance, I would be able to help Alan, that I would know how to ease my brother's tormented mind. In the mind of a child in distress, barely a gossamer membrane separates fancy from realism. With the luxury of hindsight, I'm sure my inflated sense of potency was by far preferable to the helplessness and loss that lay beneath. This grandiose fantasy is the earliest I can recall wanting to brandish the staff of psychology. My first super-power, I guess. I wanted more than anything to save my brother, when no one else seemed to know how—but my chance to try would never come.

Some time after his release from hospital, when coming home with friends late one night, the car my brother was travelling in was hit head-on by a drunk driver. It was all over. A demolition ball crashed through our lives, and for me, childhood came to a sudden halt. My family disintegrated; we were scattered to the winds. In a flash, my parents became hollow shells.

Dad and I had been travelling and had just landed in Athens when our names were called. We were rushed off the plane and told to call home urgently. And then the axe fell. Dad frantically scrambled to get us on the first flight home. Back at the arrivals hall of Sydney airport, the unearthly sound of my mother's howl let me know that my brother had not made it out of his coma. He was gone. This time for good.

Walking numbly towards the mob that surrounded my mum, I was headed off by Fred, a friend of my parents. Taking hold of my arm, he repeated this mantra several times: *Above all, you must now be strong for your mother.* And since adults know everything, I obeyed, instantly and absolutely. It took all my strength to swallow hard against the animal wail threatening to burst from my throat.

Some part of my innocence, my freedom to emote, was left behind on the cold floor at Kingsford Smith Arrivals. A cleft was opened between the 'me' that I am, and the 'me' that others expected. I dimmed my light, so as not to trouble anyone. You can get used to a burden until you no longer feel its heft. My throat still fights the impulse to cry. Was it for my mother that I learned to disappear? Or for Fred? One thing for sure; it was for shame.

But everything Alan taught me—our rich dialogues on the nature of the cosmos and the meaning of life, our shared enthrallment with all things esoteric, the love of philosophy, guitar and song—all these things have remained central to me, woven tight into the tapestry of my being. For better—and sometimes for worse—the thirst for understanding why we all do what we do continues to engross me to this day. An 11-year-old boy sits at the wheel, driving my eternal fascination with psychology and all social sciences. Maybe, in part, I am still trying to save my brother. To rescue my mother. To calm my father. To find a crumb of predictability. A scrap of order in a volatile universe.

Alan's abrupt departure also marked me with a taste of life's precariousness—a sense that our plans are puny before the mighty river of Time. That the Big Things do not happen when we are ready for them. That fate—if there is such a thing—does not wait for our approval. That all can turn on a dime, in the middle of a sentence. I became hyper-vigilant, scanning horizons for all eventualities, anticipating futures, preparing for all weathers. Pervasive childhood anxieties can become, ironically, a fuel for the planner, the organiser and the researcher. Not bad, if you want to be a non-fiction writer. But the pleasure of surrender, the exhilaration of letting go, the choice to trust—these do not come easy to me. I must yet embark on more Inner Child Journeys. This boy has more to tell me.

He will need me to hold his hand, to sit with him and listen attentively to him again.

At times I can be worry-prone, controlling and intrusive as a father. Sometimes I hear my own voice, and it sounds like one of my father's rants. I saw adolescence slide into tragedy, saw my father come apart. Decades later, when it was my turn at the reins, my hands shook. An old forgotten pain resurfaced, demanding healing, when my daughter reached Alan's final age.

In the months and years that followed Alan's death, a lugubrious shroud enveloped our home. My parents had no idea how to support each other. Back then, bereavement counselling was little more than a stigma—psychological needs a shameful disease. Their relationship sank into betrayal; it became poisoned, soured beyond repair. We muddled on, hollow people, each in our own separate worlds.

But in the midst of this bleakness came an unexpected turn that would colour our futures quite interestingly. Our close neighbour, Betty, had also recently lost her son in a tragic accident. Not surprisingly, Betty and my mother turned to each other for solace. Their shared agony was beyond the ken of most people, and it forged a special bond between them.

Anguish made seekers of Betty and Mum, both desperate for a sign that Life might offer us more than this frangible existence. Betty was to find her inspiration in Findhorn, on the harsh, windswept shores of Scotland's north. The Findhorn Foundation was one of the world's first intentional communities founded on principles of ecological sustainability and non-aligned spirituality. Findhorn had achieved a legendary status around the world, for producing unexplained horticultural miracles on its inhospitable, sandy soil. Seekers of all stripes and provenance were magnetically drawn there for a spiritual sustenance that drew from a range of traditions.

Betty would bring home mystical books by the armful, and tales of wonder from her pilgrimages. I would seize and devour any of Betty's books that my mother might leave lying around. For a while these books dispelled my loneliness, dazzled me with worlds beyond my imagining, thrilled me with soaring ideas and possibilities, and comforted me in times of discord.

By night, I would light candles and incense and let myself be transported to Findhorn, this personal Shangri-La where I would learn of auras and devas, sit in meditation among the pines, and join in pagan circle dances. These rich voyages of the imagination filled me with awe and a yen for internal adventure. Reading, learning and flights of the mind held me together in a time when the world abandoned families in distress. I loved the allure of Findhorn's magic and intrigue, with its images of oversized vegetables, roses in the snow, visitations from Pan and his satyr-like Nature Spirits. In a period of unfathomable gloom and inexpressible loss, these fabulous tales renewed my sense of wonder.

Though I am far more earth-bound and pragmatic today, the *sensation* of magic—not necessarily its substance—has never left me. I relive this thrill each time I discover a way through the perceptual traps I live with. The discovery of new possibilities always brings a tingling aliveness.

I have never lost the suspicion that what my eyes show me is not the complete picture, that when I think I have understood, I haven't. Not yet. And therein lies our freedom. Can pain be a doorway? Can fear and shame bear a message? What can be more enthralling than the study of consciousness? No doubt we are bound and limited by universal laws. But who says we've understood these laws yet?

Forty years later and out of the blue, I was to receive an invitation to speak at a conference in Findhorn. I could not believe it was real. If you had told the 14-year-old me that I would one day be part of an event—'Healthy Birth, Healthy Earth'—at Findhorn's Universal Hall, I would have jumped through the roof.

Of course, my visit in the flesh helped bring me back down to earth about this special community. But it still felt like I was walking on hallowed ground. It was a trip to the enchanted playground that gave me sanctuary in my early teens. There I was able to express my gratitude to the community that, decades earlier, helped remind me what children know best: life on this earth is redolent with magic.

I first dipped my toe in the waters of psychotherapy at 20, when quite unexpectedly I was overcome by stage-panic. My high school friend Tony and I had landed a gig at our local folk-music den—The Brewer's Elbow—a dingy upstairs wine-bar in Gordon (a suburb of Sydney). We'd given the owner our demo-tape; five or so tracks we'd pounded out in our lounge room, recorded on a Panasonic cassette player with a pinhole microphone. We were certain he'd book us for an innocuous night like Tuesday, if at all. As beginners, we hoped to cut our teeth on meagre audiences—ten or so indifferent casuals with their backs turned to us. No such luck.

To my dismay, we were asked to start on Fridays, their busiest night. We'd been thrown in the deep end and I was racked with the most morbid performance-shudders. Over and over I saw myself forgetting the words halfway through a song and getting booed off stage. So I found an ad for a psychotherapist in a crumpled issue of Betty's *Southern Cross Magazine*, of course—and I booked myself in. I had nothing to lose and I was desperate enough. I wondered what kind of wizardry a therapist might invoke to dispel the spirits that haunted me.

My first session struck me as bizarre, but also fascinating. And though I could not understand why, it also proved quite helpful. Nineteen-seventies Sydney was a crucible for every kind of social and psychological experiment, abuzz with the human potential movement and the mixing waters of East and West.

I would put David, my first therapist, and his approach, somewhere on the outer fringes of experimental modalities. We sat cross-legged facing each other, mostly in silence, inside a soundproofed, padded, womb-like chamber he had built into his living room. Frankly, everything about this felt weird, if not downright scary at first.

David said very little from behind his dark and bushy guru-like beard. But as I sat with him, eyes closed, ensconced in this uterine environment, I began to descend into an unfamiliar, deep and peaceful state. I 'heard' a kind, reassuring voice springing from somewhere inside me, counselling me to simply befriend things as they were, to accept my emotions as they came, without trying to fix or cure them.

This was nothing like what I had anticipated. I stopped wrestling with myself, I let myself just *be*. Even though I did not understand the nature of this powerful and spontaneous experience, it had profound and far-reaching effects. In subsequent conversations with David, I got my first hint that my psychological wounds were far more complex than a little stage fright over a gig, and that the fear and shame I carried had deeper roots than I realised. But for the time being, I chose to put therapy to one side so I could focus on the goal that had brought me there.

Before long, Tony and I were playing our first of many gigs at The Brewer's Elbow, singing every kind of popular folk song from the '60s and '70s, tolerated by a cider-addled mob of locals. Remembering the words to a song is not everything. Singing like your soul means it-*that* is everything! I guess my throat began to open up again, on stage at The Brewer's. I had begun to feel visible again.

My first brush with psychotherapy, exotic as it seemed at the time, piqued my interest and rekindled my commitment to the study of psychology. Disillusioned with the jaundiced, desiccated approach to psychology that university proffered, I embarked on an immersive adventure that wound through a plethora of body-oriented psychotherapies, meditation, yoga and years of encounter-group therapy. A heady mix of consciousness-expanding experiences and intense personal growth, in which I was first exposed to Inner Child work. The most exciting frontiers of psychology seemed to be outside academia, where a hands-on spirit of discovery prevailed.

A bold experimentalism was sweeping 1980s Australia that said, 'live it first, let science explain it later!' A widespread hunger for release from traditional restraints pervaded, along with a feverish search for a more emotionally liberated and authentic way of being. New therapies and healing modalities were sprouting everywhere, with workshops abounding for every pop psychology under the sun.

I was exhilarated, youthfully caught up in this radical movement for social change. Despite the occasional wrong turns, dead ends, tussles with self-appointed gurus and unsavoury experiences, this enriching and expansive time taught me so much.

I tended the wounds of childhood, learned to grieve, to reach past my isolation, to voice my feelings and to connect with others more meaningfully. I still feel nostalgic for those days. Some of my closest friendships, including that with my wife Linda, were formed during those highly-charged adventures in consciousness. I'm grateful for all I learned then, mindful of how formative those times were for me vocationally. Talking about Inner Child issues feels as natural to me now as talking about sleep, hunger, play, laughter, hopes and dreams.

Although my love of psychology burned incandescently, for the time being it was only a personal quest. The drily cerebral psychology shown to me at university seemed so tuneless, so devoid of human vulnerability. I knew in my gut that intimacy did not live in the predictable and the formulaic.

Human folly and despair were not diseases to cure, puzzles to solve or cracks to mend. I was then, as I remain to this day, offended by a dominant paradigm that diagnoses us, downplays the impact of our prenatal and childhood environments, and sees a sick individual rather than sick relationships. The orthodox psychology of the era had thoroughly—and permanently, I thought—turned me off the idea of sitting in a therapist's chair.

Nevertheless, I love much of what my two universities gave me. They did their best to show me how to be rigorous and disciplined in my searches, how to write cogently and build an argument. I thank my teachers for helping me understand the nobility of the scientific method, and for giving me a healthy irreverence and unremitting scepticism for everything; including for my own ideas. I still adore books; I think of them as holy. I still love to stroll among the majestic sandstone archways, the gargoyles, the ivy and jacaranda of the Sydney University Quadrangle. Perhaps the sharing of knowledge is the lifeblood of the human spirit, I find it thrilling.

Eventually, thanks to the experiences I was so fortunate to have outside of academia, I did what I'd sworn to never do. With reappraised priorities and a new vision, I launched my own private psychotherapy practice. Of all the guiding lights that direct my work today, one stands out in particular. I love that alchemical moment when two people can drop their guard, surrender their composure for a moment, and speak their heart's truth. Often these moments carry some hint of our Inner Child, real and unprepared. These moments are not about fixing anything, not about helping or advising; they occur in a resolution-free zone. Mutual, intentional vulnerability is a meeting of two souls, a moment of contact that cannot but transform us. We become filled with *self*, moved by the *other*, and this changes us in ways we cannot anticipate. We return then to our friends, colleagues and families tangibly renewed, altered somehow; better listeners perhaps, more compassionate, less afraid, more expressive.

People in our lives, our children especially, benefit from what happens to us when we hold meetings of the heart. And the world around us is nourished by us when we embark on our Inner Child Journeys. Voyages into deeper self-awareness bring us a greater intimacy and an expanding heart. I'm not sure that facilitating these deeper connections with ourselves and with each other can rightly be called 'work'. To me, it feels more like an adventure—sometimes perilous, at times dark, other-times difficult and almost always uplifting.

My decision to chronicle all I've learned about Inner Child Journeys evolved slowly, and this book was cooked over a low flame. Writing came in fits and starts, with many long pauses in between. Was it six or seven years, or longer still? This book snuck up on me unannounced, and it changed shape and direction many times.

I had wanted this book to come through at a fair clip but Life, as She often does, had other plans. First, the sudden, un-forecast death of my mother. It was not meant to happen, not then; so we kept telling ourselves. But on reflection, it was just as she had wanted it. Death stole her by surprise, at full vitality. Losing the woman in whose belly I was formed shook me to the core. A world without her in it–incomprehensible.

With barely enough time to come to terms with the hole left by our matriarch's abrupt exit, just 10 months later Dad called it a day. He was spared too long a time without his life-companion, his dance duo, his sparring partner. For me, the blow of losing both their voices jolted everything into slow motion. Life itself became an unmapped frontier, an empty and unwritten page. This book would have to wait while my heart rested in this strange new reality; a parentless life. Our family was again undone. This time, I felt oddly liberated, even exhilarated; yet cold and lost, all at the same time.

Before I'd regained my senses, our daughter had blossomed into adolescence. This was—as it has been since the beginning of time—an intensely challenging, tumultuous and absorbing time for us all. Who can attend to writing a book amidst the maelstrom of teenage-hood in the house? Stolen moments at my laptop were few and far between. Even then my thoughts were unsteady, my mind preoccupied with the worry, frustration and bewilderment of fatherhood.

Quite painfully, this period brought me face-to-face with the wounds and loose ends of my own adolescence. It was a time to take more inward Journeys, to have the conversations with my Inner Teen that I had put off for too long. How could I be a clear-sighted father while so much remained unfulfilled and unheard from that time of my own life? And then, when we least expected it, our daughter's moment of independence arrived. In one leap from the nest she took flight, soaring, splendid, eyes on the horizon: a formidable force of Nature. Her room, still festooned with girlhood, was suddenly silent.

I got the message. The universe does not wait until we say we're ready to let go. In an instant Life redefines us, while we look elsewhere, attending to the mundane.

Goodbye is not said only to the one who leaves. We also say goodbye to a part of ourselves. Now that I am no longer a son, nor any longer *Daddy*, then; who am I? Who is behind me? Who is before me? I want to give, but—to whom?

Writing not only slowed to a trickle, sometimes I had to stop altogether. I did not have the time for it, nor the peace of mind. Maybe I just didn't have the heart. And yet, I suppose that loss, when it is timely and natural, makes a new space. At first, the space bears the outline of the one who has taken their leave.

Then gradually, it is just a space. A new freedom. It takes a while to decode it, to figure out how to traverse this unchartered territory. Change makes us vulnerable. Alone-ness affords us room to listen to our inner voices. It also gives us more to say.

Soon enough I was filled with renewed energy; one final push and I could complete this book that had been so long in the planning and the crafting.

Teachers and Inspirations

The inside of my head is, I hate to admit, much like an unmade bed. Or rather, like a class full of clamouring toddlers when the teacher has left the room. To gain the tranquillity I need to hear my deepest thoughts, I often chose to write in wild places. Sometimes in my car, parked on one of Sydney's dramatic sandstone cliff-tops, overlooking the Pacific Ocean. Sometimes on a picnic chair, deep in the Australian bush. Always in silence, away from the ceaseless drone of my city.

This Australian landscape that had once seemed so alien to me eventually won me over; like unexpected love in an arranged marriage. In time I fell in love with this strange, adopted Great Southern Land. This most ancient of all lands finally makes sense to me.

High up, a family of sulphur-crested cockatoos makes its home in the hollow supplied by a disarmed Angophora. I watch them strive to give their young their all: a home, an education; daily lessons on how to commune with the world. These highly expressive birds have a life span comparable to ours. I wonder if they too rejoice when their little ones finally take to the sky. I wonder also, how cockatoos weep when they say goodbye. And I am sure they too gain in wisdom through what their fledglings teach them. Families are everywhere, families within families, ecologies within ecologies.

I am deeply indebted to the buffoonery of Australian bird-life. Their avian antics and raucous cacophony remind me to keep things light, not to take myself too seriously while tapping at the keys. I also owe much to the majesty of the Pacific Ocean, the reverberant *boom* of its curling swells. Its colossal, changing moods help remind me of the eternal—the things that matter. The embrace of eucalypts, the soughing of wind in casuarinas—wise trees help settle my skittish mind so my most hushed inner voices can be heard and ideas can rise.

Frustrating as my writing journey was at times, I am glad now that it took so long. This allowed me more time to take the much-needed Inner Child Journey in all its forms—simple and complex, with my clients, with groups and with myself. I've been lucky enough to offer this Inner Journey to a culturally diverse 'audience', around Australia and overseas. Everyone that I've shared this Process with has had something to teach me—with every traveller placing a new tile on the final mosaic. People's feedback has helped me to hone the Process and understand it better. The final version presented in these pages reflects the inputs from individuals that have taken this Journey with me. I am grateful for the value that each of their Journeys has added, just as I hope that these Journeys have been of value to your life.

Since the publication of *Parenting for a Peaceful World* and *Heart-to-Heart Parenting*, my work mostly entailed the topic of parenting. It became increasingly clear to me that the greatest impediment to our effectiveness as parents is not to do with a lack of knowledge. Even the most knowledgeable, up-to-date parents get stuck in old response-patterns.

The greatest obstacle to connection resides in ourselves; in the emotional reactions and projections that arise from our own childhood experiences, for which our children are the trigger but not the cause. In parenting or education, insight is more important than information; self-knowledge counts more than science. Our awareness of the Child Within is the greatest guide that I know. Frankly, I did not *want* to so much as *had* to write this book. Without it, my other writings felt incomplete, a vital piece was missing.

The greatest obstacle to connection resides in ourselves; in the emotional reactions and projections that arise from our own childhood experiences....

A Brief Explanation of Terms

From here on, when I refer to 'your child', it can apply to one of your own children, a student in your class, a grandchild, a nephew or niece, a foster child, or any other child that occupies an important place in your life.

I use the terms Inner Child Journey or Inner Child Process interchangeably, both refer equally to the guided quest that this book explains and teaches. I could not decide between the terms, so I elected to keep both. *Process* refers to the way that our emotional state and perceptions are altered as we undertake the self-reflective steps in sequence. Yet it also seems fitting to call this a *journey* in that it takes some time, it has predictable, prescribed and familiar steps, and as with all worthy journeys we are—at least in some small way—transformed by it.

And now for the gender thing. Ah, that damned gender thing! It forces us to make a call on one of two genders with every mention of a child. It drives authors mad and makes clumsy apologists of all of us. Tying ourselves in knots to avoid offending we use 'they', 'he-she', or accentuate the feminine in a fruitless effort to atone for millennia of patriarchal prepotence. Prefaces and introductions everywhere carry a laborious disclaimer; the fallout of this vexing idiomatic bug. So, until our governments procure as the Swedes have—by an act of parliament—a new pronoun relieved of gender, I'm stuck with what I've got. His and hers. As no doubt you have already noticed, I've tried to hop from one to the other at random. I'm hoping they've added up to 50-50 by the end of the book.

Origins of the Inner Child Process

My approach to Inner Child Journeying has had many influences. It is a quilt containing some of my own stitching, but the patches come from many other writers and psychotherapists to whom I owe a great debt. The idea of Inner Child Journeying, in its many forms, is certainly not uniquely mine.

Psychotherapists of all stripes have long-employed a rich diversity of Inner Child Processes around the world. Although I have set the course for the Journey in these pages according to my experience as a psychotherapist, I cannot entirely claim authorship.

My professional lineage harks from a tradition of somatic (body-oriented) psychotherapies, culminating with many years of training with Chris Campbell, PhD. My Process also benefits from John Bradshaw's contributions to Inner Child work.[1] Author, counsellor and educator, Bradshaw helped the world get comfortable with the idea that we all have an Inner Child, and that we carry the wounds and the strengths of this Inner Child into our relationships and our endeavours. Bradshaw was joined by Joseph Chilton Pearce, Alice Miller, Bruce Davis and many more eminent psychologists, thought-leaders and writers who helped to make Inner Child awareness a cultural norm. Eric Berne, MD, may have started it all when he developed the concept of the Child ego state in his psychoanalytic theory of transactional analysis (TA) in the late '50s. It was then popularized by his 1964 bestseller, *Games People Play*.

Although my adapted Inner Child Process owes a great deal to the influences I mention here (and more besides), it does not wholly or without deviation represent them. The Inner Child Journey as I present it has been modified by the most revelatory experiences that I have accumulated as a therapist. I have had the privilege of absorbing the mastery of many teachers, writers and therapists; and though all have contributed markedly to my Inner Child Process—none can be blamed for my personal adaptations and recasts.

I have been using this Inner Child Journey as a psychotherapeutic tool for around 25 years, with its many applications in relationship counselling, individual therapy, and parent coaching. I have also introduced this inquiry method via parenting workshops around the world. Across diverse cultural settings, the feedback has been very positive and I have been privileged to witness beautiful and heart-opening moments of healing for many parents. Many of those extraordinary moments have remained with me and their faces and voices continue to enliven my work.

My perspective bears the imprint of developmental psychology, and I particularly appreciate my training in body-oriented psychotherapies for their solid grounding in the brass tacks of neurobiology.

I am grateful to brain scientists; the protagonists of modern interpersonal neurobiology. They have helped us find the places where the Inner Child hangs out in our neural matrixes. They've helped bring a new concreteness to something that, until recently, seemed merely metaphorical. Science has demystified what was until recently the postulations and intuitions of psychotherapists. Like a lost city that was once the stuff of legend and speculation, finally unearthed by archaeologists, the mythical has been unearthed and it is real. Today we can talk about the Inner Child with far greater resonance.

The Inner Child is no longer mere metaphor; she is made of flesh. The persistent, automatic response-sets and thought-patterns that were conditioned in childhood are animated by cognitive webs, made of neural fibres and brain chemistry. Our beliefs, prejudices, projections, knee-jerk reactions and deep emotional currents are visible as flashes of light and colour in the paraphernalia of a brain scan.

Now that we know the Inner Child is real, what are the implications for us, and how can this knowledge help us to live and love better? Undoubtedly, this is a ripe time to write about Inner Child awareness and how it can enrich our lives.

My Vision and Dedication

Our Inner Child will not be left behind. He lives on in our memory, our reactions, our behaviour and our perceptions. She whispers about all we have lived and learned, in our mother's womb, at birth, in the arms of our elders, at school. We would not want to lose access to this body of experience if we understood but a fraction of its gifts.

We have everything to gain from becoming better acquainted with this Inner Child, his wisdom, her vibrancy, his bottomless creativity and playfulness, her resilience. If we dare to learn from remembered pain, then this pain was not for naught.

But what I love the most about the Inner Child is how she connects us to each other, making us all family. This has been the shared story of us all, since the beginning. From child to adult to elder, and back again, often. It was true for our forebears, and will be true for our descendants. Joni Mitchell was right when she sang that our 'painted ponies go up and down... on the carousel of time.'[2]

Through the eyes of a child, nothing is mundane; everything contains magic. A leaf. A shoelace. A stick. A beetle. Every moment is wondrous, filled with portent. Nothing is ordinary, everything brings awe and delight. I remember our daughter as a baby, how she'd wrap her chubby fingers around something, then drop it, watching it fall. She would do this over and over, and each time gravity had its way, she would belly laugh as if it was the first time all over again. When did we lose this capacity for wonder?

Watching our baby daughter playing nakedly on the pavers in our patio, she helped me to remember what I had become blind to: the essential magic in all things. She saw grandeur in the flow of water. She heard endless surprises in the call of a bird. She meditated on the march of an ant. She saw the miracle of each moment. Hers was an absolute absorption in each activity, a reverence for the extraordinariness in all ordinariness. How nourishing the world would seem, if we could see again, as we all once did. I had not anticipated that fatherhood would teach me so much. Our daughter helped me to rediscover my own capacity to be child-like. I have not lost this—not entirely, that is—and I can thank her for helping remind me about the magic that dwells in the mundane. More than enough beauty resides in the most ordinary moment; if we just remember how to see it.

This does not require any appeal to notions of a 'supernatural'; as if the natural is not miraculous enough. This magic has more to do with our own internal state. The kind of undefended vision that is permeable to the miracle of all things and the magnificence of all beings is entirely re-discoverable, for those of us who have temporarily lost it. It is simply a matter of re-learning how to see, and re-learning how to hear. In the palm of his or her hand, our Inner Child holds the secret to this clarity of perception, and will share it freely when we have deeply listened to his feelings, her needs.

I dedicate this book to the *re-magick-ing* of our lives; to the human right to find pleasure in our work, to have harmony in our relationships and to be filled with wonder about the world we inhabit.

 I dedicate this book to the re-magick-ing of our lives; to the human right to find pleasure in our work, to have harmony in our relationships and to be filled with wonder about the world we inhabit.

It is everyone's biological inheritance to experience peak moments of bliss and connectedness with all Life. The blueprint for ecstasy is encoded in the brain and its chemistry. Pure joy is as attainable as any other ordinary state, but it is obscured by a protective shroud that we have spread over our emotional wounds suffered in childhood. Bring compassionate attention to these wounds, give a voice to the blows and bruises of childhood and adolescence, and our capacity for joy and ease are reclaimed.

We see our own children more clearly as we bring our Inner Child home. This change in our vision invariably transforms our moods and our responses, allowing our parenting to flow more naturally and more pleasurably. This brings me to the final—but not the least—yearning that compels my writing: if we liberate the next generation from the psychological vestiges of our past, I strongly believe that we can transform the world.

My Book's Purpose

I'd like to set my own story aside to introduce you to the manual that will help you get more closely acquainted with your Inner Child. And I may share a few more of my tales here and there as you take your excursion through the text.

This book is primarily intended as a personal-growth guide; a manual to help you use the challenges of human relationship as growth opportunities. More specifically, it is a handbook designed for parents, teachers, therapists and all who have children in their lives. I believe the challenges brought to us by children are the most powerful provocations for our awakening and our development. That is why I have chosen the context of our relationships with children as the springboard for Inner Child Journeys.

'the challenges brought to us by children are the most powerful provocations for our awakening and our development.'

This book is also a manual for counsellors and psychotherapists. The Inner Child Process can go to any depth you choose, depending on how you direct it. You can usher your client through a light and conversational version of the Journey, or guide them through a deeper and more immersive experience.

My approach to Inner Child Journeying is highly adaptable to group settings. As a shared experience in a safe setting, this Journey (in its light as well as deeper versions) is one of the most wonderful tribe-building exercises that I know. I particularly encourage parent-support groups and school-teaching staff to sit in a circle and share Inner Child experiences together.

I have offered a diversity of methods for Inner Child inquiry; from deeper dives to brief introspective dips. The Journey can be done as a personal meditation, a dialogue with a friend, a process with a group or a formal practice in a therapy setting.

The Journey is by no means limited to addressing issues that arise in a parenting or teaching context. It is entirely applicable to any relationship in conflict, and I have often used it as an integral part of counselling couples, siblings or business partners. In fact, I hope you will use this Process to work through a wide range of challenges in your life—even in conflicts within yourself! So often, what we think we are fighting about is but a thin veil over an old, personal wound. Addressing the childhood issues that have been triggered for both parties can bring enormous relief, forgiveness and reconciliation. Please use the Process in any way that feels relevant for you. For the purpose of this book, I have maintained a focus on parent-child or teacher-child relationships.

Besides the instructions for the steps in the Journey, you will also find numerous nuggets of practical, everyday psychology strewn through each chapter. I am fascinated by those simple pearls of neuro-psychological know-how that clarify our steps towards growth and fulfilment. These are peppered throughout the book, both in support of the Journey and for their own intrinsic value.

This book is a map, but the walking is all yours. And although your Inner Child Journeys will be perfectly unique and unrepeatable, you are not alone; the Inner Child experience is intrinsic to human life. By daring to make this Journey consciously and intentionally, we transform what might otherwise seem scary and confusing into a gift of healing and growth.

Stories Are Teachers

To help you grasp the foundational concepts, I have infused the text with many illustrative anecdotes that depict challenging situations between an adult and a baby, a child or an adolescent. The situations I have chosen tend to occur commonly across cultures; almost as rites of passage. You are likely to find many of the anecdotes familiar—from your own life, or perhaps the life of a friend. Stories bring a concept to life by making it personal. Real-life context is best for demonstrating how our childhood wounds can so often underlie our conflicts and how Inner Child Journeys can bring resolution, healing and peace.

Although my anecdotes are loosely drawn from a mish-mash of my experiences as a psychotherapist, they are purely fictional and not directly representative of any individual. I have scrambled and re-mixed moments from my personal and work life. Any resemblance to yourself or someone you might know is entirely incidental, especially as the dilemmas pictured are commonplace. A couple of the anecdotes spring from my personal life, and I make that clear in the passage. Otherwise, the characters are all fictitious and their names are all invented.

When to Use the Process

Some moments are particularly ripe for you to make a little distance between you and your child; to take a few minutes and withdraw to your own space to do some Journeying. Inner Child Journeying is appropriate when you face the kinds of challenges that seem to come up over and over. With every fresh phase of parenting or teaching new pesky or worrisome issues arise that seem to become entrenched for a while.

Challenges come around in a cyclical fashion; we might have a 'good' day, and then *that old chestnut* comes back around to haunt—or at least daunt—us. Every parent and teacher has them: those 'Oh, not again!' moments that wear us thin, 'make us' flip our lids, lose our patience, feel like giving up, become judgemental or emotionally numb. Any parenting decision we make from that kind of space is likely to be muddied by our internal turmoil. To move forward with any clarity, we first need to pause and examine what has been triggered for us personally; what in *us* needs a little healing first.

Here are just a few common examples of occasions for which an Inner Child Journey would be both suitable and called for.

You might take the Inner Child Journey when you find yourself repeatedly arguing with your teenager about schoolwork.

Or perhaps to learn more about the root-causes of your most troubling reactions to your children's sibling-squabbles.

When you find yourself emotionally thrown off balance by your toddler's tantrums—his refusal to go to sleep, her powerful demands for attention, his clamouring for this or that toy—it might be time to take yourself on an Inner Child Journey.

When your baby's crying seems to get on your nerves, this could be an indication that your Inner Baby needs your attention.

If you are gripped with anxiety as your little child begins to explore the world and to take some physical risks, it may be time for you to examine your own experiences as a toddler.

Are you a schoolteacher? What important new discoveries might you make about yourself if you take the time for some introspection, regarding that disruptive child; the one that really seems to get under your skin?

These recurring or pattern-like entanglements in your childrearing partnership signal you that it is time; not for yet another strategy, but for some inward exploration.

Use the Inner Child Process when you feel stuck in a rut. When you suspect that your emotional reaction to your child is bigger than it needs to be. Use it also when you see yourself under-responding to your child. Most people are aware of the common propensity towards over-reaction—when our buttons are pushed hard enough. But how often do we acknowledge our under-reactions—those times when we freeze, tune-out, when we rationalise or deny our feelings? Some examples of 'under-responding' might include:

⊛ not being protective of your child when protection is called for

⊛ being unmoved by their pain

⊛ being indifferent to their longings

⊛ being lax about saying 'no' and setting boundaries

⊛ making too few demands for your child's collaboration.

From time to time, don't we all experience lapses of empathy; those moments when we just find it hard to care? Inner Child Journeying rejects pathologising; it simply brings compassion to the hidden hurts that colour—or suppress—our responses. The two anecdotes that follow illustrate quite common, everyday samples of parental under-responding. In both cases the parents' impedance becomes perfectly understandable in light of their childhood experiences.

The Boundary Bummer

A young mother struggles to be firm and to assert strong interpersonal boundaries with her 6-year-old daughter. The little girl is going through an angry phase, feeling hostile towards her mother, scratching, biting and even hitting her.

Reflecting on her own childhood, the mother recalls how intrusive and overbearing her own mother had been, and how disempowered and suffocated she had felt. She had grown up feeling socially awkward, timid and inhibited. While immersed in her Inner Child Process, she re-visits a number of moments when, as a little girl, she had silently vowed to never behave like her own controlling mother.

Bold as her commitment was, it brought unexpected collateral damage. Without realising it, her self-assertion had been tossed out along with her sweeping rejection of authoritarianism. In her resolve to not be a bully, she had overcompensated and quashed her right to stand up for herself when her daughter mistreated her. Saying 'no' with a smile and a silken, sing-song voice was as ineffectual as it was an additional irritant to the little girl.

Visiting her Inner Child sheds new light on her dilemma, revealing what she needs to develop her new strengths. This mother's healing journey involves re-learning how to be vocally assertive and how to set strong interpersonal boundaries. With practice, she learns that true self-assertion is entirely unlike her own mother's domineering style.

Soon, she is surprised to discover that, far from feeling intimidated, her daughter feels nourished by her newfound solidity, as well as more grounded and secure. Over time, the mother gains in wellbeing, while the daughter's capacity for consideration, respect and healthy self-containment grows by leaps and bounds. When mother is healed, so is the child.

Stand by Me

A young boy feels intimidated by a schoolteacher who appears to be gruff and indifferent towards him. His father has avoided speaking to this teacher on his behalf, even though his schoolwork has begun to suffer. The father rationalises his inaction by telling himself that his son will be 'better off learning to fight his own battles'. Deep down, however, this father is painfully aware that he generally leans towards conflict avoidance.

While doing an Inner Child Process, the father gets in touch with how vulnerable he felt as a schoolboy whenever the classroom or playground felt like a hostile environment. He contacts a deep well of sadness and helplessness about how unprotective and distant his own father had been. His deepest wish would have been for his father to come to his school and speak in his defence, at least once. He also uncovers a yearning for a paternal figure to teach him the skills of assertiveness and conflict resolution.

With new resolve, the father reaches out for assistance with communication skills, and challenges himself to move into his zone of discomfort. He finds new determination to replace his tendency for appeasement and avoidance with non-violent communication skills. With time as, the father begins to feel more empowered, his role modelling also empowers his son.

The following anecdote offers an example of a parent's over-reaction.

Tantrum vs Tantrum

A mother screams at her 4-year-old boy when he has a tantrum. She grabs his arm roughly and drags him to his room, closing the door and snapping at him to stay in there alone until he 'finds his manners'. She tells herself that this is necessary 'discipline', to reign-in the boy's 'bad behaviour'. This story repeats like a broken record, until a close and concerned friend points out how closely the mother's reactions resemble her son's out-of-control emotions.

In the course of an Inner Child Journey, the mother recalls for the first time how terrified and humiliated she felt as a child when her father would punish her for her own tantrums. She remembers how her body would freeze in shock when he would rage at her, and how bitterly unfair she thought her father was when he smacked her. In a world that normalised punishing attitudes to children, her heartbreak found no voice and was soon benumbed. She had learned to grow a thick skin to conceal her pain. But so long as she rationalised her quick temper—

putting it down to her 'personality', or to her son's 'naughtiness'—her Inner Child remained lonely, ashamed and unheard.

Going deeper into her Journey, she recalls how abjectly impotent she was, as a toddler, to meet her father's impossible demands for emotional self-control. She sees how desperately she'd needed space to express her feelings, and how acute was her need for comforting once the flood of emotion had passed. It becomes clear to her that her explosiveness is a leftover from her own past, and how unhelpful her over-reactions have been for her son. She now knows that she needs all the support she can get to heal her own stagnant anger before she can help her son with his.

The foundation of effective parenting is self-knowledge; that's where the Inner Child Process comes in. It is the best self-reflective tool that I know to sharpen our intuition and insight. We cannot hope to understand our children's feelings and their emotional needs unless we closely understand our own. But every time we take the time to experience life from the child's frame of reference, our effectiveness as guides flourishes.

Ultimately, you practise this Inner Child Process because you are as interested in yourself as you are in your child. As you uncover the personal wounds brought to light via the challenges your child brings you, some of the most valuable opportunities for healing will come your way. Redefining childrearing as a path of personal growth will nourish and empower you in ways you could not have anticipated.

Even if you only have half a minute or so every now and then to pause and check in with your Inner Child—especially when parenting seems to be wearing you down—this is an excellent self-care practice.

Checking in with your Inner Child will often revolutionise your experience of childrearing. We are doing nothing less than re-imagining childrearing as a spiritual pilgrimage, a path of unfoldment that can bring out strengths you did not know you had. Inner Child awareness can make sense of pain, bring purpose to chaos and find meaning in despair.

Far from being an exercise in self-preoccupation, attending to your personal growth needs will always benefit others in your life. This holds especially true for your children. When we embrace Inner Child awareness collectively, we liberate the next generation from the burden of our history.

The more you use this Process, the more you will come to trust that even the most frustrating and confusing ordeals are in fact rites of passage, replete with precious teachings. Pain is no longer for naught when we choose to see its purpose; and the burdens of parenting seem lighter in a context of personal growth.

Increasingly you will come to recognise that the non-catastrophic trials and conflicts your child brings you hold gifts of incalculable worth.

Where to Use the Process

Light versions

You can employ a light version of the Inner Child Process when you are alone, even if you only have a minute or two. Sometimes all it takes is to ask yourself, 'How was it for me, when I was roughly my child's current age, and I behaved a little bit like she does?' You may be surprised how helpful the answer can be. If you have space to go deeper and take longer, better still—but when you need a simple, short version of the Process, refer to Appendix 3, and even shorter and simpler Appendix 4.

Ideally, a private and quiet space would be more conducive to contacting what can potentially be tender or perhaps fiery emotions. But sometimes I have spontaneously delved into inner inquiry while sitting in a crowded bus, looking out the window.

At times I might ease into silent dialogue with my Inner Child, in a contemplative state that feels like musing or daydreaming rather than a focused reflection. There is no reason why a Journey can't sometimes be approached as a mosey rather than a trek. You can visit your Inner Child while sitting with a cup of tea, lying in bed before falling asleep, even while taking a shower.

When you are using the short and light versions of this Process, it is exceedingly important that you give yourself permission to pull out of the experience, if it feels like the emerging emotions might be too big at that time and place. You can bring yourself out of the Journey by distracting yourself with other thoughts, standing up and moving about, or engaging in some new activity. (See 'Create a Safe Experience', page 145.)

Deeper version

When you feel ready to undertake a deeper, more sustained and revelatory Journey, find a comfortable and quiet space to sit where you will not be disturbed for at least half an hour or so. A designated time and place where you feel safe is essential for you to engage with all the steps of the self-guided Inner Child Journey as explained in Chapters 6–10. Use Appendix 2 for this purpose; you can simply read the steps if you like. Once you have completed your Journey, consider writing down your discoveries, 'ahs', inspirations and new commitments in a journal. This can be a wonderful way to embed your learning and allow you review it with fresh eyes, at a later date.

Sharing with a friend

Close and trusting friends can use this Process in tandem by taking turns guiding each other through the steps of the Journey in the right sequence. Appendix 2 provides an ideal format for working easily in pairs. Alternatively, it can be equally supportive to share the 'Light' and 'Super-Light' versions of the Process, along the lines shown in Appendices 3 and 4. Sharing stories of childhood and opening-up to each other about how we felt as children can be a singularly bonding experience between friends, an especially heart-expanding kind of dialogue. The point of sharing this Process is not so we can find answers for each other or to 'fix' each other's dilemmas. The sharing has a far more important purpose, and that is to *connect*. The most special people in our lives are likely to be those whom we know and who know us at this level of intimacy.

Co-parenting relationship

An entire book could be written about how you can integrate this Process into your co-parenting path with your partner or spouse. Sharing the Inner Child Journey in turns with your partner can bring wonderful new understanding about each other's strengths and vulnerabilities. This can synergise you as co-parents and pave the way for a mutually supportive parenting adventure.

The closer we feel to each other's Inner Child, and the more we understand each other's wounds and triggers, the less likely we are to blame one another when we fall short of our best selves. Sharing our childhood experiences makes us emotionally vulnerable together. We fall into a deeper intimacy and trust. When we can feel the world as it once felt for another, it is hard not to forgive their foibles and mistakes. By knowing their wound, you can see through offending or disappointing behaviour.

Disputes over childrearing choices are almost never resolved through argument—no matter who thinks they possess the best 'evidence base' or who claims to have read the best 'research'. Childrearing disputes are almost always driven by the impacts of two vastly different childhood imprints, and therefore can only be resolved through the shared vulnerability of an Inner-Child-based dialogue. Before we can resolve what appears to be a philosophical dispute, we need to unmask the old fears and hurts that drive our convictions. I believe shared Inner Child Work is essential for couples, especially those planning to have children together.

Group Journeying

One of my favourite applications of the Inner Child Process is for communal parenting groups. This can be a wonderful and effective way to create a tribe-like, emotionally supportive 'village'. I know of no better ritual to connect people deeply and generate waves of group loyalty and compassion. Taking turns sharing our stories and strivings in a non-judgemental, empathic circle can be one of the most life-sustaining and regenerative experiences. Intentional vulnerability is the key to generating trust and safety. A group of people who get to know each other at this depth can engender a profoundly supportive and nourishing environment. I'll have much more to say about this in Chapter 15.

Therapist-led

If you ever feel stuck, frightened, or overcome with the intensity of emotion that this Process brings up for you, please explore this difficult terrain with a qualified counsellor or therapist. Even if your therapist is unfamiliar with this kind of work, but willing to usher you through the steps of this Process, your Journey will be safer and more comfortable.

Whatever you do, don't be alone; be well supported when things feel scary or too intense. Traumatic early memories and emotions may surface, and that's why I have detailed a number of measures to make this Journey as safe as it can be (see page 145).

Safety is paramount if this Journey is to be of any benefit, so it is okay to slow—or entirely stop the Process at any moment.

Usually, the most optimal way to undertake this Journey is while being patiently guided through each step by someone you trust.

Inner Child work does not always bring up painful emotions and in fact, the Journey can be a pleasurable, calm and profoundly fulfilling experience. When someone else takes over the guidance so that you feel held, it can free you to let go and potentially travel to deeper layers of your mind. An empathic interpersonal connection can intensify the healing.

Health Professionals

I especially invite counsellors, psychotherapists and all those in the helping professions to use this Inner Child Process—the Light versions as well as the more intensive form—when it seems appropriate as part of work with clients. The Process is highly adaptable to a broad range of therapeutic settings, from one-on-one sessions to group work.

The Book's Structure

Our Inner Child Journey can be a little more intricate than many of the guided processes commonly used. The Journey's destination is not prescribed; it emerges organically from within. The longer versions of the Journey help you to devise an appropriate response to your Inner Child's needs in real time. Learning to listen to your Inner Child's deepest yearnings does not always come easily, at least not immediately. But the most enduring and relationship-transforming changes are set in motion when we answer our core developmental needs.

Finding a salve for the wounds of our Inner Child can be more fruitful with a little psychological know-how. For this we'll need to understand the stages of childhood psychological development, and how these rites of passage affect our continued development as adults. The sections covering developmental psychology will help prepare you for the deeper Journeys so you can gain the most profound and lasting benefits from your Inner Child work.

Finally, we look at how you can support others as they travel on their own healing Journeys. Being a guide for another's Journey can be a profoundly uplifting and bonding experience, whether you do this as a friend, colleague, counsellor or therapist. Much in these pages will satisfy your interest in psychology, whether you are a 'lay person' wishing to broaden your understanding or a practicing counsellor seeking to diversify your toolkit.

You can of course skip to the progressively simpler instructions for the Journey as they appear in the Appendices 2, 3 and 4. You can always delve into the deep-dive sections later as your need and curiosity arise. Whichever your preferred pathway, if you want a deeper Journey that brings you more far-reaching changes, you will want to explore the full text. The information that makes advanced Journeying possible—particularly that in Part C—will help you navigate through the impasses and blind alleys that we commonly encounter in personal growth work, paving the way for deeper and life-changing outcomes.

Let's take an overview of the book's contents. Part A—Chapters 1, 2 and 3— explains the principles and concepts that you need to use the Process meaningfully and safely. Please don't think this is just an entrée before the main course. These chapters—charged with helpful bytes of psychological wisdom—are an end in themselves, not just a stepping stone to the rest of the book. They are applicable to you and your relationships. You'll find practical exercises that will bring you invaluable new insights about you, your Inner Child, and how he or she manifests through your interactions with your children. Think of these exercises as important navigational equipment that will contribute to the most successful Inner Child Journeys.

Part B—Chapters 4–10—contains all the steps in the Inner Child Journey. Each step is accompanied by a full explanation, so you can understand its purpose.

Part C—Chapters 11–15—guides you through the deeper and more complex aspects of the Journey. Here you will discover how psychological healing and growth follows a stage-by-stage sequence that parallels childhood stages of development. You will learn to work with subtle aspects of body-memory, understand the nature of resistance and use the Journey for your own liberation and healing as well as that of your children. Finally, you will also learn how to guide others safely through their own Journeys, and how to facilitate Journeying in a group setting. Inner Child work in groups is a beautifully bonding and tribe-building exercise.

The steps of the Journey appear again, user-friendly and without explanatory text, in the Appendices. The diverse approaches in Appendices 2, 3 or 4 are adaptable to a range of settings and purposes; from 'in-depth' to 'super-light'.

Let's now get into the nitty gritty of the Inner Child Process. See you on the Journey.

CHAPTER 2

The 'who' Behind our choices

This workbook contains no advice about how to raise your children, what to say to them or how to be with them. This workbook is for you, and about you. But first, let's examine why anyone, when faced with a parenting challenge, might pause for inward reflection and self-examination instead of just reacting to their child.

why Take a Journey?

When engaged in the everyday dance of parenting, the child is traditionally the focus of our attention. But how often, and how honestly, do we look back at ourselves? We the adults are the agents, the children are the acted-upon. Our sights are set outward, towards the child. Our concerns encircle them. In conversation with friends, we tell stories about our children, perhaps only superficially making mention of our own internal experience: what our children 'put us through', how proud we are of them, how we fear for them, how desperate we are for more sleep, or a moment's peace.

But how often do we examine our reactions, to be curious about the stories that drive us and the life-experiences that, without our realising, have shaped our parenting style? How well do we understand the internal forces that govern our parenting decisions? I wonder how many of us have met the adolescent, the child and the baby dwelling inside us? Inside each of us lives a Child, and this internal Child never ceases to whisper instructions, fears and longings in our ears.

Parents, carers and teachers universally strive to *get it right* for the children. And so it should be. But if this is all we do, then we miss an important aspect of ourselves. We are so much more than that. Interpersonal contact of the kind that moves us, changes us, and opens our hearts requires something more than a problem-solving approach to life. True connection requires us to lower the bucket deeper into the well. Connection asks for emotional vulnerability; a little emotional risk.

And here is the most wonderful of all paradoxes. When for a few moments we ease up on our strivings to *get it right*, when we drop prescribed techniques and opt for an emotionally authentic connection—when we embrace the Child who lives inside us—we become a far more powerful influence for our children. They are so intuitive, our kids. They know when we have found humility; they know when our voice carries the wisdom borne of our remembering that we were once as vulnerable and innocent as they are. They sense when we are open to the presence of our Inner Child; they can smell it—and they listen. They settle. They follow.

When we drop prescribed techniques and opt for an emotionally authentic connection—when we embrace the Child who lives inside us—we become a far more powerful influence for our children.

Why does my work seem to come back to this Inner Child Process, over and over like a homing call? Because when we connect with ourselves this deeply, we connect with others in a whole new way; more profoundly, more satisfyingly. And what could be more important?

Why not receive more from life when it gives so abundantly? Childrearing and education are not just a job, these relationships were not meant solely for our children's benefit. Our work as parents, grandparents, carers and teachers offers us many more gifts than most of us realise. In every challenge and struggle, in each moment of strain, confusion, worry and bewilderment, lies a key to our own healing and growth, should we decide to grab it.

Please don't think that Inner Child Journeying is about self-obsession. I would not enjoy seeing a parent or teacher remove him or herself into an introspective sanctum, there to remain. I doubt our children want to relate to our meditations and monastic remoteness. They want our engagement. They want vibrancy, heartbeats, warmth and all our senses involved in dialogue. The Inner Child Process uses the flame of crisis as a foundry for personal renewal, but then it brings us back to our children with more compassion, more respect, more capacity for love, play and learning. The Journey ends hand-in-hand, heart-to-heart.

An intentional and conscious Inner Child Journey is an adventure into yourself. When you come out from this immersion into your inner world, your outer world will seem to have changed. In other words, though your environment might objectively remain the same, you will *experience* it quite differently. You will feel as if you have more room to move, to act, to give and to receive.

Returning from our Inner Journeys, we view our relationships from a whole new vantage point.

The Inner Child Journey leaves you with a map, full of clues on how to move forward, showing you steps you can take to heal, grow and have richer experiences in your world. Don't be surprised if on occasion you find yourself feeling grateful that your child has pressed your buttons and thus pushed you into your Journey.

And meanwhile, what happens for your children? They pick up on your vibes. How lucky is the child whose parents take ownership of their own over-reactions and under-reactions! How special for that child to get to know you more intimately, to see your personhood beyond the roles you play, the rules you espouse and the authority you wield.

Before we launch into the instructions for our step-by-step Inner Child Journey, I have provided an explanatory introduction that elucidates the whys and wherefores of this reflective practice, and an examination of the principles, concepts and science from which this Journey is curated. The preparatory sections are intrinsically useful.

You can gain much by merely exploring the terms used, contemplating what they mean for you and doing the practical exercises, before you engage with the Inner Child Process. I encourage you to periodically revisit these early chapters as a useful reference and reminder of the concepts that give meaning to our Journey.

Where Does the Inner Child Live?

Our bodies are more than fleshly vessels in which we travel. They are also our character. The full complexity of our unique personalities is visible in our posture, our gait and how we carry our frames. As we sit, stand, breathe and move, so do we relate to the world around us.

Each layer of our multifaceted self, down to our deepest unconscious, has its home in our nervous system and in the varied textures of our musculo-skeletal system; the knots, tensions and collapses that we carry. Today, we are also beginning to understand how the bacterial ecologies that populate our gut play a significant role in regulating our mood states, our reactions and our perceptions. In every way, our body is our mind is our body.

Our most persistent beliefs, attitudes and emotional responses are not just fleeting shadows darting through our heads. They are total-body phenomena, rooted in neural circuitry, sinew, fascia and viscera. Even our parenting style, our usual and personal manner of teaching or guiding children, is grounded in flesh. Our characteristic and unique pattern-like ways of responding to the challenges and the joys that our children bring are animated by complex webs of neural circuitry.

Our Inner Child is far more than a concept. He or she—like every other 'she' or 'he'—is alive and made of flesh. This Inner Child is most clearly evident in our unconscious, spontaneous and automatic behaviours, in our habits, in our characteristic, pattern-like responses. Many of our deep-set reactions, life-beliefs and emotional dispositions were conditioned by key moments we have lived—nourishing and hurtful, thrilling and terrifying—during our formative years. Powerful experiences change us because they alter our brain, heart and gut. And since in childhood our brains were most malleable and sensitive to our environment, childhood experiences affect us most of all.

Our behaviour is our memory; it reveals our story. It's not that we necessarily reproduce a facsimile of how we were treated as children, but rather that our manner demonstrates how we adapted to our childhood environments. Is that a scary prospect? Maybe.

Our behaviour is our memory; it reveals our story.

At first it can be unsettling to discover how transparent our body language makes us, how poignantly our actions tell our tale. We wish to leave our past behind, but our past will not let us go; its imprint remains in our neurology, our neurochemistry, our gut microbiome and our behaviour.

In that regard, our past is present. We speak it, we think it, we see the world through its lens; we feel it every day. It colours our relationships and touches our choices. But—does this mean we are trapped? Destined to repeat our histories? If these ideas have stirred up some discomfort, please take heart: the purpose of this book is to turn this into a most empowering realisation.

Certainly, our *actual past* is behind us, but the way we personally adapted to our past remains with us here and now, encoded in our neural pathways. Some brain scientists use the term 'cogwebs' (cognitive webs) to refer to the matrix of neural pathways that underpin our deepest mental associations, belief-systems and attitudes.

If our Inner Child—with all her longings and reactions—is wired into such cogwebs, this certainly explains why she endures through the term of our lives, and does not easily change.

But today we know that the brain remains plastic and responsive to new experiences for as long as we are alive. Personal growth is a matter of changing the brain. It results from giving ourselves the appropriately nourishing developmental experiences.

The Inner Child grows like any other child. Not overnight, but according to an orderly sequence, and according to how he is nourished, supported and empowered. By understanding the embodied nature of our Inner Child, we gain clear indications on how to grow, develop and renew ourselves whenever needed.

While the denial of our past is the greatest block to healing and an impediment to close relationships, embracing our past and its lessons is ultimately freeing. Exploring our childhood histories through Inner Child Journeying is the opposite of wallowing; it means using our past experiences dynamically, mining them for wisdom and compassion.

Our very wounds, when we tell the truth about them, offer us vital clues about the way towards personal healing. Letting go of our past does not come through a simple act of the will. Helping our Inner Child to heal where she might be wounded, or grow where he might be stuck, requires a sequential, step-by-step process.

I found it reassuring to learn that the cognitive webs that give life to our Inner Child remain receptive to growth and change. Psychological growth is much like the growth of a plant. Metamorphosis is not instantaneous, but with the right nutrition, it is inevitable. However, our thirst for change requires a little temperance. Our cogwebs can't chop and change according to any caprice. Our nervous systems are not like a Lego set, ready for us to retrofit for a custom-designed, brand-new personality.

Personal growth follows a natural pathway in accordance with our Inner Child's developmental needs. As we will see later, once we learn to hear what our Inner Child needs, the way forward is illuminated. A path of healing and growth opens, with clear and successive steps.

All we need for personal growth is to understand the Inner Child's programmed developmental trajectory. But this developmental code isn't like the clinical, algorithmic entries that go clickety-clack on a keyboard. It's more like an adventure—rich with feeling, story and risk. Our adult self and our Inner Child go forth on a Journey together. A greater happiness awaits them both at the terminus.

A Deeper View of Parenting

Being a parent is so much more than the act of parenting itself. The same can be said about being a teacher: there is more to it than simply teaching. You are so much more than who and what you become in either of these roles.

Adopt this vision, and you have begun a revolution that expands parenting or teaching far beyond the ordinary optics. This perceptual revolution lifts us from drudgery, self-sacrifice and worry about how our children will 'turn out': to a grand mutual adventure through which you grow as extensively as your child does, in which your growth and your children's growth are marvellously intertwined.

Parenting and teaching are not only about what we do for our children; both are equally about what we learn in the process. Our students teach us, our children grow us up—as long as we pay attention. If we dare to look inwardly at ourselves—and not just outwardly at the child—our journey becomes enriched with new meaning and purpose.

If we let them, our children can teach us some of life's greatest lessons. The trials and frustrations of childrearing serve as a spotlight on our old and perhaps forgotten unresolved hurts. So it makes sense that resolution of conflict with our children must begin on the inside; with us.

What if we cease to view the hardships of childrearing as interruptions to our plans? The travails of childrearing are not necessarily about something gone 'wrong'; they can be opportunities. Children bother us, they worry us, they chafe at our skin. They spur us to complete our own personal development where it has been arrested— to resolve the unfinished business of our own formative years. If we dare to pay attention to our own emotional processes, we can begin to reclaim lost pieces of our own childhood.

Your child's maturation is intricately tied with your healing and growth. Your own personal healing and unfoldment cannot help but cause ripples in your child's consciousness, liberating him, enabling her to expand.

These days, a growing number of people understand this principle. A new generation of parents and teachers have begun to view childrearing as a path of personal growth. There is a new commitment to self-inquiry, in which we dare ask the question, 'Might my reaction to my child have more to do with how I was raised, and less to do with my child?' I believe we are witnessing a new willingness to re-evaluate our past and to learn its lessons, in order to create a better future.

Parents and teachers the world over are becoming more comfortable with Inner Child awareness. It is no longer taboo to ponder how our most painful and most pleasurable childhood experiences have shaped us. We have become more willing to talk openly about our childhoods because this can be intrinsically fulfilling. In the right company, sharing these formative stories can create the most wonderful bonds of trust and friendship. It is deeply satisfying to get to know ourselves and each other better—the root causes of our responses and our deepest drives.

Through the eyes of a child, nothing is mundane

Who Is the 'Problem' Really About?

Our assumptions are not random; they usually spring from unexamined personal experience. When confronted with the often-baffling behaviours of our children, usually we make a declaration *about the child*. We might say, 'This kid needs more discipline' or, 'That kid needs more encouragement'. But if we don't pause to examine our own childhood learning and re-evaluate the source of our convictions, can we be sure we are really talking about the child that stands before us? Or might we unwittingly be talking about ourselves?

Sometimes, almost automatically, we merely repeat what our elders once said about us. As a typical example, children are often judged to be doing things '*just* to get attention'. What if our perceptions about our children say more about our own childhood experience and our self-image, than about them?

When friction occurs in a relationship, we tend to play responsibility-volleyball. Whose fault is it—yours or mine? Who is supposed to take responsibility—you or me? When it comes to responsibility, we either divest too much to the other person: 'It's up to you to make things better.' or we shoulder more than our realistic load, 'It's all my fault' or, 'I must have done something terrible.' How often do we see responsibility as shared?

We tend to assign our parenting dilemmas an *aboutness*: 'Who is the problem *about*? Is it *about* you? Or is it *about* me?' Instead, can we look at how each of us has pushed the others' buttons? It can take courage to really examine how we—perhaps without realising it—have contributed to the eruption of a conflict, its escalation, or the logjam that blocks resolution.

Responsibility is not the same as fault. Think of it as *response-ability*; when you assume response-ability you see yourself as 'able to respond'. Self-empowerment should not be confused with accepting culpability. True response-ability is a blame-free and guilt-free zone.

In a moment of trouble with your child, instead of asking 'whodunnit?' look for what your child might be able to learn from the situation (appropriate to her age), and how you can make her learning environment safe, as well as optimally challenging.

Just as importantly, look for what the situation can teach you about yourself. What is your learning opportunity here; how might this trial be pointing towards potential healing and growth for you? Could this dilemma be showing you a pathway to deepening your compassion? A way to improve your assertiveness? Could it be calling you to be more open and honest about your feelings? Or perhaps to slow down your frantic life and re-prioritise? Might your reactions be signposts; revealing the presence of deep, old and personal wounds?

As the Inner Child Journey supports you in your quest to embrace response-ability, it guides you toward a deeper and truer source of personal power. We begin the Journey with the intent to discover to what extent the dilemma we face is about *us*, about *our* personal history. The willingness to invert the age-old perspective that says 'it is all about the child' takes much courage, but it brings us many rewards.

A common trap is to cut responsibility into portions: 'How much is the problem about my child and how much is it about me?' Response-ability is not about percentages, so this question is as futile as it is unanswerable. In taking the Inner Child Journey you are asking something different, '*In what way* are my responses (or lack of them) a part of the dilemma? How are my emotional wounds being exposed through this parenting challenge, and what inside me wants healing right now?' Taking the Inner Child Journey is about curiosity, self-interest and the yearning for growth.

To portray problems as being 'about the child' is so common and traditional for parents and teachers that we barely question the habit. Collectively, we tend to say 'That is a problem child', or we characterise children in terms of their *behaviour*, 'That child has a behaviour *problem*'. Diagnosis targets the individual and downplays the role of context, and in this way it resembles blame.

Granted, external behaviour is what can most readily be seen. But pointing a finger at behaviour creates more problems than it solves. When we think about a child in terms of his behaviour, it is like thinking of the ocean in terms of waves— as if the surface turbulence exists without regard to the currents beneath, the seismic activity of the ocean floor, the winds above. Can waves and swells move independently of the streams, rivers and glaciers that flow into the sea?

If we end our conversation about a child's behaviour without thinking about how her environment affects her, our conclusions about her are both meaningless and misleading. For instance, if we simply say, 'That child is oppositional and defiant', without trying to understand the root causes behind her resistance, we hamper our ability to help. Our responses might be quite different if we discovered how the child has been disempowered, shamed or frightened; thus making sense of her challenging behaviours.

Child health professionals too often diagnose and categorise children by assessing their behaviour. I wish more 'experts' would ask, 'I wonder why this child behaves in this or that way while they sit in *my* office, with *me*? Could there be something about me—my demeanour, my body-language, the way I speak to this child, the appearance of my office—that triggers this child's seemingly aberrant behaviour?' The world would be a more peaceful place if we all did a little more of this.

At best, narrowing our focus to our children's overt behaviour makes us ineffectual, at worst it can hurt or alienate the child. Reality is *relational*; responsibility is shared very widely. Freedom comes to us when we stop looking for where the buck stops, and start looking for learning opportunities—for ourselves as well as for our children.

We are all subject to falling in the blame-trap from time to time. The voice of blame speaks abruptly; we either blame ourselves, we blame the child, perhaps we blame the child's peer group. This tendency is so common that I like to call it the 'automatic blame reflex'.

The blame reflex runs roughly along these lines: 'If I am upset, someone must have done this to me.' It's not that blame is never a fair call—you could say blame is reasonable if and when we are entirely helpless victims.

When it comes to our children, however, we are usually co-creators of the predicaments we face together. No parent is their child's universe—influences come from all directions—but we certainly are an important part of it.

So, I invite you to challenge yourself, and when you encounter your parenting trials, practise asking yourself, 'In what way might this also be about me?'

An inspiring example of responsibility taking and its powerful effects comes from the work of Australian psychologist, Vicky Flory, DPsych, (author of *Your Child's Emotional Needs*).[3] Dr Flory's team was able to substantially help children suffering from severe and chronic psychiatric disorders, not by treating the ailing children, but by helping their parents.

The support aimed at increasing the parents' empathy for their child, and challenging their negative judgements about their children's behaviour. Even though these children presented with serious psychiatric disorders, their symptoms were much reduced by a program that focused on the parents.[4]

Today, psychological health professionals should be put on notice to discard the old approach to diagnostics and labelling. For the longest time, we had been asking the misguided question, 'What is wrong with you?' This question makes no sense in light of current science.

Now we are learning to ask, 'What has happened to you?' Even the most bizarre and maddening behaviours have a context. This new and far more compassionate perspective that asks for your story, rather than your flaws, springs from new scientific insights about how children develop.

One of the most enlightening studies—and the largest of its kind spurred this historical turning point was carried out at the Kaiser Permanente Hospital in San Diego, California, in which the health and wellbeing of around 17,000 patients was traced to key elements of their childhood environments.[5]

A host of traumatic, adverse childhood experiences (ACEs) were confirmed as key drivers of behaviour, as well as a surprising range of addictions, psychological disorders and life-threatening diseases.

The results of this study are stunning in their scope and are driving a revolution in the way we view and treat children; at home, in schools, and in every professional setting.

Beyond this ground-breaking ACE study, a huge body of multi-disciplinary research today shows how commonly occurring stressors in-utero, during childbirth, the early years at home or in the classroom can disturb behaviour for the long term.[6] Children's reactions and behaviours can no longer be validly seen as entirely about them.

Taking ownership or responsibility can too easily be confused with self-blame or guilt, and that is why so many people at first feel uncomfortable with this orientation. Additionally, looking at our own issues can put us in touch with our emotional vulnerability. No wonder this takes courage, and considerable self-care.

The simple question, 'What is this issue about for me?' is really a foundational, paradigm shift that reverses generations of old customary attitudes. If this fundamental shift in response-ability is the only thing you gain from this book, by itself this will revolutionise your relationships and open new vistas for you. You will also begin to notice exciting changes in your relationship with your children. Lastly, far from being an inducer of guilt or shame, the Inner Child Journey—as you will later see—is the greatest generator of self-forgiveness that I know.

The Part of You that Is Your Child

The attributes we resist most in others are those we resist most in ourselves. What we judge most about others reflects an aspect of ourselves that we seek to disavow. Perhaps even more poignantly than the adults in our lives, our children hold a mirror to us. What most appals us in our children is—much as this makes us squirm—a faithful reflection of those bits of us that we would rather disown.

At some level we are, each of us, holographic representations of all humanity. We have inside us at least a little bit of what we admire most in others, and at least a morsel of what we despise in them. As parents and teachers, we become particularly reactive to facets of our children that we do battle with inside ourselves.

Perhaps it is more than figurative to say that somewhere in your bodymind, you *are* your child. This would be especially true with regard to your biological child, who carries your DNA and has osmotically absorbed much from your way of being. But it is also true, if only to a lesser extent, in relation to others' children in your care. When I say, 'You *are* that child', I am saying that in some small way at least, you embody some of that child's essence.

What we tussle with in others is a signal to us; pointing not only to what we have suppressed, but by implication, to a part of us that wants healing. Our children, just by being themselves, do this signalling for us especially well. They reflect a comparable aspect of our nature that has been longing to surface—an aspect of our Inner Child that wants to come home and be embraced.

In human conflict, problems arise because we feel alienated from each other. If you say to yourself, 'I would never behave like this child', you become the driver of conflict with this child. To declare 'I am not like you' is in a fundamental way to deal the first blow.

Reconciliation arrives with an empathic moment—when we can finally say about the other person's ways 'I can relate to that'. So, imagine this as a practice: each time you see something in your child that irks you or provokes you, say to yourself 'That is *myself* I am looking at.' The first step in the dance of interpersonal healing is to recognise ourselves in the other. Indeed, a part of you *is* your child.

For example, you might be struggling to accept a child who seems aggressive or hostile. Even if only in a small way, a part of you can also offend. You will be able to connect effectively with this child if you begin by asking yourself, 'When I speak aggressively, what do I really need?' or 'What is it that I fear, when I am having angry thoughts?' Get to know this part better; listen to this part of you and learn its longings and you will be much closer to helping the child before you in a meaningful way.

That seemingly 'lazy' child who irritates you—well, what have you done with the part of you that wants to be lazy sometimes? Are you sure you have understood what lies beneath the superficial appearance of laziness? Hold a conversation with that part of you, embrace that part, it won't necessarily mean that you adopt a life of slothfulness. Heal the rift inside you, and become a powerful guide for the child before you.

Heal the rift inside you, and become a powerful guide for the child before you.

If your child's behaviour feels bewildering to you and you are lost as to what to do, painful circumstances in your early life may have made you lose touch with that part of yourself that *is* the child before you. In other words, you have lost contact with a part of you that feels similarly, has comparable longings and impulses to those of your child today.

This alienation from our Inner Child makes our children's behaviour seem foreign or confusing to us and complicates our ability to respond effectively as parents, teachers and guides.

But as we move deeper into our Inner Child Journey, we ask what has happened to the part of you that *is* your child. Reclaiming that part of you will do more than heal you, it will also help you immensely to understand your child—from the *inside*.

Great Tool—Wrong Job!

There are so many reasons why I recommend that parents check in with their Inner Child before they decide how to respond to their children. Not the least of these reasons is that sometimes, if we reach too quickly for a parenting technique, we might be altogether misreading our child's needs. That is one of the most common ways to set ourselves up for a struggle.

Bedtime Blues

A mother once asked me if I could offer any new ideas to help her get her recalcitrant 3-year-old daughter to sleep at night. She had tried everything; bedtime stories, bedtime songs, avoiding screens and sugary foods in the evening, keeping the home quiet, the whole kit and caboodle, but nothing seemed to work and she was at the end of her tether. We could have dug around for more helpful tricks, but this would have meant glossing over some of the most important needs and feelings of both mother and child.

To begin with, I invited the mother to explore her deepest feelings about bedtime and to look at what she had learned about this ritual when she was a child. She recounted how her own mother had imposed a strict bedtime routine—no deviations, no explanation. As she recalled her own transition through this early life passage, she remembered feeling estranged from her mother's rule-bound ways. Having her light switched off no matter what, and being forced to remain quiet, had felt quite torturous. Today, the same routines that her mother had employed were being rehashed by her friends, doctors and nurses.

How often we are told to narrowly interpret our children's difficult night-time behaviours in terms of 'tiredness'. The only answer, so they say, must be a rigid night-time routine. But recalling how this treatment felt to her as a little child was a game-changer for this mother. She'd been desperate for her mother to show an interest in her feelings, to include her in two-way dialogue—to share with her why saying goodnight was so important. She remembered how she'd longed for conversation, rather than an imposition.

Reconnecting with her own childhood helped this mother see that she did not have to abandon her night-time ritual to help her daughter feel included. She could vary lights-out time just a little according to normal daily fluctuations in sleepiness. Even more importantly, she would hold her daughter close and explain carefully how a good sleep would help her not to be cranky in the morning.

But the main deal-clincher turned out to be a little truth telling about her own needs and feelings. She opened-up to her daughter and shared that she too was tired, yearning for rest, and that she was struggling to keep entertaining her daughter into the night. Mothers have needs too. They also have limits. The need for a bedtime was as much hers as her daughter's, and it was the first time the little girl had heard this so directly. This conversation made a big difference. The daughter now felt more connected to her mother as they eased into the tender moments of pre-sleep.

When the mother spoke her own truth, the daughter finally felt *met*. There is something deeply satisfying about shared emotional authenticity; it fulfils a hunger for intimate, heart-centred connection. Without knowing it, the daughter had been doggedly fighting sleep, until she could feel her mother's heart one last time before giving-in to the darkness. She'd been hanging out for the kind of contact that only an interchange of emotional truth can bring—so she could finally surrender, let her head ease back into her pillow, and drop into a peaceful slumber.

A brief Inner Child inquiry helped the mother in the 'Bedtime Blues' story above access the voice of her heart—her simple emotional truth. As useful as a handy, parenting technique can sometimes be, techniques do not necessarily produce the rich interpersonal contact that children need in order to settle. In fact, since techniques can sometimes be manipulative, they can get in the way of a deeper connection. That's why even our best parenting techniques can backfire. Once they are no longer babies, our children do not want us to be technicians. They want us to be authentic or *real*; that means being transparent about our needs, feelings and limits. And they want us to find appropriate, non-threatening ways to show them how we truly feel. Ironically, our best interventions—such as bedtime stories, rituals and songs—are much more readily received and welcomed by our children when we make this kind of connection with them first.

Here are some further examples of why tools and tips and techniques can sometimes miss the point.

Piano Practice Doldrums

A father and mother are worried because their 14-year-old son, who has been learning the piano for some years, has stopped practising. At a loss about how to persuade the boy to keep honing his hard-won musical skill, they decide to offer him a small sum of money for each half-hour of practice. Of course, the lad welcomes the stipend. True to his agreement, he buckles down at the keyboard for the required time. But he drags himself through the practice session, eyes on the clock. Though the amount of playing has increased, the feel and creativity of his playing suffers and his musicality fades.

Both parents had formally learned to play musical instruments as children. Following-up with some Inner Child Journeying, they recalled the agonies of practise-by-compulsion, hour-after-hour, past the point of soured enthusiasm. In fact, for both of them the joylessness of enforced repetition had dampened the spirit of the music, leading them both to sideline their instruments in the end.

The parents resolved to do everything to help make the piano fun again for their son, until he could find himself thinking, 'I want to play', rather than 'I should play'. They helped him explore new styles of music and to take a chance jamming with various bands, until he found a natural source of inspiration and intrinsic motivation.

Recapturing the feel of being a child and reconnecting with their deepest childhood wishes showed these parents an easier, more pleasurable way to rekindle their son's passion for the piano. It was memory, rather than bribery, that brought music back.

Café Follies

When her 5-year-old daughter causes a ruckus in a café, a mother loudly counts, 'One... two... three...'—her voice forewarning un-named woes, should the hullabaloo dare extend to 'four'. The restless girl is momentarily cowed to silence by the spectre of implied punishment. But now that she feels distanced from her mother and her threatening tone, pressure builds inside her again and she becomes even more agitated.

A moment of introspection might have shown the mother what her irritable reaction prevented her from seeing—that her daughter would have soon settled if she'd paid her some attention first. Sitting still for any length of time in an environment designed for adults is beyond a little girl of her age. In part, the mother's tetchiness is a flashback; an echo of how strict her own mother had been towards childish exuberance. Her mother's glare had once filled her with shame until she'd learned to choke-off her own spontaneity.

Understandably, her spirited daughter today makes her cringe, especially in public places. It's no wonder that her first impulse is to control instead of connect. But as she remembers what she would have wished from her own mother, she withdraws her menacing tone and turns to play with her daughter for a minute or two. A little inclusion, rather than a threat, proves far more effective in helping her daughter to settle.

The Attention Deficit Fallacy

A teacher proposes a child be screened for attention deficit disorder because his concentration often seems to wander in class. However, reminiscing about his own time as a schoolboy brings back how he'd hated being forced to pay attention to those subjects he'd found unpalatable or irrelevant. This helps the teacher to view his pupil in a fresh light, making room for a new plan. The child's learning environment is modified to permit him to move around as he learns. He is given learning modules more closely aligned with his natural interests and affinities. It works! A little recollection has helped this teacher tap his own past as a source of intuition. His body memory has freed him to let go of pathologising—opting instead for a child-centred, intrinsically motivating approach.

To reach for a tool without first understanding the emotional landscape can be like trying to build a house without first surveying the land. First taking the time to dip into our own lived childhood experiences gives us a whole new reference. The perspective of the child's heart, seen and felt from the inside, helps us choose responses that come from a more empathically informed vantage point.

What the Process can't Do

At this point I'd like to issue a note of caution about the limitations of the Inner Child Process. This Process should not be applied to every crisis. Parenting, childcare and teaching will always bring situations that call for a quick response. If your toddler looks set to run across a busy road, it's not the time to work on your personal insights. Faced with a bout of sibling warfare, you might need to intervene first and reflect later. The time for prompt action is not the time for an introspective trance.

This Process is not about holding yourself back. On the contrary, it enables you access more of your wisdom and intuition so that when it is time to act or speak, your new insights will make you more effective and you will feel yourself becoming a stronger influence in your child's life. But this only holds true as long as you use the Process when appropriate, to bring more mindfulness—and heartfulness—to your responses, rather than to censor yourself.

No doubt, Inner Child Processing can be overused. I doubt our children would enjoy waiting patiently while we scrutinize our every parenting interaction. Not everything we think, feel or perceive springs from an old body-memory. Not all our behaviours are driven by our history, or coloured by our childhood wounds.

This Process does not replace the need to hone our practical parenting skills. For parents, carers and teachers this would include leadership, negotiation, assertiveness and listening skills—in other words, pretty much the same skillset that makes for loving and transformative human relations in every area of our lives. If communication skills comprise the toolkit, then our understanding of children's developmental needs and norms would be the manual that informs us when to use these tools. In the meantime, our Inner Child Process helps us choose our tools more wisely and to employ them more effectively. It also shows us when we are better off using no tools at all—instead simply being present and connecting.

The Inner Child Process is not a panacea. Its purpose is to help us tease out the difference between projections that spring from emotional memory and true perceptions about our children. From time to time, every one of us is prone to viewing our children through a muddied screen. But even if we can never achieve perfect clarity, the more emotional memory we wipe from our screens, the more clearly we can see. The more we distinguish memory from actuality, the freer we are to choose new ways to respond to our children.

Inner Child work involves listening to ourselves and paying deep and careful attention to our innermost thoughts, perceptions and emotions. It is above all a self-reflective venture. It does not substitute the occasions in which we need to look outwardly; to listen to our children and mindfully observe them. Nor does it replace the support we need from others so we can remain grounded and attentive.

If after taking an Inner Child Journey you find yourself needing to supplement your learning quest with a specific communication skill, you will find useful guidelines in my two prior books, *Parenting for a Peaceful World* and *Heart-to-Heart Parenting*.[7]

The Inner Child Process is certainly not a stand-alone, complete source of parenting wisdom. However, I believe it is an essential foundation because listening to yourself more deeply will make you a much better listener toward your child.

How Your Child Benefits

The Inner Child Journey is one of the most powerful ways I know to sharpen your innate intuitive abilities as a parent. Practising this Process attunes you to the still, quiet messages that spring from the depths of your consciousness; from the sum-total of all you have experienced as a child plus what you have witnessed in the lives of others.

The more you practise this Process, the more intuitive you will become. Parents can learn to use this Inner-Child Journey to help them better understand their child's complex and often hard to decipher communication. Hear the voice of your Inner Child, and you learn to *get* what your actual child is trying to tell you; as if you are hearing her *from the inside*. Now you are far better equipped to respond: not to the projections your mind creates about your child, but to what your child needs in actuality.

There's more. When a parent undergoes a healing experience, children pick up on this immediately. Even when we don't know it, a moment of growth transmutes our thoughts and feelings, bringing about a host of involuntary body shifts. The way we look at our children and the tone of our voice are no longer the same. The change may be subtle or it may be remarkable. Our children immediately feel this; their senses tell them something about us is different—even if they cannot put their finger on it. Bodies communicate with bodies through a simultaneous profusion of multisensory cues that fly below the radar of conscious attention. We are changed by each other's changes.

The flow-on effects of our healing and growth are beyond our control, and it's precisely because of the spontaneous and involuntary nature of our changed demeanour that our children know we are genuine; they trust us and they accompany us to our new space.

Never underestimate how accurately our children sense our shifting inner states, our moments of heart opening and release. Like one weather system affecting another, they change with us. They relax, they let go, they open-up and listen to us a little more; our peace becomes theirs.

In my parenting groups I have seen a roomful of babies jointly settle into contentment when one parent moved through a Process, shed a tear or two and felt healed by the emotional release and the group support. Just as our children are susceptible to our stress, they are equally absorbent of our wellness. This energetic contagion can be so powerful, that at times babies and little children can catch serenity from us without direct touch or a spoken word.

Your Inner Child connection can be immensely helpful when you need to set boundaries with your child, when you find yourself having to say 'no'. Once you have come to empathise with the nature of your child's desire—no matter how 'irrational' their desires might have seemed at first—your 'no' will sound and feel quite different.

It's one thing to limit your child's behaviour, such as putting a stop to more sugary sweets, more screen time, or the rough treatment of a sibling. It's quite another thing to be judgemental of your child for the fact of *wanting*. Here lies the difference between saying 'no', and saying 'hell, no!' When our 'no' is abrupt and without consideration for our child's experience, we are usually met with resistance.

The 'no' that comes with validation for our child's right to have a need or a desire, is a 'no' to which he is far more likely to listen.

The Inner Child Process puts us in our child's shoes. We relive a little of our own childish longing, and learn to see ourselves in the child we interact with. Our children more readily accept the boundaries we assert when they can sense that we are on their side.

In other words, they can better handle us saying 'no' to behaviour when we can say 'yes' to the emotion that was driving it. This kind of understanding cannot be conjured or faked. It can only come from our connection with our own childhood feelings and longings.

Television Antics

At the tail end of a TV viewing marathon, a boy nags his dad to let him stay up later and watch one more show. His father is well aware of the detrimental effects of screen-time overuse, but he has fond memories of his own childhood indulgences: 'Lost in Space' and 'Land of the Giants', his favourite after-school series. He remembers the magic of these shows, how fervently he anticipated each episode, as well as how crushed he felt if ever he had to miss one.

With these feelings close to the surface, the father can easily empathise with his boy's bottomless excitement for extended viewing hours. For the sake of his son's health and wellbeing, the father sticks to his guns and says 'no'.

At the same time, he assures his son that he knows only too well how he feels and that he understands his disappointment. He was once a boy too, in love with his heroes and their fantastic adventures.

Feeling met by his father's validation, the boy tolerates his disappointment; though not without a passing grumble. Empowered by his father's respect, he more willingly acquiesces to wise parental guidance.

> *Our children listen to us much better when we have listened to them. And we listen to our children far better when we know how to listen to our own Inner Child.*

The gains for your child do not stop there. Inner Child work helps you to differentiate what is yours from what is your child's—what is true for you from what is true for your child.

The vital function of *differentiation* deserves a little explaining. At times we might worry unnecessarily for our child because we imagine he might be feeling something alike to what we most dreaded when we were his age. When our own pain has been triggered, we are all prone to forgetting that, for instance, our child's boredom may be different from ours, that a moment of loneliness might affect him differently to how we once felt—that his fear may not necessarily bite the way it did us.

Our children may have inner resources quite different from those we had as children—especially if they have had a more emotionally secure start in life than we did. Inner Child Journeying helps us disentangle what is ours from what is theirs.

Whose Pain Is It?

Cassie felt devastated as she watched over the preschool fence while her 4-year-old daughter Angie played silently, all alone. Unknown to her, Angie was in fact quite content with her own company. But that's not what Cassie thought she saw.

Cassie's Inner Child Journey helped her reconnect with the acute loneliness she had often felt as a pre-schooler. The brief revisit to her early days at school helped Cassie distinguish her own pain-memory, triggered by seeing Angie playing alone, from Angie's actual experience.

Speaking with Angie's teachers some time later, they confirmed that Angie was in fact quite unperturbed in her own space, fulfilled with her own company. Cassie was able to verify this further, much to her relief, by watching Angie more closely.

Cassie's Inner Child connection allayed her fears and prevented her from becoming overly protective.

When our own past gets in the way, it is just as common for us to *under-respond* as it is for us to *over-react*. Painful experiences in early life are sometimes covered by an emotional scar that can leave us desensitised to our own feelings. This can in turn desensitise us to our own children's messages.

Like Father—Like Son?

Alex started drinking when he was 15 years old. Sometimes he even invited his friends home in the afternoon where they would practise mixing cocktails of increasing strength.

Alex's father, Liam, knew about all the drinking, but said very little and largely ignored the son's bingeing. Liam rationalised his passivity, telling himself, 'This is what teenagers do, they just need to get it out of their system—to work it out for themselves.' This father was ignoring his own deepest concerns, while Alex continued abusing liquor without guidance or boundaries.

Liam's Inner Child Journey helped him see that his rationalisations were little more than a cover over feelings of abject helplessness. His own father, also an abuser of alcohol, had been remote and abandoning. As a teenager, Liam had felt utterly lost and angry at the world. Growing up, he had forgotten how badly he'd once wished for a strong male presence in his life, a supportive elder who could help ground his adolescent impulsivity. He had suffered much for the lack of a loving structure.

Liam needed to connect with the anguish of his youth—to give a name to his loss—so he could recognise that Alex was now in real trouble and needing his fatherly involvement.

In summary, sometimes we project onto our children what are in fact our own Inner Child needs. The Inner Child Process can help us to differentiate ourselves from our children, freeing them from our projections—so we can give them what *they* need—not what we once needed.

At other times, we fail to see that our children need our help, and that we can be desensitised to their plight.

The Inner Child Process can help us awaken to the tenderness and naiveté of childhood so that we can become more attuned and responsive to our children. Further, bringing to consciousness the vulnerability we felt as children puts a powerful brake on the human tendency to blindly pass on what was done to us. In all these ways and more, each time we listen to the Child that lives within us, we become better at listening to the child we are raising.

The greatest parenting method of all is to regulate our own feelings. This does not mean always having to remain calm. Healthy self-regulation involves the appropriate expression of all our feelings—with ownership of our emotions instead of blaming our children for how we feel. It creates the internal space that enables us to be empathic listeners. Our willingness to cultivate our own emotional intelligence has a cascade effect on our children; they grow as we grow.

Benefits for You

Sometimes even the most painful and protracted family conflict can point the way to that place inside you that is crying out for healing—a deep emotional need that had been long buried and forgotten. There can be immense relief in the discovery that a painful situation might have a larger purpose—that perhaps it contains a gift. But the path to healing is not guaranteed and requires a little persistence, some risk and the willingness to learn new things. The Inner Child Process offers a framework for moving forward, for the benefit of your emotional health and wellbeing.

Emotional health is intertwined with relationship health. This Process takes you deep into the realm of the heart, so sharing it with a partner or in a group can be a beautifully moving experience. The innocence and raw emotionality of the Inner Child magnetises compassion and engenders a most soulful depth of interpersonal contact. I have been awed by the trust and the intimacy that it generates among participants in workshop settings. A palpable sense of human family pervades the space as we get to know the Child who lives in each of us. Some people's stories would rock your soul. Your own heartfelt stories are likely to move others. I know of few rituals that can so evocatively unify people. Many barriers are lowered and new tribes are created with the sharing of childhood story.

The value of becoming more open to ourselves and to each other cannot be quantified—it can only be directly experienced. In this context we realise that parenting means much more than raising a child. Parenting grows us—if we let it.

There is gold hidden inside the tests our children bring us and we can be grateful to them for this. Parenting—and indeed all work with children—pushes us to the edge of ourselves, and dares us to jump. Children can trigger in us greater depths of emotion—from agony to elation—than we have ever felt before. The pain, the madness and the joy of parenting make us more real, more human, more available. Parenting prises us open if we let it, making room for deeper and more mature friendships.

Childhood is meant to end, but the positive qualities of child-likeness are not supposed to leave us. Life intends us to retain the vital faculties that children so beautifully express—well into our old age. Human suffering so often results from the repression of our most valuable child-like qualities. But the gifts of our Inner Child are liberated for use if we dare to remove the barriers imposed through enculturation, shaming, punishment and neglect.

We are all the poorer when robbed of the child-like faculties that are our birthright. If we are fortunate enough to retain them (or determined enough to reclaim them), these qualities enrich us and empower our work for the rest of our lives.

Babies possess a capacity for ineffable, delicious bliss. They see a world of wonder, without judgement.

Toddlers are endowed with a fathomless well of uncontainable joy, tireless play and untamed laughter.

I love the fierce capacity for friendship and loyalty that school-aged children display—their indomitable spirit of discovery and their stubborn persistence when they set their minds on a goal.

With adolescence comes the disposition for delicious romance, the fearless spirit of adventure, the raging fire for change and a motherlode of defiance to hurl at archaic customs and prejudices that no longer serve anyone. The young are the frontline of audacity when social change is urgently called for. Their strengths can also be our strengths when we tune in to our Inner Child and our Inner Adolescent.

Evolution intends that we continue to draw from our babylike, childlike and youthful capacities whenever we need to—throughout life. Being the full span of ourselves is what helps us become self-actualised individuals and in turn give our community the best that is within us.

Our Inner Child does not know when to give up. Whenever she feels hurt, frustrated or incomplete, she will nag us and tug at our sleeve relentlessly until she is finally heard. No Inner Child will accept being left behind. Whether it is through conflict with others, illness or mishap; when we neglect our inner voice, Life seems to find a way to chaff at us without letup. The aggravating 'problem' persists until we finally listen and give the Child Within what is rightfully hers.

Some of our most adaptive faculties—including curiosity, wonder and awe— spring directly from our child-likeness. The essence of child-like traits is vital for the thriving of our species. Science, engineering and exploration could not exist without people's insatiable thirst to see what is under that rock, to pull things apart and see how they work, to discover what lies beyond that ocean, behind those mountains. The kind of playfulness that children so freely indulge fuels the creative potential that has driven human progress for millennia.

Only when we let go of old rules and limitations so we can play like a child, can we become infinitely inventive. Now we can imagine the unimaginable, boundlessly design new solutions, produce divine music and sublime art. Without an open channel to the Child Within humanity would have been lost.

In a child's game there is much grit, often to the point of obsession. You need only consider the litany of injuries and embarrassments a child racks up to master a skateboard, ride a horse or play an instrument in public, to know exactly what I mean. The youthful spirit of 'never say never' gives us the undefeatable perseverance by which we master the difficult and overcome the insurmountable.

The ability to laugh like children preserves our sanity in dark times. Without childishness we get stuck, depressed and angry, even our physiological health deteriorates. To lose the Inner Child is to lose ourselves. But when we play at life we live longer, love more deeply and bring more sunshine to the world around us.

The true luminosity of Life is obscured by our accumulated perceptual guard. So it is no coincidence that the world's diverse wisdom traditions all invite us to be as children again. Undeniably, something alluring radiates from us all when we unfetter the natural, spontaneous warmth we once evinced as guileless children.

What intrigues me most is that much-reported ecstatic experience that befalls people—of every language, across the ages—when for an uncharacteristic moment we suspend our jaded, adult way of seeing things, and look outward as freshly and innocently as a baby would.

Spirituality and child-likeness seem irrevocably linked. Little by little, as we free ourselves from our ossified perceptions, we become sensitised to the interconnectedness of all beings—a blissful and peace-inducing state of awareness. I believe that far too many of us sorely miss this way of seeing. Perhaps we are lost, and want to come home.

What if childhood is a rehearsal for some of the most vital strengths required for human thriving? What if it is part of evolution's master plan that our children trigger us again and again until we reclaim what we have lost—that they poke and prod us until we fulfil what remains unfulfilled in us?

What if it is part of evolution's master plan that our children trigger us again and again until we reclaim what we have lost—that they poke and prod us until we fulfil what remains unfulfilled in us?

In one way or another, we have all distanced ourselves from some aspects of the child that dwells within. We suppress, disavow or entirely forget the parts of us that were punished, shamed, ignored, neglected, exploited or simply not helped to develop.

Although these aspects of our natures might be buried temporarily, they are never entirely gone. Our Inner Child Journey is about calling these parts of ourselves home. The happiest, most self-responsible and most fulfilled adults I have known are those whose Inner Child is never too far away.

Perhaps we can come to accept that the children in our lives bring us needed provocation so we can be reconciled with ourselves. I wonder if we might learn to welcome the difficulties our children and our students bring us. Without knowing it or consciously intending it, they push us to become whole again.

CHAPTER 3

Building-block concepts

If the Inner Child Process were a house, our key building-block concepts would be its foundation and frame. Reading about each of these concepts will do more than prepare you for using this Process; it might also prove to be an enlightening self-discovery tour in itself.

As you read about each of these key concepts, pause to reflect how they might apply to you personally. I have provided some anecdotes along the way; short vignettes to illustrate how the phenomena described here commonly apply in people's lives. I have also provided some simple exercises designed to help you learn more about yourself, your inner world, and how the building-block concepts apply to you personally.

The Bodymind

I have borrowed this term from psychologist Ken Dychtwald, PhD,[8] as it most adequately expresses my belief that the ideas of a human body and an independent human mind are a false dichotomy. Body-oriented (or somatic) psychotherapists have known this for decades. Today brain science is continually finding more evidence that nothing happens in the mind without it also happening in the body, and vice versa. Our constructs of 'body' and 'mind' are really just two aspects of one entity.

We have become so used to separating the body and mind in our day-to-day thinking, that Western dialogue nearly always treats them separately. But the mind and the body are no more extricable from each other than waves are from water.

Our bodies have their own way of thinking—quite different from the thoughts that we seem to hear inside our heads. The thoughts that occupy our ordinary awareness are those that are couched in language; we refer to these as our 'self-talk'. We seem to 'hear' these thoughts as *voices*. Ordinary consciousness also includes imagery, as if there is a screen inside our heads on which a movie is projected. Those are the audiovisual streams of thought processed by the brain's frontal lobes. These thoughts pass through our minds slowly enough that our ordinary attention can capture and view them. While this is going on, deeper thoughts emerge from the emotional centres of our nervous system. These thoughts are generated faster and more powerfully than the thoughts arising at the frontal lobes. The language of these thoughts is the language of emotion. This is our emotional mind.

Our emotional responses are generated in the limbic system, at the core of the head-brain—in concert with the neural cells that reside in the heart (the heart-brain) and in the lining of the intestines (the enteric brain). It is no accident that we speak about heart-felt feelings and gut feelings there is a biological basis to these expressions.

This complex system that powers our emotional life is usually dominant over the sequential and rational thinking system in the frontal lobes of the head-brain. First we feel, and then we think—according to neuroscientists, Lewis, Amini and Lannon, authors of *A General Theory of Love*.[9] In their words, 'A person cannot direct his emotional life in the way he bids his motor system to reach for a cup', and, 'Emotional life can be influenced, but it cannot be commanded.'[10]

The thinking that powers our choices, our longings, the many twists and turns of our lives and who we fall in love with is primarily emotional; it is the bodymind thinking super-rapidly according to the sum-total of our memories. The emotional centres of our neurobiology inform the frontal lobes of the head-brain; the slow thinker. The frontal lobes adroitly rationalise and filter a decision we have already made on emotional grounds. More often than is justified, our so-called 'rational' mind gets the credit for our beliefs and actions, when in fact we are largely driven by emotion, and emotional memory. It's often said that we should not let the heart rule the head, but unless we can re-wire ourselves, we have little say in that matter. Far from being a cause for concern, this is a welcome discovery. To begin with, it explains why emotional intelligence appears to be the most important asset to our success in every aspect of life.

Our wisdom depends on our ability to listen deeply to what the bodymind is saying—the whole body does the thinking. This means we need to pay close attention to the sensations and emotions that arise in our bodies, and validate the messages our feelings bring us. To influence our destiny, we need to work with our emotions. Healing cannot take place simply by working with our conscious thoughts. Since the mind is really a bodymind, to change our minds we must change our emotions. The Inner Child Process offers a developmental approach to changing how we feel and think.

Neuroception

The term 'neuroception' is a combination of 'neurological' and 'perception', coined by neuropsychologist and professor of psychiatry at the University of Illinois, Stephen Porges, PhD.[11] It explains why most of our instant perceptions and reactions seem to be outside our immediate control, as they involve deep and primitive brain regions that operate beneath conscious thought. You could say that our neurology perceives the world first, prepares a reaction, and informs our conscious mind later. And this spontaneous neuroceptive response can be highly conditioned by the formative experiences of our early lives.

If you have ever been in a situation that called for immediate action, when you would have been well advised to leap before you look, and not the other way around, then you will have no trouble understanding why our body's capacity for neuroception is so adaptive—crucial in fact. Neuroception—and the emotional and behavioural reactions that it gives rise to—is powerful because it has been critical for our survival on this unpredictable planet.

However, it becomes increasingly problematic or maladaptive when the after-effects linger long after the original stimulus has passed. But here is where the brain's frontal lobes come in handy. With the right information and a little training, the conscious and rational mind can come to the rescue—once it has learned how to liberate us from obsolete, out-dated or inappropriate neuroceptions.

Snake in the Grass

Walking in Sydney's eucalypt forest as a child, I saw an Eastern Brown snake lunge at my friend Gary a few yards ahead of me and narrowly miss biting his forearm. A bolt of energy shot up my spine and before I knew what was happening, my legs were running helter skelter in the opposite direction. As my body had spun around, I had heard a rustle in the leaves behind me—and I 'knew' the snake was chasing me. I doubt I have sprinted that fast before or since, and I was simply unable to stop until I thought I'd put a football field between me and the reptile. (The Eastern Brown snake is the third most venomous snake in the world. It is aggressive and has been known to give chase and lunge repeatedly when it feels threatened.)

When I came to my senses and ran back to check on him, I was relieved to find Gary safe and well; he had hotfooted in the opposite direction. Neither his nor my number was up that day.

It's quite feasible that our choice-less burst of speed may have saved one or both of our lives. Was the snake in fact chasing me when I heard the rustle? Was it definitely a deadly Eastern Brown? What if I am still here because I did not take the time to look behind me to verify, nor to contemplate my actions? As I said, my legs ran all by themselves and asked for no permission. Neuroception, an ancient evolutionary asset, took care of things that day.

Sometimes our perceptions are so coloured by experience that we can barely see the present at all; we are in fact seeing our past. This effect can feel so real and so convincing that no logic can penetrate to loosen its grasp on us. When we see the past, we react to the past—no wonder human relationships can be so messy.

Our life experience shapes the way we see and understand the world. Instead of seeing the object in front of us, we see a story about that object. That story conditions our visceral responses—how we feel towards the object—and therefore how we react to the object. This process of neuroception happens faster than we can notice. A boy who was once bitten by a dog is automatically repelled by dogs years later. A woman who had gone to boarding school as a child cannot sleep if she has to share a room with a friend. And I once knew a man who felt safest in a wild storm, because as a child, the only time his father would hold him is when thunder and lightning tore through the sky. The dog-and-boy story here is one of danger, the shared-room story is one of oppression, the storm-man's is a tale of love.

Neuroception affords us an adaptive edge in many ways. It can be very helpful for us to get a quick, gut-felt sense of a situation; to accurately perceive the difference between danger and safety. Neuroception is only problematic when it is excessively loaded with history and when it gets in the way of our healthy self-expression or loving interaction. It can be pathological—as with anxiety disorders, phobias or explosive tempers, and as extreme as a psychotic breakdown. But a little bit of this phenomenon affects us all enough to complicate our relationships—and of course this includes our relationships with our children. This gives me pause to think: when do I see my child as his true self, and when do I see in him an extension of my stories ?

Neuroception and the reactions that follow it are automatic, involuntary and unconscious. As Porges explains, '…the neural evaluation of risk does not require conscious awareness'.[12] Understanding that neuroception is rooted in biology can be life-changing, since it demonstrates that even our most bewildering reactions are forgivable, worthy of compassion and respect.

Every one of us can be prone to misreading other's intentions. The memory layer that obscures our perception can cause a parent, for example, to view a toddler's tantrum as a manipulative ploy. Or perhaps a schoolteacher might view a child's assertiveness as a direct assault on her authority. The child who forgets to say 'please' or 'thank you' might be seen as 'rude'.

Each of those visceral responses to children springs from a maladaptive neuroception that is probably untrue about the child, while revealing something important about the childhood history of the perceiver—in other words, the parent or teacher. You could take a rough guess that in childhood, the adults in question felt disempowered, shamed or perhaps too strictly controlled. Their neuroceptions expose a vestigial hyper-alertness to power dynamics in relationships.

You may have heard that our judgements—the conclusions we draw about others, and this includes our children—say much more about us than about the person that we are describing. Today, neuroscience has begun to shed light on how this principle operates in the structure of the human bodymind. Richard Gregory, PhD, former professor of neuropsychology at the University of Bristol, estimated that our perception can, at times, be made up of up to 90 per cent memory and as little as 10 per cent signals from our senses. In a series of audio lectures entitled 'The Neurobiology of We',[13] neuropsychiatrist Daniel Siegel, MD, explains how our sensory perceptions are continually bombarded with a barrage of emotional memory arising from the limbic brain, the brain stem and deeper cortical layers. Humans struggle to see the here-and-now. We tend to smother the world we see around us with past experiences, old feelings and stored emotions.

Our bodyminds remember the sum-total of everything we have ever felt.[14] The body remembers *how* we felt, without necessarily remembering *what* happened; it remembers not only our experiences, but also how we reacted to those experiences.

It has benefitted our survival to retain automatic response-sets, so we can react immediately to the *semblance* of something toxic or threatening. But it benefits our quality of life, our wellbeing and our ability to love and be loved, if we can learn to discern neuroception from perception—to differentiate our past from the present that surrounds us and accordingly to develop new relating skills.

If sometime in our lives we prevailed over stressful times by taking flight or by making a fuss about our distress, we might find ourselves anxiety-prone, struggling to relax our guard even years afterwards. Similarly, if we survive a hostile environment by learning to be aggressive, we might find ourselves stuck in high alert and combat ready thereafter.

Difficult as it is to release these vestigial reactions and the thought patterns that accompany them, we need to come to terms with neuroception because it is integral to the human condition. Today we embrace the idea that children should be seen *and* heard. As parents, teachers and carers, we can get much closer to this goal once we accept that much of what we seem to 'see' and 'hear' is, in fact, our own past.

Today we embrace the idea that children should be seen and heard. As parents, teachers and carers, we can get much closer to this goal once we accept that much of what we seem to "see" and "hear" is, in fact, our own past.

If Looks Could Kill

Having grown up in one of the toughest neighbourhoods of his city, Nikau had survived adolescence by forging a tough-guy persona. Just the daily walk to school meant facing gang-related attack. Abandoning school at the earliest opportunity, he became a gang member himself. In his youth, direct eye contact often signified a threat and could lead to a physical fight.

For many years after Nikau had moved to friendlier climes, this learned battle-readiness was so embedded in his demeanour that he was scarcely aware of it and how it frightened others. His gruff and defensive manner made friendship difficult. On many occasions when someone looked at him with simple curiosity, he would misread the signs and react with suspicion. Neuroception showed him hostility in others' eyes, even when there was none.

Another common example of neuroception involves phobic reactions. Have you ever tried to reason with someone in the throes of a phobic reaction? You probably soon discovered that you were making them more afraid, more isolated, and probably angry with you. Neuroception and the body-flashback (explained below) need our *respect, patience and empathy*. We cannot undo a neuroception, and the reactions that follow it, with a few words of reason. A strong and seemingly inappropriate reaction based on body-memory can at times be underpinned by years of built-up neural networks in brain regions that have re-organised themselves in adaptation to trauma.

Neural wiring cannot be neatly dismissed with a stroke of logic. Releasing yourself from the thoroughly convincing grip of a trauma-related neuroception involves a step-by-step, developmental process. It involves repeated healing experiences to stimulate a reorganisation of the neural connections that sounded the alarm.

Our propensity for seeing the past is embedded in biology, and is therefore not to be trifled with. As Porges explained so well, there is a neurological basis for our most quirky behaviours and ideations.

Without this humanising information, people are too often shamed and given unrealistic expectations. A lack of understanding permits the unkind injunctions we sometimes use against ourselves, and against each other to 'get over it' or to 'let go of the past'. Although most of us can control our *behaviour*, controlling our *emotions* is another matter. Judgement is ruinous and perfectly unhelpful. Ultimately, we do need to find release from our past if we are to be fully present to the moment. Our emotional wellness and our capacity for loving relationships depend on this. But we need a developmental pathway that it is both graduated and kind. Release from neuroception can't happen by merely wishing it so. It takes time, and it requires a careful, step-by-step healing process.

Tunnel Vision

I have felt extremely uncomfortable in enclosed spaces for my whole life. If my destination is not at least 20 floors up, I'd rather take the stairs any day. This claustrophobia flared up quite seriously for me in the early 1990s. For the first time, I could not even bear to drive my car through a tunnel. This was particularly bad timing since a new tunnel had just opened as an alternate crossing of Sydney Harbour. In a city riven in half by a large body of water, not being able to drive in a tunnel was a major handicap.

I tried to force myself to face this alone, and each time my car neared the entrance I was overcome by the most unbearable panic. The dark, gaping mouth of the tunnel would suddenly become the entrance to an ever-narrowing and ever-deepening pit. No exit! Each time I circled and made a new attempt, my heart would race, my breathing came in gasps, and my vision would narrow to a point. Just metres from the tunnel mouth, my arms would seize the wheel and veer my car off the target, across the lanes.

A freeway with cars zooming all around is no place to do self-therapy, and in the interest of public safety, I gave up. I was trapped in neuroception, seeing some horrific memory ahead of me, and no amount of common sense would dissolve the body-memory that told me I was driving into an asphyxiating death trap.

Psychotherapists would probably suppose that my phobia is a body-memory of birth trauma—a tempting guesstimate since it certainly has all the trappings. In this instance, my Inner Child work did not yield an absolute certainty on the root causes.

However, even without exact clarity about a source trauma, I did connect with a deep sense of terror from very early in my life, a time before language and narrative memory. The terror was coupled with a paralysing aloneness with no comforting on offer and the foreboding of impending doom.

Since this had a distinct flavour of earliest infancy, I sensed that the way through might involve being warmly held in my terror by someone I trusted. Baby steps for baby fears. Perhaps the most difficult challenge would be to allow myself to receive this.

Some weeks later, I was in the backseat of my car, with a good friend who had agreed to be the driver (babies should not be at the wheel). My wife, Linda, was sitting with me as I lay curled up with my head across her lap. I had a strong sense that my head needed to be cradled, so she placed one hand on it. My friend in front had agreed to drive us into the Sydney Harbour Tunnel, no matter how I felt.

The moment the driver called out that we had crossed the point of no return, I felt a ringing in my ears—a flash of utter despair. And then surrender. I shut my eyes tight and my hand gripped Linda's knee. For the first time in my history of claustrophobic episodes, it felt safe to feel unsafe.

Halfway through the longest tunnel journey in the universe, I felt able to open my eyes and look out the window. I felt myself move in and out of numbness, and a tolerable edge of panic. Moments later the unimaginable happened: I began to feel traces of enjoyment. An entirely unfamiliar sensation of pleasure at being in a dark tunnel with billions of litres of water just metres above.

We chose the tunnel rather than the bridge for the homeward journey. This time I sat up, eyes wide open all the way, almost exhilarated at the freedom to enjoy what had previously been an ordeal.

My next trip through the Harbour Tunnel some days later saw me at the wheel and alone in my car again, tense but also trusting the process.

Today, the phobic response has not completely left me, but it has never gone back to its most debilitating levels. A new body-memory has become the reference point; one of comfort and togetherness in the face of fear, and also one of pleasure and triumph. A carefully crafted new experience has given me new and freeing body-memories, and my neuroception at the entrance to tunnels has been transformed.

Exercise 1: 'I'm not Crazy! This Is a Neuroception!'

Think of a time when you were seized by an emotional reaction that felt beyond your control. It might have been a sudden feeling or discomfort that seemed unrelated to what was going on around you. It might have been an inexplicable anxiety. Perhaps you over-reacted, or even under-reacted to a certain situation.

Pay close attention to that experience as a neuroception, and even if it seems irrational and baffling, take careful note of what it appears to be saying about the place you are in, or the people you are with. When your feelings don't seem to make sense about the present, they do make sense about a past experience that is being evoked.

Have you ever felt this kind of reaction before? Is it familiar?

Do you see a pattern in the kind of conditions that trigger this neuroception?

Even if your surroundings cannot account for the reaction, what in your environment might be acting as a *reminder* of an earlier time that really did make you feel this way?

How might your reaction to that present moment serve to alert you to a deeper issue? Something important that has really upset you in the past?

Can you validate these emotions, even if they seem out of place for now?

What might have helped you in the original situation?

Does this give you any clues about what might help you to feel settled when these feelings are triggered again?

The Inner Child Process is designed to help us unravel problematic neuroceptions by getting to the roots of the emotional memory from which they spring and finding a developmental pathway to a more open state.

How does our neuroception affect our relationships with our children? All too often children are judged and labelled. They are commonly said to be selfish, naughty, lazy, obstinate, hyperactive, rude, devilish, even angelic and a thousand more tags (both positive and negative) that only limit our understanding and block our connection with them.

As with other examples of neuroception, our judgements about children tend to pop up quite automatically. Our bodyminds produce both positive and negative neuroceptions about our children—about ourselves and in fact about *all* people—repeatedly.

When faced with challenging behaviours in our children, those of us who were shamed as children are likely to judge our children as shameful. Those who were ignored are prone to judge them as unworthy of attention, and those who lived in fear might see children as overly fragile. Neuroception and the imagery it casts is not always that simple and straightforward, but it does redirect our parenting choices according to our unexamined past.

Evolution has elaborately programmed our bodyminds to refer to body-memory when trying to make sense of a challenging present. When we see the world through history-coloured glasses, this is because an emotion-laden body-memory has been triggered at the neurological level. I hope you are beginning to realise that there is therefore no cause to judge yourself for being judgemental! What the judger needs is self-compassion and self-understanding.

This can only begin once we become honestly willing to look inwardly, to examine and unpack our neuroceptions, to trace their origins, and thus to disentangle our internal reality from our external, present-moment reality. The world around us and the people in our lives begin to take on a very different appearance—as if they are unveiled for the first time—when we free our vision from old interpretations.

Since neuroception and body-memory so deeply pervade our perception and behaviour, the most empowering and freeing thing we can do for ourselves is to take an interest in our emotional histories, and in the continuing unfoldment of our emotional intelligence. I think that these discoveries about memory and perception point to something very reassuring for all of us. It means that the harsh self-judgements so many of us suffer from are little more than shadows of painful body-memories. The toxic shame we carry is not real; it is a memory. Many of our long-held fears do not accurately represent the world that surrounds us in the present; they too are memory. Our feelings never lie to us, but they often speak to us of real, past experience; rather than present-day reality.

As we let this discovery sink in, we find the key to our liberation from a great deal of what ails us in human relations. The moment we awaken to the intrusive nature of our neuroception, our spirit breathes a sigh of relief. In this watershed moment we are freed to become more of ourselves, and people around us— especially our children—are freed from our narrowed view of them.

So, what about free will? Are we trapped in our bodies, destined to be endlessly confused by a ceaseless stream of body-memory? There is always an exit. But to leave a room, you can't leave any old way; you can't walk out through a wall. You need to know where the door is, and how to use a key. Then you can have freedom of movement, and enjoy coming and going.

Humanity has developed a broad array of methods to release our bodyminds from the hold of our past; meditation is one of the better-known examples. Body-oriented psychotherapy, hypnosis and cognitive-behavioural therapy are but a few of the offerings in the marketplace of methods available for gaining freedom from our histories.

Inner Child work is a particularly powerful method at our disposal. It helps us make sense of the roots of our reactions, and then it lights a path for a developmental way forward.

Daniel Siegel, internationally renowned professor of psychiatry and director of the Mindsight Institute explains, 'Research reveals that the more coherent a narrative we have of our own attachment issues in childhood, the more we make

sense of how our early life experiences have shaped us—the mor
children will have a secure attachment to us.'[15]

In other words, understanding our history can free us from it, and in turn,
free our children from it. Denial, and the avoidance of our history places us at
risk of reliving it, repeating it and passing it on to the next generation.

> *Understanding our history can free us from it, and in turn, free our children from it. Denial, and the avoidance of our history places us at risk of reliving it, repeating it and passing it to the next generation.*

Projection

Projection is a basic phenomenon of human relations that was first identified by
Sigmund Freud. The understanding of projection has been continually updated
and refined and today this term has become commonplace in our day-to-day talk.

Projection refers specifically to the mental imagery and descriptive thoughts
we hold about others, tinged by our own internal associations, expectations and
past experiences. Our projections about others can be compared to an internally
created image superimposed over an object that we are looking at, thus altering
the way it appears to us. In the same way, we may imbue another person with
presupposed qualities that have little to do with them.

What we see are replays of people, events, thoughts, feelings and wishes that
spring from our own past. We look at life through personal-history-coloured
glasses. What we project onto others says little about them, but reflects much
about our personal life experiences and how we have processed these.

It can be surprising to discover how frequently we view people in our lives
through the lens of our own emotional history. We think we see the present, yet
we see the past, or a combination of the two. The first step to freeing our vision
and gaining clarity is realising that our internal image of others is distorted.

Neuroception involves a complex combination of emotional and sensory
(bodily) reactions mixed with the ideation that accompanies them. Projection is
simply the set of ideas that accompany neuroception and a far more familiar and
commonly used term. We all project continually—and we can't help doing so. As
Porges explains, this is because neuroception operates automatically; it's a
neurological reflex.

Although we can't seem to switch off the mind's projector, we can certainly wake up and realise that we are watching an old 'movie'. Naming the illusion is what frees us, and the people around us, from the illusion's grip.

Our projections are multimedia; they involve mental imagery, feelings, and verbal statements we say to ourselves. We tend to judge ourselves and others as 'good' versus 'bad', 'positive' versus 'negative'. This part of our mind likes to flatten the world into a one-dimensional space that loses depth of meaning and flow.

Our judgemental mind freezes our image of people into the illusion of predictable patterns. Predictability might offer us some comfort and security in times of anxiety and confusion, but it comes at a cost.

When we lock in our projected image of others, our responses to them become automated, inflexible and stuck. If we don't regularly challenge our own projections, growth becomes stultified or impossible. A heart-to-heart connection with others is blocked, the wonder and the fascination that we could feel for one another becomes like a distant signal made scratchy by interference.

Most of the problems we have with relationships spring from our projections because our perceptions shape the way we act. Perception is like the viewfinder on a camera; it determines the frame through which we see and interpret the world around us. Once you have framed your child as *defiant*, for instance, you are more likely to respond by trying to restrain her behaviour, or to react with annoyance. That will impact your openness towards your child and affect your ability to listen and understand her motivation. In that moment your projection becomes your prison, sharply narrowing your range of responses. Projection keeps us all stuck.

Never underestimate how convincing our projections can seem. At times, we can feel utterly certain that a person is one way, only to be surprised or even shocked to discover that they are quite different. I'd like a dollar for every person who has exclaimed, 'You are not the person I married!'

Sometimes our projections can hold a kernel of truth, but by giving us an incomplete picture, they lead us astray. Being spot-on about one aspect of another person does not mean you have the full picture in all its depth—and that may seriously limit how you behave towards that person.

You might have a deep hunch that someone in your workplace is a petty thief, for instance. Later you discover that you were right all along. Yes, he is a thief, but you know nothing about why he steals. Our behaviour towards another changes once we look beyond our assumptions. All too often, our negative projections lead us to attack another person—with our thoughts, the way we look at them, with our words or with our deeds—when a strong self-protective boundary would have sufficed.

Our positive projections can be just as problematic as our negative. In both cases, our ensuing decisions and behaviours are dubitable. A positive projection can be like going outside on a cold rainy day dressed for warm sunshine. 'Positive thinking', the much-lauded elixir of self-help and motivational coaches, can be little more than a disabling trap.

With rose-coloured glasses affixed under our brows we can walk off many a precipice. Think of all the people who have remained in abusive relationships despite years of injury, assuring themselves over and over that they can 'see the good' in their partners. Many more place their partners on a pedestal and refuse to see them as flawed and vulnerable persons. Multitudes are caught in the thrall of charismatic cult leaders, 'healers' and gurus, rationalising their most violent and duplicitous behaviours. Celebrity itself is a cult; we idealise human beings and make stars out of them. We exalt leaders as saviours, we romanticise our heroes—sometimes even our villains. I am not sure that the sum-total of humanity's negative projections outnumbers the positive.

Adults can sometimes erupt in a blaze of positivity and children don't escape their elders' propensity to gush. A parent who is convinced that their child is an 'angel' who'd never hurt anyone might fail to set strong boundaries or make firm demands for respect. Sometimes adults can be blind to the struggles—perhaps even the aggressiveness—of a child who is perpetually viewed as a *wunderkind*.

Another example: I often hear early childcare workers say of a child that she has had a great day because there was 'no crying'. This lack of expression is anything but a complete picture. In fact, strong evidence suggests that some children become very quiet and hold their emotions deep inside when they feel particularly unsafe and bereft. These children will show alarmingly high levels of the stress hormone cortisol even though nobody detected their despair. Inside, they were yearning for their parents to come and pick them up, or at least for someone familiar to give them a cuddle. What the carers should be looking for as evidence of wellbeing is the full range of emotionality; including joy, mirth, warmth, playfulness and shared affection. The quiet child is not necessarily the contented and secure child. All projections are disempowering—that is, until we become aware that we are projecting, we fail to open to opportunities for a truer connection.

Projection

Common examples of projections, and how they become problematic, are listed in Table 1.

Table 1: Examples of Commonly held Projections

Projection	Resulting behaviour towards the child
They are just trying to get attention'	We turn our backs
The 'good baby'	We praise and reward—*conditionally*
The child who is 'so fragile'	We overprotect
The baby who 'tries to rule the house'	We ignore
The 'little tyrant', the 'terrible twos'	We judge, we shame, we punish
The child who is a 'cry baby'	We shame
The 'little angel'	We overindulge
Tantrums are 'misbehaviour'	We punish or reject
The 'lazy' child	We coerce and pressure
The little grown-up	We over-empower and praise
The wise child or 'old soul'	We make unrealistic demands
The precocious, genius child	We over-expect, put-on pressure
'Boys will be boys'	We set no boundaries
The 'rebellious' teenager	We condemn and judge
'Oppositional defiant disorder'	We 'treat' the 'patient', employ manipulative behaviour modification tactics, and prescribe drugs

Many people understand the principle of projection well; we have come to accept it as a reality of human life. But how often do we apply this knowledge to ourselves? When we hear ourselves thinking, 'This child is naughty' or 'That child is lazy', do we ask ourselves what that projection tells us about ourselves? When we hear ourselves thinking, 'That child is a saint', do we ask ourselves to what degree it reflects our wishful thinking; our need to idealise? The point is not to chide ourselves for projecting, but to understand that the content of every projection holds vital clues about the inner world of the projector, while skewing or narrowing the image in front of us.

How do we identify our projections? How do we know our judgements about our children (and generally about other people) are not accurate representations of them? Shouldn't we trust our hunches, our gut instincts? How do we learn to tell a projection from true detection?

On the one hand, we may never know with perfect certainty whether our vision is a true intuition or the biased result of a triggered body-memory, at any given moment.

On the other hand, we needn't invalidate our every perception; sometimes we make a good call and see things as they are.

The point is to ask ourselves honest questions about the source of our perceptions. It never hurts and it often leads to enriched self-knowledge, wisdom and self-acceptance. The more we explore the historical source of our perceptions and reactions, and the more we uncover how our childhood has shaped our minds, the easier it is to differentiate between our projections and our true gut-feelings.

I have seen this ability grow for countless parents; the rewards are abundant and satisfying. A parent's willingness to self-observe and to do Inner Child work is a major factor behind co-operative, empathic, vibrant and transformative family relationships.

Our children don't need us to be perfect; they need us to be honest with ourselves and with them. They feel most deeply cared about when they see that we are willing to allow our perceptions to evolve.

Food Battles

Whenever Sylvia's daughter Elena refused her food, Sylvia thought her 'rude'. At 6 years of age, Elena could be quite forthright about her varying appetites, and at times blunt about what she did not like on a given day. For some time Sylvia had taken it personally each time Elena blurted her displeasure at something on her plate. When Sylvia projected that Elena was being 'bad-mannered', a battle of wills would ensue; one defending her pride and the other her right to self-assertion and choice.

A much easier partnership developed around mealtimes when Sylvia began to include Elena in choosing what they would eat, providing a little flexibility to accommodate Elena's shifting nutritional needs. This required Sylvia to see past her own projections about 'rudeness'—an overlay from her own childhood—when faced with Elena's inexpertly-voiced grumbles and druthers.

Over-attached

Even though Samara was an exhausted young mother, she refused to allow anyone else to look after her 1-year-old daughter, even for brief periods. A devoted reader and practitioner of 'attachment parenting', Samara insisted that her baby must remain closely attached to her day and night, lest she be traumatised by premature separation. Seeing how terribly drained Samara was, her friends would sometimes plead with her to allow them to care for her baby while she took some time out to rest and renew herself. But Samara clung to her child; the thought of parting with her would flood her with anxiety. So, while meeting all of what she thought were her baby's 'attachment needs', Samara got progressively more run-down and morose.

Samara had overlooked advice that babies thrive on multiple attachments to familiar, trusted and warmly responsive individuals. She had also omitted her baby's need for a mother who is well supported and able to take pleasure from their time together. It eventually became clear to Samara that she had been projecting her own anxieties onto her child. Little wonder, her own time as a baby had been filled with insecurities—a wound that remained unhealed and unresolved. Although she remembered very little of her early childhood, she was nonetheless afflicted by it. Her own unconscious attachment needs, rather than her baby's, were driving her maternal clinging.

Without a working (and expanding) understanding about how our childhood experiences have impacted upon us, we risk parenting from our own blind spots and acting out our unresolved childhood issues on our children. In my experience, at least half of all childrearing predicaments, and half the psychological afflictions that children carry, are the result of unexamined emotional wounds in the parents.

Exercise 2: Zeroing-in on Projection

Think of one of your children's behaviours that you find most difficult.

Listen closely to the voices in your mind, and pay special attention to the things you say to yourself internally about your child's behaviour. Notice if labels or descriptive words about your child pop up in your mind.

In particular, pay attention to your most automatic and spontaneous thoughts about your child and his or her behaviour—rather than the thoughts you would *like* to have, or the thoughts you think you *should* have. Try being as honest as you can be with yourself about this.

You might also like to note any automatic things you hear yourself thinking about you as a parent, about how you see yourself managing the behaviour you find difficult in your child. Do you sometimes hear, even if only fleetingly, your mind giving you labels about *you*?

Write down these automatic descriptive thoughts about your child and/or about you. Perhaps you could even share and discuss these confidentially with your partner or a trusted friend.

Do these automatic thoughts sound familiar to you? Where and when might you have first heard these kinds of things said, about you, or about another person? Who did you first hear make these particular kinds of remarks?

What is the antidote for projection? Curiosity and some self-examination. All that is required is your genuine interest in peeling back superficial layers and remaining open to what lies beneath. As we take ownership of our projections about our children, two powerful things happen.

First, a healing opportunity opens up for us. The Inner Child Process offers illumination on the pathway through which we can reconnect with lost parts of ourselves.

Secondly, the more you free your mind from projections, the more cleanly you wipe the screen through which you see your child. Even if you think it would not be possible to love your child more than you do now, releasing your projections does bring you closer to your child; you find yourself appreciating your child's essence more deeply. Your intuition sharpens and you begin to understand even your child's most baffling behaviours and emotions. I know of no more powerful tool in a parent's kit, than to take this Inner Journey whenever it is needed.

It is pointless to blame ourselves for the human tendency to project. This process is unstoppable and no one is entirely free of it. You would rightly wonder why it is so universally human to project, given that it can appear so maladaptive. Remember that there is a clear evolutionary purpose to neuroception and the projections it produces. For millions of years our survival has depended on a hair-trigger level of preparedness to react in the face of peril, even if the signs of danger are not perfectly clear. If it looks like a sabre-tooth tiger, run now, ask questions later. The approach-avoid impulses, just like the fight-or-flight impulses, are wired to bypass the reflective region of our brains, at least to begin with.

Stored as implicit memory (a scientific name for emotional memory or body memory), our brains retain the sum-total of our vital experiences, and the strategies that have been most successful in getting us through situations of perceived physical or psychological threat. Life will always present us with situations that demand a quick, automatic and spontaneous response. We need to be able to act with spontaneity, whenever urgent action is demanded. Just as with our automatic, defensive and protective behaviours; projections are generated automatically (see the section on 'neuroception', above). That is why our projections about ourselves and about each other, both negative and positive, flow thick and fast.

So, are we destined to act out against each other based on primordial reactivity? Not at all. Beside our off-the-cuff impulses, Nature has also endowed us with a very powerful balancing tool; the faculty of self-reflection. The ability to cultivate mindfulness is what sets us apart from other species. Self-reflection has evolved in human beings so we can self-examine, absorb new impressions, adapt to new discoveries, deepen our vision, and thus develop new responses. Our Inner Child Process begins by disentangling perception from memory so we can move on and develop new choices.

When do we project? When something or someone in our environment has triggered an old emotion, a body-memory that causes our perceptions to be altered. Let's take a closer look at how these triggers operate.

The 'Trigger'

Many of the feelings we seem to feel *towards* our children are not necessarily entirely *about* our children. And sometimes, some are not about them at all—we have confused the source (see page 40). These feelings are in fact *memories* that arise in us, even when we seem to have forgotten their origins, and they are prompted by our children's behaviour. The child is not the *cause* of what we feel, but the child's behaviour has acted as a *trigger*.

When we are triggered, the feelings that arise are absolutely real and valid but often inappropriate for the context. What has been momentarily confused with present time is the real source of these feelings. While we may think we are reacting to a situation in the present moment, our bodies are re-experiencing something from the past. The *now* has triggered a body-memory from *back then*.

Speaking at a conference in Sydney, psychologist Janina Fisher, PhD,[16] explained the phenomenon of triggering by using fear as the example: 'When emotional memories are triggered, we experience overwhelming feelings, sensations and impulses. For instance, this feeling of danger is misinterpreted as meaning "I am in danger" instead of "I am *remembering* danger".' We tell ourselves, 'I am under threat', instead of 'My body is remembering a past, threatening situation'. In the same way, sometimes we say 'I am offended', when in fact we are reliving an old offence, or 'I am angry' when we are reliving an old frustration. The trigger induces a kind of emotional time travel. Until we awaken to the fact that we have been triggered, the present moment—or someone in it— gets the blame for how we feel.

Why do triggers operate on us the way they do? Emotional memory (implicit memory) is the memory of feelings and bodily sensations, and it works quite differently from narrative memory, which is the audio-visual memory of events that enable us to tell a story about what happened. These two types of memory are organised by different brain regions and therefore can operate independently of one another.[17]

For example, on the one hand you can remember an important event without recapturing any of the emotion that accompanied it. And on the other hand, your body can remember powerful feelings and sensations without any awareness of when and where these feelings sprang from. As Siegel puts it, sometimes we can 'act, feel, and imagine without recognition of the influence of past experience on our present reality'.[18] Little wonder we so often get confused and locked into unnecessary conflicts.

One of the principal features of emotional memory is that it is *state-dependent*. In other words, one bodily or perceptual state is likely to trigger the body-memory of another similar state. Let's look at a few examples.

Say you sit down to join a committee meeting and your chair happens to be lower than everyone else's. You might for a moment, or perhaps longer, be triggered into feeling child-like and disempowered. Entering a physical state in which you are looking up at others around you, your body is triggered into the feeling-state associated with being little. In fact, that is why so often people in authority sit behind a desk. The unspoken objective is to trigger you into feeling somewhat intimidated, disempowered or of lesser social status. The clever device of furniture arrangement exploits the principles of emotional memory by recreating a bodily state similar to being hauled off to the principal's office at school. And most of us know how a sudden noise can trigger panic in a war veteran.

For me, the smell of cinnamon cookies evokes the warmth of being with my German grandmother at Christmas—a happy time of family sharing when the smell of her baking permeated our home. The very same state-dependent mechanism, the smell of hospital disinfectants immediately gives me the heebie-jeebies. Clearly, my body retains no memory associating hospitals with pleasure.

A specific physical position, smell or sound—in fact any bodily or sensory state— can trigger a similar body-memory.

Our interactions or communications with others can also be powerful triggers. Arguably, the most potent triggers of all are our babies and children. Body-memory or body-flashbacks are regularly activated in us due to a similarity between some aspect of our child's behaviour and something impactful that we have witnessed or directly experienced in our past. Any cue from our child; the sound of their voice, a look in their eyes, their little feet … can be enough to evoke a rush of emotion, and much of this emotion has memory content.

Most often the triggered body-memory moves us toward caring; the urge to be protective or playful. Sometimes what is triggered in us is an old pain, old resentments or long forgotten fears; giving rise to negative projections and misaligned parenting responses.

Exercise 3: Body States as Triggers

This exercise explores how different body states or body positions can act as triggers for body memory.

For this simple exercise you will need to work with a partner. Make sure you explain the instructions and the purpose of the exercise clearly to your partner and ask them if they are comfortable to share this experience with you.

Begin by asking your partner to simply stand silently two or three feet in front of you, for a few moments. Then sit on a low stool facing your partner, or crouch on the ground. Slowly and mindfully, lift your face upwards until you are making eye contact with your partner, and for the duration of a few breaths, hold their gaze in silence.

As you do this exercise, pay very close attention to any emotions or bodily sensations that arise in you. What happened to your breathing as your eyes travelled up your partner's body until you met their eyes? Take careful note of all the emotions and sensations you experienced, and the changes to your breathing patterns.

Then gently close your eyes and lower your head, entering your own private inner space for a few moments. Here, pay close attention to any images that come to you spontaneously. What emotions, sensations or images arise when you have entered a body state in which you are looking up at someone?

You might then swap places and repeat the exercise. Then afterwards, share together what you each discovered; you might be surprised what this simple exercise can demonstrate about the powerful effect of postural states on state-dependent body-memory.

Exercise 4: Identifying Triggers

The next time you experience a surge of emotion or a tension in your body while in conversation with another person, take careful note of these emotions and sensations. Ask yourself, 'Could this reaction be (at least in part) a body-memory that has been triggered from my (recent or distant) past?'

When have you previously felt similar feelings in interaction with others?

What about this person and the present interaction might have acted as the trigger? Is it the other person's body language? The expression in their eyes? Their tone of voice? Or perhaps something they said to you?

In what way is the current trigger similar to the original, source-situation?

Note: Often, our bodies remember an emotion or sensation without recalling the accompanying event. Sometimes you may feel that a triggered emotion is only vaguely familiar—as if you have been here before without being able to put your finger on when or how. Let it be OK if you have no explicit recall, but merely a sense of having felt this way sometime before.

Why do our children trigger us so powerfully? Partly because they are so close to us and we are so open to them. But since triggers work via similarities, our child's voice, physical movements, facial expressions and behaviours are extremely potent invocations of all we once felt at their age. The vulnerability and innocence of a child, as much as their wildness and unbridled behaviours, pull us inexorably back to a time when we were the same.

As powerful and universal as this phenomenon is, however, none of us need be imprisoned by triggered reactions and projections, forever destined to recreate and relive our past. Evolution will not settle for a Groundhog Day-type of existence. Whoever said, 'The more things change, the more they stay the same' knew little about human nature—and was probably feeling a little bitter that day. Liberation begins at the very moment we awaken to the trigger and unravel what is memory from what is present-time. By acknowledging that our child has triggered us, we emancipate them from our blame.

This awakening uncovers a pathway for our own healing that would have otherwise remained concealed. It also makes us more effective guides for our children, as we learn to see them instead of our projections about them. We are thus saved from being at the mercy of our projections, and from opting for a behaviour-modification technique that misses the point.

People in Glasshouses

I remember a day when I was 9 years old, hanging out with a friend in one of our neighbourhood streets, when an interesting stone on the ground caught my eye. I stooped to pick it up to examine it more closely, just as an elderly woman happened to be walking by. She suddenly stopped, barked at me to put that stone down, and lectured me about the evils of children throwing stones. I was dumbfounded, since throwing the stone could not have been further from my mind.

She saw in me an intent that did not exist (at least not on that day). Clearly, the elderly woman was immediately triggered by what she was convinced was a threat to public safety. In her view, she had done something good and important. I hate to think what kind of ordeal she must have experienced that left her in such a state of hyper-vigilance.

To Help or not to Help?

A little girl is busily climbing a rope web in a public playground. Her mother sees her child struggle, wobble and waver—though her grip on the ropes remains strong. Startled, the mother rushes to the daughter's aid, gently heaving her to the next level on the climb. The child is thus prevented from finding a way to overcome the difficult moment on her own steam.

A body-memory of danger and injury, stemming from an accident in her own childhood, had been triggered in the mother. She had, with the best intentions, been protective beyond her child's actual need.

Boys Don't Cry

A father sees his little boy, who is playing with friends, start to cry when one of his buddies hurts him. This triggers in the father a body-memory of being shamed for crying when he was a boy of a similar age. The father offers no comfort, ignoring his son. Ashamed of male emotional vulnerability, he does not respond to his son's need for support.

The above examples are not, by any stretch, a sufficient cross-section of the myriad ways in which we are all triggered by our children and by each other. Triggering happens every day, and the themes are as diverse and infinite as the complex life histories of all humanity.

So, we should learn to say, 'let's look at what the child has triggered in me', rather than 'that child *makes* me feel annoyed, exasperated, worried, etc.' Over recent decades, we have begun to say that a child 'presses our buttons'. This is another very apt and useful phrase that acknowledges that we, not the child, are responsible for our emotional reactions. We would not have been so upset by our child's behaviour—or unmoved when their plight warrants our empathic response—if we did not have personal buttons (old wounds) to be pushed in a relevant area.

At this point, I'd like to reiterate that not all of our responses to our children are the result of a triggered body-memory and the projections that ensue. There probably is no more paralysing enterprise than to examine every one of our responses with a fine-tooth comb, looking for traces of neuroception. Not all responses are about the past, and you don't need to drown your spontaneity in a self-analytic morass. Soul-searching, yes; navel-gazing, nooo.

The Inner Child Journey is designed to help you differentiate between *reaction* (to a triggered memory) and *response* (to a real, present situation).

Exercise 5: Tracing Triggers to their Source

Think of some ways that you are triggered by your child, or by children in your care.

Take note of both your over-reactions as well as your under-reactions— that is, when you feel the biggest emotional charge, as well as when you find yourself detached from your child's feelings and emotional needs.

While thinking about each of these triggers and your resulting reactions, ask yourself:

✲ What similar experiences do you have from your own childhood?

✲ How were you treated when you felt or behaved similarly to your child?

Write down the childhood experiences these triggers have highlighted for you.

Consider sharing these discoveries with a trusted friend or counsellor.

Body-memory and the Body-flashback

Narrative memory enables us to tell a story about what happened to us and around us. It helps us—more or less—see a movie of events playing out in order, in the cinema of our minds. Body memory, on the other hand, is quite different from our storyteller memory. It is simply about emotion, feelings and bodily sensations, whether or not these are accompanied by recall of actual events. Our bodies are able to recall everything we have experienced emotionally and physically, independently of narrative recall. We might not remember being born, for instance, but sometimes we can recapture how it *felt* to be born. The *sense* of it comes back to us.

It is very important to understand that body memory affects us even without our consciously recalling the event; our bodies remember feelings and sensations whether or not we remember *what* happened and *when*. Very few people have any narrative recall of their lives before age two or three, for example. And yet everything we experienced as babies affects us deeply in one way or another for the rest of our lives—remaining an important part of the complex patchwork of our character.

Body-memory presents itself as a complex of emotional states and bodily sensations. I use the term interchangeably with 'emotional memory' or the more scientific term 'implicit memory', to emphasise different aspects of the same phenomenon. Body-memory can sometimes arise without an immediate sense that something from the past is being recalled. We subsequently act from this body-memory without realising that we are responding to the past and not the present.

In *Mindsight*, Siegel states, 'Such implicit-only memories continue to shape the subjective feeling of our here-and-now realities, the sense of who we are moment-to-moment....'[19] A constant companion in human life, body-memory is triggered daily, pervading our perceptions, our decisions and our behaviours.[20]

At first, we might feel dismayed at the suggestion that so much of what we see and feel is our past relived and projected. But this phenomenon is so intrinsic to being human that we do well to come to terms with it. Wisdom traditions the world over have offered this same counsel for thousands of years; that what we *think* we see is illusory.

The good news is that we are only trapped by body-memory, helplessly repeating history, if we don't take notice that body-memory is what's affecting us. From the moment we become willing to ask the question, 'Might this be triggered body-memory?' the gears of our release are engaged, and new avenues of response become apparent. To be free to create the new in our lives, we need to recognise what is old.

So, 'body-memory' refers to the general sense in which our bodies carry the memory of all that we have felt. But within that general body-memory potential are single, powerful moments in which a strong trigger floods us with an upwelling of old emotion, old thoughts and bodily reactions. I call this striking moment a 'body-flashback'. Sometimes a body-flashback can be quite dramatic, overwhelming or even paralysing. It can seize us unexpectedly, such as with a sudden phobic attack or an irrational fear or an explosion of rage. And a body-flashback can also be subtle, even easy to miss.

Ordinarily, we say we are experiencing a memory flashback when a narrative memory flashes suddenly onto the screen of our minds. Perhaps you hear a long-forgotten song on the radio that triggers memories of a high school dance, and all of a sudden you recall what you and others were wearing, who you danced with and who played in the band. A body-flashback, on the other hand, can come with or without any narrative recall.

Sometimes we can be aware that our emotions spring from an old experience that eludes our conscious recall, because the feelings seem familiar somehow. We feel a sense of déjà vu. But a body-flashback can equally be triggered without our knowing it, so that we mistakenly attribute the entirety of our reaction to the present moment. During a body-flashback our perceptions about ourselves and about others are significantly altered. The flashback distorts the lens through which we perceive the world; this is when we are most likely to have the strongest projections about ourselves and about others.

A body-flashback can be a welcome signpost that points the way to an emotional wound in us that wants healing. It is the *unrecognised* body-flashbacks—the ones that we have without knowing it—that cause us problems by clouding our perception. When we fail to acknowledge that an old emotional state has been triggered in us, we are disempowered, at the effect of our environment and likely to blame others for how we feel. Many of our frustrations and irritations in response to our children, or the fears we feel for them, contain elements of a body-flashback.

Another example of a commonly experienced body-flashback involves those occasions when physical contact with someone we love and trust can make us feel invaded. Closeness can feel 'too close'; and for some people proximity or touch at the wrong time can even bring up feelings of revulsion. Of course, this can simply be due to tiredness, and for most people the normal cycles of intimacy include a natural and periodic need for personal space and alone-ness. But when aversive reactions persist to the point that they interfere with the normal enjoyment of close physical contact, this can feasibly be the result of a triggered body-memory.

Many kinds of toxic or frightening experiences of bodily contact can leave a mark on us in childhood, adolescence and also in adulthood. By some definitions, surveys reveal that up to one in three women and one in six men have experienced some kind of sexual molestation in childhood. Owing to the reluctance to report and the reality of abuse amnesia, some argue that these are underestimates.

Beyond violations of a sexual nature, the memory of bodily intimacy can be unpleasant in plenty of other ways. For instance, many of us know what it felt like to receive sticky and smothering hugs, or touch that was cold and stiff. Some of us were denied hugs and comforting touch entirely, so that our bodies no longer know how to receive it. Most people know too well what it is to have been smacked, slapped, belted or caned; corporal punishment has been a stubbornly enduring practice in most cultures. In today's image-obsessed society, far too many of us have experienced humiliation of some kind for our physical appearance; such is the strength of the lingering shame that sometimes we cannot bear to be seen or touched.

The unpalatable truth is that in one form or another, these kinds of experiences are extremely prevalent. Given the scope and size of the pain, shame or fear that so many of us carry in relation to our bodies, is it any wonder that the physicality of relationships can be such a minefield?

The human body retains the implicit memory of its intimacy history, and both pleasurable and aversive body-memory is apt to be triggered through the stimulus of our close relationships. And here is where our children come in. Our children are not born with a highly developed sensitivity to our boundaries. From birth onwards, babies and children demand a huge amount of closeness, and they are not particularly reverent in their approach. They cry for us, grasp for us, and protest bitterly if their hunger for contact is denied. Babies don't ask if this is okay right now; they behave as if the maternal breast—or the paternal arms—are their entitlement. Toddlers clamber into our beds without asking how we feel about it. They jump all over us, they kiss us and unceremoniously grab at us in the tender moments of morning awakening. They squeal to be picked up without a thought for the state of our backs. It takes a considerable reservoir of inner security and wellbeing to meet, with any sense of enjoyment, the full physical passion and need of a human child.

A child's undomesticated appetite for contact can be, and often is, a powerful trigger for body-flashbacks. Sometimes their reaching out triggers pleasurable feelings in our hearts and this enables us to embrace them affectionately. But when an aversive body-flashback is triggered, we might find ourselves feeling overcome, irritated or repelled. This can impel us to push the child away—to be impatient, distant or cold.

Though of course not all of our reactions spring from body-flashbacks; it is always worth exploring whether our excessive or pattern-like responses might be about our past and not about our present reality. Once we identify a body-flashback for what it is, it opens us up to healing or restorative experiences (that's the goal of our Inner Child Process) and the way is clear for a truer connection with ourselves and with our child. Both adult and child can be relieved of suffering simultaneously and the emotional needs of both are thus served.

Wherever I travel for my parenting workshops, I like to take a simple survey. The responses are the same everywhere I go—whether in Australia, New Zealand, North America, Indonesia or the UK. First, I ask for a show of hands of anyone who ever vowed to themselves that, as parents, they would never sound like their own scolding parents or teachers once did. Almost everyone in the room raises a hand. Then I say, 'Please leave your hand up if you've already found yourselves sounding *exactly* like one of your parents, when you are under stress.' Laughter. But none of the hands come down. We are fundamentally the same all over the world. We carry body memory wherever we go, and are vulnerable to being triggered. Despite all our best-laid plans for the most modern and peaceful of parenting styles, under great stress, our reactions often come from body-memory—our childhood scripts. Much as we aspire to be the 'zen' parent, when Life presses our buttons intensely enough, that's when we fall short.

Here are some more commonly occurring roadblocks to parenting that are often not understood for what they are: the result of a body-flashback.

Flashback at Childbirth

While lying on her back at labour with her legs apart, a mother's contractions stop and her cervix ceases to dilate. Unknown to the staff or the mother herself, the open vulnerability of her body position has triggered a body-flashback related to a traumatic and unresolved memory of sexual abuse. Since there is no conscious processing of the flashback, the alarming body-memory is somaticised (it causes her body to seize up and her contractions to cease). This is misinterpreted as birthing complications, and obstetric interventions are imposed.

Flashback at Breastfeeding

The pleasure of breastfeeding can also be blotted out by feelings of invasion or overwhelm that arise as the passionate child latches on to the mother's breast. Body-flashbacks can, for some mothers, reduce or impede the pleasure of breastfeeding and potentially contribute to early cessation.

Perhaps a mother has experienced sexual molestation at some time in her life. Perhaps as a child she felt emotionally drained by a demanding, overpowering or needy person. Or perhaps she had been denied her infantile needs, and her baby's pleas for nurturance trigger her own despair memory. Many kinds of adverse experiences relating to bodily intimacy can later interfere with the pleasure of breastfeeding.

If the body-memory content is not recognised and acknowledged, healing and resolution is less likely. The suffering mother risks blaming herself for the bodily discomforts and obstacles she encounters, or defensively downplaying the value of breastfeeding in general.

Fear of Pleasure

Breastfeeding can also confer streams of pleasurable sensations in the mother's body. It is a sensual as well as intimate act, designed to be entrancing and bonding beyond its nourishment value. When a woman has been shamed or given guilt-inducing messages about bodily pleasure, the act of breastfeeding can make her squirm with anxiety and shame. This too is a body-flashback; the threat of pleasure is the harbinger of all the admonishments she has heard about the enjoyment of her body. The human body has a tendency to withdraw its energy and to tense up in the face of a perceived threat. When pleasure-anxiety is triggered, this not only limits enjoyment, it can at times also interfere with milk supply. Becoming aware that a body-flashback has taken place is the first step to our release from its hold.

Jealousy as Flashback

Many fathers find it strangely upsetting to see their babies being breastfed. All kinds of distressing emotions are stirred up: jealousy, envy, resentment, or an urgent sense that their child should be soon weaned and become more 'independent'. In their provoked state, some fathers begin to agitate for an early cessation. There have been countless rationales given to these triggered feelings, but most miss the mark. Healing and relief are possible when the father is helped to understand the source of these feelings—which can include painful experiences from his own infancy. It can be deeply provocative to watch, on a daily basis, one's child joyously and sumptuously receiving what was denied us at the same age.

Touch-Aversion

Some parents feel awkward around the physicality of hugs. They hold back demonstrations of affection or become tense when someone reaches out to hug them. Perhaps they were never hugged as children and their bodies do not retain comforting hug-memories. Perhaps they were shamed as children for their need to be held. There are all kinds of historical reasons why many adults avoid closeness, since it has the power to trigger so much childhood emptiness or shame. The mere suggestion of a hug can at times be enough to trigger an automatic recoil.

Flashback about Abandonment

The sound of our baby's cry can powerfully evoke the rage, panic or despair we felt as babies when our own cries went unheard. The similarity of the sound acts as the switch that re-opens a channel of feeling, which may trigger a distressing body-flashback in the parent. In some parents this produces an over-anxious response, in others an aversive reaction towards the baby.

Flashback about suppression

For many of us, when as toddlers we tried to be forthright and assertive—in our clumsy, toddler-like way—we were hushed, told not to 'back-chat' or scolded for being 'too demanding'. It is not uncommon when we become parents to be triggered by our own toddler's stridency. Their protests can trigger a body-flashback of powerlessness or shame. Alternatively, they can trigger a flashback of the bottled-up rage we felt towards the parent that suppressed us. These body-flashbacks colour our perception of the child and we project. The child is now at risk of being seen as 'spoilt', 'manipulative' or 'trying to get his own way' in much the same way as we were viewed as children. It can be hard indeed to let our children have their personal power when this is precisely what was denied us at their age.

The teen trigger

Adolescents can sometimes sound brash and overconfident. If our own fledgling opinions about life were harshly quelled when we were their age, teenaged cockiness can come across as particularly irritating and even outrageous to us. If we aren't mindful of our own flashback-driven reactivity, we too often and too soon douse our young's passion and outspokenness.

Sexual abuse flashback

A mother who had been sexually abused in adolescence becomes hostile towards her teenaged daughter when she begins to dress up and experiment with make-up. Her daughter's emerging sexuality rings powerful, historical alarm bells. She harshly rebukes her daughter, unaware of the body-flashback of shame and fear that fuels her censure.

Shame flashback

A father who was often humiliated for showing any vulnerable feelings in adolescence refuses to respond protectively when his teenaged son tells him he is being bullied at school. As his son's story triggers a body-flashback of humiliation, he tells his son he needs to 'man up'.

Exuberance-Allergy

Sometimes when parents punish or berate their children for their rowdiness, it springs from a body-flashback of anger that does not actually belong with the children at play. Perhaps the parents themselves were once punished for their childlike exuberance, by their own strict and overbearing parents.

So, can we distinguish our body-flashbacks from responses that are uncomplicated by old, unresolved hurts and frustrations? We can certainly get better at sifting what comes from our wounds from what comes from our hearts. With courage and practice, we can develop and sharpen our tools for honest insight. And it begins with knowing where to look.

The body-flashback is most discernible in your most immediate, spontaneous and automatic responses. But most of your automatic and spontaneous responses, verbal or otherwise, do not bloom into overt behaviour. Part of you evaluates each raw impulse, regulates and modifies it, and filters your output. Most of your behaviours, including your responses as a parent, carer or teacher, are highly regulated. Some of your responses are completely withheld, others censored and edited prior to expression. Thank goodness for that! It is a sign of our psychological health as adults when we reflect before we act; that's what protects us and our loved ones from all kinds of hurt and embarrassment.

Kathleen Taylor, PhD, an Oxford University neuroscientist, calls this the 'stop-and-think' function, and it is regulated principally via the prefrontal cortex.[21] But does self-regulation work perfectly every time? The answer to that is a resounding 'no'.

The sum of your impact on this world includes your raw, uncalculated responses and the things you say and do after a bit of quality control. But all too often your automatic and unmodified impulses leak out or burst through, as water from a fissured pipe.

For example, despite your best effort to project a reasoned tone, your anger might show in your brow, your jaw, your body language, the timbre of your voice. Another example, for all your attempts to speak with confidence, the cadence of your speech might betray a lingering self-doubt.

Hard as we might try, our deepest feelings are rarely entirely hidden. In one way or another, they alter the course of our self-expression. No feeling is neutral, and none is without some effect. At the very least, our reactions tinge our actions, and that is why it is so helpful to understand our deeper impulses and their origins.

The search for our body-flashbacks begins by listening to our inner voices and self-talk—those things we wish to say or do *before* we apply self-censorship, *before* we filter out what we deem 'unacceptable'. These emotionally-loaded internal impulses and reactions are hardly reasonable or rational. Nor should we expect them to be, since they emanate from long-past, highly charged experiences.

To listen openly to your body-memory you need to suspend self-judgement and be willing to acknowledge those regions of your self that are not necessarily 'nice', 'good' or 'mature'. Exercise 6 is designed to help you tune-in to body-memory.

Exercise 6: Observing your Body-memory

This mindfulness exercise asks you to pay close attention to the most *immediate* and *automatic* inner responses you have towards your child's behaviour.

The next time you are about to respond to your child, take a few moments to pause, reflect, and allow your attention to scan inwardly. Whether you are moving to comfort your child, to set boundaries, to help her, to join her in play, to teach her a new skill, to help her sleep— irrespective of whether this is a pleasant or difficult interaction—listen carefully to the inner voices that pass through your mind before you speak aloud or act.

If you don't hear words internally, then notice your first and most automatic bodily impulses towards your child. For instance, you might notice what your hands begin to do, what happens around your jaw, or around your eyes and brow in response to your child's behaviour.

At first it might take a little courage to look inward, particularly if your initial impulses seem punitive, avoidant or in some other way unpleasant. Remember that we all have realms of Self, some call it the 'shadow', that we'd prefer not to know about.

Thinking about these impulses, whether you think they are 'positive' or 'negative', what might they reveal about your own past?

Are these impulses in any way familiar, or reminiscent of someone you know?

Where, and with whom, did you learn these responses?

If any of these deep-seated and spontaneous impulses ring a familiar note for you—sound like one of your parents, or one of your schoolteachers?—it is most likely a body-flashback. Take note of the body-flashbacks that are triggered, as these can be ideal opportunities for an Inner Child Process that could bring you healing and a deeper and more effective connection with your child.

The more we familiarise ourselves with our personal 'buttons' and the types of triggers that push them, the sooner we recognise a body-flashback as it comes up.

Psychotherapists, especially body-psychotherapists, understood and worked with the body-flashback long before modern neuroscience laid bare its biological inner workings. The body-flashback has been observed, documented and worked with therapeutically for over a century. So many of the things we say and do contain at least some thread of an old emotional state. This is especially true of the habits and addictions that we feel powerless to influence. Here are some typical examples of how body-memory and body-flashbacks can silently drive impulsive behaviours, as well as choke-off healthy responses:

❋ **Our addictions to substances or to particular experiences.** That feeling of *must-have-or-bust* is not necessarily about the object of addiction. It can be a triggered burst of despair related to a past-unmet longing.

❋ **The people we are attracted to.** In an aggrieved tone, many people say, 'Why do I keep being attracted to the same kind of partners—even when time-and-time-again I keep getting hurt and disappointed?' We cannot readily control who we become attracted to. That is, until we begin to unpack and understand how our earliest relationships—the people we bonded with in infancy and adolescence—affected us at the core.

❋ **Freezing, numbness or mental blankness in the face of a perceived threat.** This can be the result of a triggered post-traumatic response. The 'freezing' response can be a life-saving reflex in the face of an overwhelming threat, as are dissociation and collapse; especially in early infancy. If this self-protective reflex was evoked often enough in early life, it becomes neurologically habituated and easily triggered as a body-flashback.

❋ **Our temper**—our explosive over-reactions to life's frustrations and irritations.

❋ **Our social inhibitions**—our embarrassment or shyness. Examples include: fear of public speaking, awkwardness at social gatherings, self-consciousness about dancing or other forms of self-expression.

❋ Our automatic judgements, prejudices or bigotries.

❋ Our lapses in empathy.

There are plenty more examples; see if you can think of more that might apply to you or to people you know.

Fortunately, the body-flashback can equally be helpful to us as parents, grandparents, teachers and guides. Our children's voices, their body language and facial expressions can trigger flashbacks of our own childhood feelings and needs, which can drive and shape our most nurturing and protective responses. Our bodies retain every moment of affection, comfort, security and playfulness that our carers gave to us and this fuels the desire and capacity to pass it all on to our children. Our hands yearn to pass forward the fullness of our hearts. The strength, encouragement and conviction with which our elders guided us continually inform our responses during key moments of parental instruction. Like an underground watercourse, our inner reservoir of loving memory feeds and sustains our parenting and leadership—even without our conscious recollection. The body-flashback is an adaptive function that serves a vital evolutionary purpose.

Until we take an interest in our inner-world and begin the voyage necessary to trace our reactivity and our empathy-lapses to their source, we remain trapped in cycles of repeating history. Ordinarily, a person's behaviour is put down to their 'personality', and that is that, no questions asked. We can do better than that. We need not run on the spot, eternally bound by our past.

Sometimes a little awareness is all that's needed; the moment we acknowledge that our emotions and perceptions relate to a past situation, we are freed to see the present moment in an entirely new way, empowering us to respond in a fresh manner that writes a new future.

And sometimes we need a little more: a healing internal dialogue that brings comfort or relief to the wounded Inner Child. If we listen carefully, our Inner Child wants to tell us what we have long been wishing and waiting for, so that we can grow. This inner voice deserves our trust. The body-flashbacks triggered by our children are the markers that show us where our wounds are. We have much to thank our children for; the awareness they provoke in us, by simply being themselves, offers us release from our past; that is, if we accept the opportunity.

As we saw earlier, body-memory is *state-dependent*. When something in our environment—an odour, a sight, a sound or even a physical position—puts us in a bodily state similar to that of an earlier life experience, we sometimes have a body-flashback about the original experience. By *looking* like us and *sounding* so child-like, our children are immensely powerful triggers for us. Each day their presence triggers in us a bodymind state redolent of our own childhood—usually without us knowing it. Like wafts of smoke, our emotions, thoughts and perceptions are signals of body-memory; they point to the embers of our personal history.

Fortunately, we can make use of this   state-dependent feature of body-memory to bring ourselves out of any overwhelming or unpleasant body-flashbacks at will. Remembering that body-states are potential triggers, we can deliberately move ourselves into a new body state that would lift us out of the body-flashback and into a calmer, more grounded experience.

This might simply involve mimicking the body-state of an adult who feels in control and at ease in his or her surroundings. Sometimes all it takes is for us to stand up, walk around slowly and take a few longer breaths, with emphasis on the exhalation. It might help even further to make a cup of tea or coffee, for instance; since these involve bodily movements that we generally associate with normal, day-to-day adult existence. These are just some of the many methods we can use to resurface if we ever feel swamped by a body-flashback. We will be exploring strategies for emotional safety in greater detail in 'Create a Safe Experience' (page 145).

Emotions 'come up'

Much of human emotional life seems to escape our notice. At times—if we are to identify what we are feeling—it seems to require some moments of tuning-in with body-centred attention. If you bring your attention to sensations in your body when you feel emotion welling up, you will usually find that emotions seem to rise as a sensation from deep in your belly, or in the centre of your chest. That's why we call them *e-motions*—they *move;* up and *out*. Emotion travels vertically towards your throat, face and arms for expression, and up towards your head for evaluation. Emotions seem to travel upwards and that is why popular expressions such as 'notice what *comes up* for you', or 'what is your child's behaviour *bringing up* for you' make so much sense.

This way of looking at your experience acknowledges that what you feel in response to your child was already inside you, stored deep in body-memory, and rises to consciousness when *triggered* by your child's presence. For example, you might notice that when your child questions your authority or challenges your decisions, some emotion comes up for you. Or, when your child makes strong demands for your attention, beyond what you can pleasurably give—notice what emotions come up for you then. What about when your teenager makes life choices that are very different to those you had envisioned? When you witness your child excel at something, what arises in you then? And when you see your child surrounded by loving friends, what comes up for you then?

> **Exercise 7: Emotional Self-awareness**
> Pay close attention to what happens in your body when you find yourself most challenged as a parent, grandparent or teacher. Notice changes in your breathing, sensations around your belly, your chest, or your throat.

Notice any muscular changes in your arms or hands, in your jaw, around your eyes or elsewhere.

Emotions come up in diverse ways: as tension, tightness, physical pain, a rush of energy, heat, tingling, even nausea. Emotions can also come up as strong physical urges: to strike out, to yell, to cry, to kick out, to hold on or to embrace, to protect, to hide or to run away. Those bodily changes are evidence that emotions are coming up, triggered by an interaction with your child.

Many emotions—sometimes conflicting—can come up at once. Take careful note of, and respect what arises. Notice in particular those emotions that seem to come up repeatedly in response to similar triggers in a pattern-like manner. You may even want to write these emotional responses down as a valuable way to get to know yourself better. These emotions spring up for a reason, whether from your present or your past.

What can you learn about yourself, when you observe the nature of emotions that come up inside you? What might these emotions be saying to you about key formative experiences you have had in your life?

As you learn to pay close attention to the emotions that come up for you when triggered by your child, you can better separate what is yours from what is your child's. It helps you to differentiate more clearly between your own needs and your child's. This prevents you from using a parenting technique that may not necessarily match what your child actually needs.

My Baby, My Mother

A mother works hard to train her baby to sleep at the same time each day and night, ostensibly because she has been told by nurses that babies need to be put into exact routines. The sleep-training programme is a battle from the beginning. Sometimes her baby falls into line with the imposed schedule, at other times the little one cries inconsolably without end.

Listening carefully to her own body, the mother makes contact with a long-standing, bone-wearing fatigue. She becomes aware of a breathless dread that comes up whenever she's confronted by her baby's seemingly endless demands. Allowing her attention to rest on the heavy feeling across her chest, she begins to recall how emotionally needy her own mother was. For years, she had tried hard to forget that suffocating feeling that would overcome her as a little girl, when her mother would swamp her with constant demands for attention. With no end in sight to her mother's complaints, she had fallen into a pit of despair.

Thinking again about her baby, the mother realises how powerfully she is triggered by her plaintive and dependent cries, how the abject wailing feels just like her own mother's martyrdom. No wonder she finds her baby's changing needs so scary. The need for predictability, in this instance, is primarily—and understandably—hers; less so her baby's.

A new tack is clearly needed if both mother's and baby's needs are to be met. Happily, taking ownership of her body-flashbacks has made room for new perspectives. The mother realises that what she really needs is more hands-on help and support from close friends and family, so she can restore her energies. When she feels more rested and supported, it frees her to understand that her baby's natural routines are not rigid; they shift with time. A more flowing and strain-free daily rhythm is thus restored to the mother-infant relationship.

By the Book

A young couple, whose 5-year-old son is struggling to learn to read, is pressured by school staff to accept remedial assistance. The reading program the boy is given is worthy enough. But then the parents discover that in some of the world's most successful academic systems, children do not even begin learning to read until their seventh year. They realise then that when they'd witnessed their son struggling with literacy, it had brought up unnamed personal fears about his future competency. They decide to look into the matter more deeply.

With a little more introspection, the parents both recognise that they are affected by the emotional memory of having felt ashamed and unworthy during their respective primary school years. They had both panicked, dreading the thought that their son might suffer the same fate. The parents' fears had been further stoked by a currently pervasive but unfounded cultural bias towards imposed, universal standards of educational attainment. While their alarm for the boy is widely shared, it is not a true reflection of their child, who is in fact doing exactly as he should according to his unique developmental trajectory.

This young boy does develop his literacy eventually—and more playfully—once the worried adults allow him to follow his natural course.

At times it is important to evaluate a childrearing intervention before implementing it, by pausing at first to differentiate the child's need from the adults' need. It's not always easy to tease apart your own issue from your child's; so there are helpful questions you can ask to facilitate this process of healthy separation. For example, before you intervene in your child's behaviour, ask yourself, 'What is my child's behaviour triggering in *me*?' or 'What is coming up for me right now, when I see my child behaving in this way?' If we don't take ownership of the emotions that come up for us, we are more likely to misread our children's needs and risk blaming them for the challenging moments that childrearing brings.

Regression

Regression is an old psychological principle that harks back to Freud. Over the years, many more psychologists have studied this most human propensity, adding their own insights and refining its meaning. Regression indicates that when we are triggered, we travel back in time emotionally, re-experiencing feelings, thoughts and longings from a younger period of our lives. Though it might not necessarily seem overtly apparent to us or to people around us, a triggered regression returns us to a younger *emotional age*. Sometimes this is only a momentary phenomenon and we soon spring back to present-day consciousness. At other times, these childhood feelings and perceptual states might linger for hours, even days.

You could say that regression is an aspect of the body-flashback. When we are partially immersed in a body-memory, experiencing the emotions, perceptions and needs of a younger age, it is as if we *are* momentarily that age. For as long as the body-flashback lasts, our emotional age can be much younger than our physical age. For instance, it is an entirely ordinary experience to be 30 years old, while at the same time, for a few moments, being at the *emotional age* of three. Or 40 years old and regress to the *emotional age* of 17. Or 60 and regress to the moment of birth. The emotional age that we regress to depends on the nature of the trigger, and it also depends on both the wounds and strengths that we carry from our childhoods.

Regression is rarely pathological; it is an integral and normal aspect of human experience. Except in the case of a psychotic break, when we are triggered we don't regress so completely as to lose all contact with our present-day adult reality. Regression is almost always partial—as if a *part of us* has gone back to childhood, while our awareness of our adult age remains. We don't necessarily end up having a tantrum on the floor, throwing our food or crying for our mothers. That is, unless the trigger is powerful enough to send us into a deep, regressive tailspin. We hear stories of young soldiers in trenches doing exactly that; becoming incontinent and whimpering for Mummy. Horror does that, and so does intense terror. The depth of our regression depends in part on the size of the perceived threat and on the gravity of our childhood emotional wounds and unmet needs.

Regression is such an ordinary occurrence; it is as if on any given day we are on an *emotional age elevator*. Imagine an elevator in which the top floor represents your current age, the ground floor is our first year, and the basement is your time in your mother's womb. The fourth floor represents when you were 4 years old, the 13th floor represents your 13th year, and so on.

On most days we travel up and down this emotional-age elevator a number of times. We tend to stop at the floor to which we have been triggered, and at times we get out onto this floor and hang out there for a while. Usually, we take the elevator back to the top floor after each descent. Our time in the penthouse becomes more sustained and more fulfilling after each time we do a little healing work at whichever lower floor we have paused.

I find it a great pity that regression is so often considered a cause for embarrassment, even a target for judgement and contempt. It is all too easy to deride people for not acting their age, when in fact, regression affects every one of us from time to time. So much has been said about the process of regression, how it works and why it happens. But have you ever wondered what regression's evolutionary advantage might be?

My sense is that regression may provide more than one evolutionary benefit. One key purpose is to alert us to the need for healing. Regression shows us where our emotional wounds are. We tend to revisit these wounds over and over again until we have felt validated enough, until we answer the unmet developmental need. We travel back in time, seeking to rescue the forgotten Inner Child. We do this so we can bring that Inner Child forward towards a healing experience—and thus expand into a more complete state of self. Telling someone who has regressed to just 'grow up' is the very opposite of the healing experience that would help that person's emotional-age elevator return to the top floor.

Did you ever notice that sometimes, catching that elevator down several floors can be pure joy? Regression provides yet another wonderful, life-enhancing gift. When we feel safe, sometimes we partially regress in order to draw from a particularly helpful faculty that we were lucky enough to have gained as children. Think about the joy of letting go of your adult, task-oriented mind-set for a while so you can play like a child. We might catch the lift down to the sixth floor to borrow from our inner 6-year-old the skill of being free and unscripted. Perhaps we go even lower, and borrow from the third floor the skill of being silly and uninhibited. Can you imagine all the ways in which this Process magnifies our lives? Some of our healthiest and most creative moments owe their existence to our ability to recapture the unbounded playfulness of childhood, or the vitality and courage of adolescence. Our Inner Child can be an enormous repository of inventiveness, spontaneity, renewal, freedom of thought, affection and other invaluable qualities too numerous to mention. These qualities, to the degree that we have gained them, are stored for us in these lower 'emotional age' floors.

I believe that regression's powerful evolutionary purpose is something we are better off coming to terms with. That our modern cultures have failed to accommodate this natural phenomenon comes at a loss to compassion and respect for one another. We need to elevate the fact of regression from a therapeutic phenomenon to something that is culturally accepted and respected.

We don't usually recognise our moment of regression—certainly not right away. Not that it is difficult to become conscious of our regressed states; but a descent in our emotional age elevator tends to happen suddenly, the moment we are triggered, and thus it often escapes our immediate attention. And though we might seem to be speaking and acting in an adult fashion, the mannerisms of maturity camouflage a more childish motivation. Exposing our Inner Child can make us feel vulnerable and most of us are adept at veiling our regressions in adult garb. Meanwhile, with our elevator stuck on one of the lower floors, our behaviours are geared to serve the interests belonging to the younger state to which we have regressed.

So many of the behaviours we take for granted as regular human foibles in fact spring from a regressed state. Our defensiveness, our grasping and clinging, our moments of narcissism or greed, our manoeuvring for power—these and more are reactions that stem from the wounded Inner Child. When we act in an authoritarian manner, when we blame, shame or intimidate our children, when we over-control their explorations—this can also be a sign that we have been triggered and are, though we may not initially know it, in an emotionally regressed state.

Emotional Contagion

Bella did not want to leave the playground. Climbing and sliding just seemed so especially thrilling that afternoon that she simply could not hear her mother, Lucinda, calling to her when it was time to go home.

But Lucinda could wait no longer. There had been so many demands on her that day, and many more important tasks awaited her at home. Lucinda was feeling strained and exhausted. With mounting urgency, she called Bella again, each time more stridently. Seeing that her 4-year-old daughter was not registering, Lucinda strode onto the playground to seize Bella by the hand.

Furious at being pulled away from the games she was so absorbed in, Bella exploded into a full-blown tantrum. She screamed and wailed, tugged against her mother, dragged her feet and battled all the way back to the car.

When, after a prolonged struggle, Bella was finally strapped into her child-seat, Lucinda forcefully slammed the car door shut. The stress of this onerous day boiled over for Lucinda. Inside the car, she in turn exploded in helpless anger. She yelled in frustration, fitfully throwing her belongings all around the front seat and floor. Lucinda had her own tantrum to match Bella's, as the startled girl watched in silence. Overcome with the day's difficulties, Lucinda had regressed to the same age as her daughter, emotionally. Just as it happens to so many in her position, her 'emotional age elevator' had descended to the fourth floor.

Fountain of Youth

Alberto had been feeling trapped in his management job for years. It no longer stimulated or challenged him, and a promotion or sideways move kept slipping through his fingers. With three school-aged children and a big mortgage, Alberto felt he could not risk quitting and shifting to a new career. His prospects seemed dreary and every day seemed to run into the next with circular monotony.

One evening Alberto snapped. When a group of younger colleagues invited him to join them for drinks at a nearby club, he said, 'What the hell, what have I got to lose?' He phoned his wife and told her he had been asked to work late. Alberto swung his jacket over his shoulder and sauntered out, throwing caution to the wind.

Alberto had not felt so carefree for an eternity. Or so drunk. At the bar he flirted with an attractive younger woman and they kissed. Barely able to walk in a straight line, he joined her on the dance floor where he spent the next few hours in Bacchanalian abandon.

When it was almost daylight, Alberto staggered out to his car. He barely managed to remember where he had parked it. He crawled onto his front seat, giggling and mumbling to himself. Unable to fit his keys in the ignition, he gave up, and fell asleep with his face pressed against the window.

Alberto had not acknowledged to himself the depth of his depression, how stuck, directionless and unappreciated he had been feeling for a long time. On this night, his 'emotional age elevator' had dropped him off at his 18th floor.

Father's Approval

Just a few years before he died, my father and I had a very candid conversation that has stayed with me always. Though he was now well into his 80s, he confessed that sometimes he still found himself craving the approval and acknowledgement of other men. He sensed that this had something to do with the approval that he missed from his own father as a boy. My father lost his dad to a terminal illness when he was 8 years old. It was amazing to hear, from someone not usually inclined towards introspection, how he saw himself seeking acknowledgement for his career successes, just as an 8-year-old boy might fish for a salutary pat on the back. For 28 years my father lectured at symposia around the world, and was lauded for his unique area of expertise in civil engineering. He loved his craft and was thrilled to receive such kudos, but this did little to satisfy his deeper longing. It felt very special that my father chose to share his heart with me on that day. I was deeply touched to see his Inner Child—not so different from my own—and this brought me much closer to him.

I doubt any of us reach a stage in which we cease to regress from time to time. Perhaps the definition of personal growth is that we get better and better at recognising when we are emotionally regressed.

As we learn to become more mindful of our regressions, we witness ourselves consciously as the regression is unfolding. We learn to say to ourselves—and when it feels safe, to say it to others—'I am feeling like a child right now.' With time, we get better at sensing what floor our 'emotional age elevator' has delivered us to. 'I am feeling just as I did when I was in the classroom, as a 9-year-old', or perhaps 'I am feeling scared as a baby', or 'I am feeling as reckless as a teenager!'

Becoming mindful at the moment of regression is a revolutionary step—quite literally a life-changing skill. Our self-awareness stops us from acting out in ways we—and those around us—might later regret. Bearing witness to our regressed states enables us to discern our adult needs from those of our Inner Child. In turn, this distinction prevents us from conflating our own needs with those of our children.

As we become more cognisant of our regressions, we get better at identifying the developmental need that our Inner Child is seeking to satisfy. And as we learn to validate our Inner Child's need and in some appropriate way respond to it, we naturally return to a fuller, more compassionate, more grounded and more creative adult state.

Regression is never for naught. It points the way to that place inside us that needs healing. Children are the best lift-attendants! They seem to have a knack for pressing just the right floor-button, delivering our 'emotional age elevator' to the level where our next lot of work needs to be done. Indeed our children, just by being children, help us to grow.

 Children are the best lift-attendants! They seem to have a knack for pressing just the right floor-button, delivering our 'emotional age elevator' to the level where our next lot of work needs to be done.

Exercise 8: Finding the Inner Child Behind the 'Adult' Behaviour

It can be interesting to try to guess the emotional age of public figures when they are in a regressed state.

When you observe a public figure who appears to be out-of-control emotionally, think about what age their behaviour reminds you of. For instance, what was Adolf Hitler's emotional age when he made his podium-thumping speeches? What emotional age was Tom Cruise when he was jumping up and down on Oprah's couch? What emotional age were the songwriters when they wrote the lyrics, 'I can't live, if living is without you'?[22] (Hint: at what age is someone's life actually threatened should a familiar loved one abandon them?)

What is the emotional age of a CEO who feels perfectly entitled to pillage the natural environment and then evade paying taxes?

In the zero-sum game of financial speculation, what is the emotional age of a hedge fund manager or corporate raider who boasts about his triumphs?

Sometimes people complain bitterly about laws that restrain their behaviour, even when these laws are reasonable and clearly in the public interest. Quite tellingly, they might grumble something about 'The Nanny State'. What emotional age might this kind of indignant self-entitlement spring from?

Can you think of other examples?

Exercise 9: What Is your Emotional Age at this Moment?

Think of the last two or three times you momentarily felt out-of-control emotionally. Perhaps you had an angry outburst. Perhaps you felt numb, unable to act or to speak. Perhaps you were consumed with worry or anxiety, or even experiencing a panic attack. Perhaps you were euphoric with excitement. For just a few moments, recall just a little of how it felt to be in that state. How old did you feel emotionally? In other words, what do you suppose your emotional age might have been at that time?

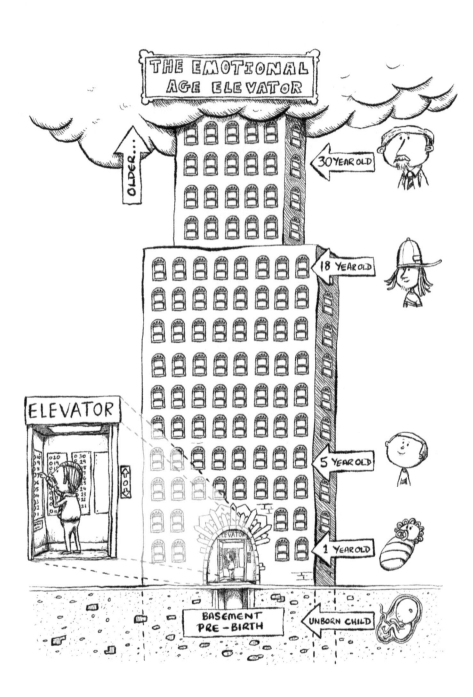

Taking ownership of our emotions

Taking ownership of your emotions is the opposite of blame. For parents, carers and teachers, this means recognising that your emotional reactions are not at the effect of your child's or your student's behaviour. The emotional reactions you experience in the presence of your child are a composite of empathic responses plus body-memory triggered via your child. Sometimes your reactions are a cocktail containing traces of regression.

You know you are not taking ownership of your emotions, for instance, when you hear yourself thinking or saying that your child has made you angry, that your child has aggrieved you, that your child has offended you, that your child has frightened you, or that your child has burdened or exhausted you. To say that too readily is to blame your child, to give your child an unfair share of the responsibility for how you feel, and to give your personal power away to your child. Taking ownership of how you feel is the first step to claiming your personal power as a parent, teacher or carer.

When you take ownership of your emotional reactions, you don't cease to make the necessary requests from your child, nor cease to assert the all-important behavioural boundaries. In fact, from the toddler years forward, your child's social development depends on your showing that you have needs, feelings and limits.[23]

Let me make an important distinction here between what our children can learn to take responsibility for, and what we adults should take responsibility for.

One of the principal goals of childrearing is to teach our children how to take responsibility for their behaviour and its consequences. Personal responsibility-taking is a difficult and long-term project; it is the definition of becoming an adult, and for many of us it is a life-long enterprise.

But as much as we want to teach our children to be responsible for *their actions*, it is an entirely different matter to make them responsible for *our feelings*. As adults, we need to be mindful of the complex source of our emotions, which often includes an element of triggered body-memory.

Taking ownership of our emotions does not necessarily come at the flick of a switch; it is a process that we need to learn and cultivate. Our capacity to take ownership seems to come and go. Sometimes this capacity seems to slip through our fingers: we regress into a younger version of ourselves and we fall into blame. But the rewards of self-responsibility are great, and it is a capacity that we can strengthen over time. Our best hope for our children to learn self-responsibility is for *us* to role-model it for them.

The business of taking ownership begins with a change in narrative; shifting from the customary language of 'I am feeling this because my child did that' to 'When my child does that, these feelings are triggered *inside me.*' Ownership is the recognition that our children are not the drivers of our emotional experience; we are.

Children are too often given power over adults' feelings; I believe this to be a culturally dominant perceptual state. We say we are tired or stressed *because* the children are 'rowdy', *because* they are 'too needy' or 'too demanding', *because* our baby is 'too fussy'. It is not dissimilar to saying that we are contented *because* our children are 'good'.

Whether we respond with irritability, disappointment, warmth, pride or joy, our responses say more about us than about our children. Our responses—both pleasurable and painful—reveal what we have lived, what we have learned and how we have adapted to our environment.

Nonetheless, as empathic human beings we do feel some emotion in tune with our children's expression; this is the very essence of connection and empathy. Akin to a stringed instrument; we ring in concert with their vibrations.

Owning our emotions does not mean mimicking the rhino with his tough, leathery hide; indifference is not the cure for enmeshment. On the other hand, if we assign too much of the *cause* of our feelings to our children, this means we see ourselves as a windsock to be blown about by the little ones in our lives; we are at their mercy. If we look too much to our children for fair weather, we sidestep our capacity to self-regulate; to seek support from other adults, to self-care, and to learn the craft of personal healing and growth.

When instead we take ownership of our wellbeing, we become generators of wellbeing for our children. We declare ourselves as the drivers of wellbeing, rather than dependants on our children's ever-shifting moods.

Taking ownership of our emotions is not easy. We all occasionally get dragged into our child's emotional whirlpool. We are permeable to their mood states in varying degrees—especially when we are tired or over-stressed.

Taking ownership is easier when other adults are nearby to support us and at times, to take over for us.

In a moment of stress, our minds often begin with a blaming thought; we tell ourselves the child is *making* us feel uncomfortable. This is okay. Most of us do it automatically. Think of ownership as an invitation—a welcome to transmute our reactive blame into a new and more empowering vision.

Begin by simply reminding yourself, 'Though this child is behaving in a way that is difficult for me, how I feel is about me, not about the child.' Sometimes this simple thought is enough to help us feel centred again.

But often another step is required; we may need to undergo some kind of healing process to disentangle ourselves from our child's vortex of emotion. The methods are plentiful and diverse, depending on your circumstances. Perhaps you need the help and support of others, perhaps you simply need some quiet time and rest.

Taking ownership must be learned; it needs to be rehearsed as an art or a language. Like a muscle, it strengthens with use. And like all human beings, each one of us swings like a pendulum; from ownership to blame and back again. Growing up is something that continues for the duration or our lives.

When we perceive ourselves to be at the mercy of our children's state, we make value judgements about them. Children are uncanny detectors of our judgement and blame; they sense it in us before we do. Instinctively, our children resist us by becoming defiant, obstinate, avoidant or superficially compliant. What we don't at first see in ourselves, our children's behaviour shows us in a mirror.

But when you ask for co-operation, or set boundaries while owning your feelings, your child is far more likely to listen, to respect you and to *want* to follow your lead. Telling your child what you need from him while owning your emotions is an art. It helps to view some examples of what this might sound like, while contrasting that with commonly used blaming statements.

Table 2 shows examples of statements commonly made by parents, carers and teachers about children in their care. In the statement on the left, the commentator makes it all about the child. In the statement on the right—based on the same situation—the person takes ownership of his or her emotional response.

Table 2: Blame vs Taking Ownership

Blaming the Child	Taking Ownership
That child is messy	I really don't like disorder
That child is lazy	I feel worried for this child I don't know how to find what motivates this child
That child is irritating	I'm feeling sensitive to noise right now, and I need some peace and quiet
That child is impudent	I feel hurt. I feel offended
That child is a whinger	I have trouble listening to helplessness
That child is ungrateful	I would like some recognition or acknowledgement for what I give

You may have noticed that taking ownership is facilitated by making an 'I statement'.[24] Hopefully you will also have noticed that taking ownership of your emotions in no way devalues or minimises your needs. When you've acknowledged that your feelings come from within, and not from another person, your child is free to hear you, to be co-operative and perhaps even show concern for you. Your child cannot do that when she feels blamed.

It is easy to forget to take ownership of our emotions, and to act as if our children are responsible for how we feel around them. This is not surprising; few of us have had good role models in this area. Many of us were brought up with traditional models of leadership (authoritarian), in other words, 'do as you're told because I said so', and 'I'm okay, you're not okay'. As we learn to take ownership of our emotions and perceptions this not only benefits our relationship with our children, it enhances all our relationships.

The Developmental Need

The developmental need is a building-block concept that begins to illuminate a pathway out of repeating our histories.

In this workbook the term 'developmental need' will refer exclusively to fundamental *emotional* needs, specific to each stage of childhood development. (The scope of this book concerns our psycho-emotional needs, rather than our cognitive or physical needs.) By stressing that some of our needs are 'developmental', I hope to emphasise that they do more than merely satisfy a passing desire. Developmental needs prepare us for a step forward in maturation, they are essential elements of our emotional and social intelligence and they need to be met if we are to reach our fullest potential as human beings.

Our core developmental needs are universal. They follow the same biologically prescribed sequence for all babies, children and youth, across all ethnic groups. In the same way that we all need clean air and water and a balanced diet, the core psycho-emotional developmental needs, are shared by all.[25]

For example, as babies we need to feel safe, promptly and tenderly responded to, closely held and protected. Having these needs met is essential for acquiring the deepest layer of emotional intelligence, which is about emotional security and trust.

As toddlers, the attachment needs continue, though to a lesser extent. Now we find ourselves driven by a new set of needs; to express ourselves, to play and explore. This next layer of emotional intelligence involves freedom and autonomy. The inner security and strength we bring to our growing autonomy as toddlers is dependent on how consistently our baby needs were met.

There are further, distinct developmental stages to follow (as you will see in Table 3 page 108), and the nature of our passage through these two early stages influence how we fare through our primary school years, our teenage years, and so on.

When our stage-specific developmental needs are met, a new layer of emotional intelligence is attained, and new relationship skills are embodied. Additionally, this needs-fulfilment at each stage is what produces an organic progression into the next stage of emotional maturation. In other words, our strength and success at each of these stages builds on the accumulated strengths of the previous ones.

It is an existential fact, however, that our stage-specific developmental needs are not always fully met. Emotional wounding at one stage can undermine the fullest expression of our passage through subsequent stages. Though we continue to grow physically and cognitively, the strength of our progress through each successive stage of *emotional* development depends on how well our *emotional* needs were met at the preceding stages.

As children and adolescents we suffer when a core developmental need is not met, or is inconsistently addressed by our carers. Sometimes the need involves something from the outside world—such as security, holding, protection, acknowledgement, being heard and validated, or being shown clear interpersonal boundaries. And sometimes it's about our inside world—something we need to be allowed to do for ourselves; such as explore the world around us, express our emotions, protest, disagree, voice our opinions, make up our own minds, reject mistreatment or escape a toxic situation.

Researchers from fields as diverse as epigenetics, neuropsychology, human attachment, learning theory and psychotherapy have contributed to mapping the stage-specific developmental needs of childhood. Accounts of this developmental map vary in detail but they are largely compatible with each other, and share common themes. So, what are the universal, keystone developmental needs of childhood and how do they change from stage to stage, through childhood and adolescence?

For your ease, Table 3 (page 108) lists all the core psycho-emotional developmental needs in stage-by-stage sequence. If you'd like to explore these needs in more depth see: Table of Developmental Needs (page 206), repeated in Appendix 5.[26]

Research into human development will continue to evolve. Table 3 shows you my proposed list of core, stage-specific developmental needs, expressed as rites of passage in childhood and adolescent development. (Note that psycho-emotional development begins *before* birth.) My list is not exhaustive; it is drawn from years of reading, research, training and experience. You may be able to think of more needs that I have left out.

Table 3: Developmental Stages

Developmental Theme	Developmental Stage (Ages are approximate, with some overlap)	Developmental Needs
Existence	*In-utero*, birth and the perinatal moments	To be wanted. To be held. To feel safe.
Primal need	The first 18 months after birth	To trust. To feel secure. To have bodily and emotional needs met promptly.
Autonomy	18 months to 3 years	To have support without expectation or manipulation; on our own terms.
Freedom	3–5 years	To explore our environment. To voice all our feelings. To be shown interpersonal boundaries without shaming or punishment.
Passion	5–7 years	To express passion and sensuality. To give and receive affection physically, without invasion, judgement, or exploitation. To explore and discover the pleasure of our bodies.
Competence	7–12 years	To learn playfully without coercion or shaming. Freedom to pursue our interests and affinities. Support to develop competencies without expectations.
Belonging	12 to early 20s	Social acceptance. Vocational development. Support for our uniqueness. Respect and support for exploration of our sexual identity, privacy, love and desire.

I strongly doubt that *any* of us have had all our developmental needs perfectly met at every stage. In varying degrees, we all have a modest level of built-in resilience to Life's disappointments and frustrations. But at some point an unmet need can become a developmental arrest, sometimes even a trauma. The unmet developmental need alters our behaviour, our self-image, our stress-response and our neuroceptions for the long term.

As renowned psychiatrist, Bruce Perry, MD, PhD, points out, children are less resilient than they are *adaptive*.[27] Trauma demands adaptation; it changes us just as a storm or a drought leaves a discernible storyline in a tree's formation.

Chapters 24–29 in *Parenting for a Peaceful World* offer an account of the various ways in which the developmental needs that go unmet can manifest in adult behaviour, mental health and relationship difficulties. The chapters also speak of the strengths and emotional intelligences that are gained when these needs are consistently and well enough met as they arise.

For most of us, one or more developmental needs were incompletely met in childhood and adolescence. These are our developmental wounds and they can affect us and our relationships for the long term.

In one way or another, as adults we unconsciously try to play catch-up with our unfulfilled developmental needs. There are those who, even as adults, keep looking for someone to make them feel as safe and secure as they needed to be as babies. Others keep intimacy at bay, searching for a sense of personal space and boundary that was robbed from them as children. Yet others compulsively seek the carefree escapades in mature adulthood of the kind that should have been satisfied in adolescence.

Unfulfilled developmental needs tend to place us in a state of developmental suspension. We seem to continue forever seeking restoration—to be listened to as we should have been, to be held as we should have been, to be free as we should have been. This is the major underlying source of conflict and discord in our relationships until some form of healing or growth can be achieved. The bodymind never forgets; it seeks to complete the incomplete. We continually regress to our wounded Inner Child places, hoping to finally repair and break through our developmental arrests. Life's strains and conflicts—with our children, in particular—trigger the body-memory of unmet developmental needs as we strive to fulfil each unfinished developmental task. Each time they trigger us, our children alert us to our own next layer of unresolved developmental need.

Plants are not so different from us, in that they require the right nutrient for each stage of their growth. Without the right nutrient for the right stage the plant might still grow, but something will be incomplete in its structure. When the plant receives the specific nutrient corresponding to its life-stage it can grow to its fullest potential.

Just as growth seems to be the imperative in Nature, so it is in human nature. The impetus to grow, expand and unfurl towards maximum radiance seems to keep nagging us, to keep prodding at our edges, to create conflict and disturbance in our lives without letup, until we make the conscious decision to answer the call of psycho-emotional development.

Our Inner Child will strive forever to complete her developmental quest, even when we ignore her voice. The Inner Child that breathes within each of us is a lot like Loki, the Norse god—wily trickster notorious for his incessant pranks and mischief. Together with the significant people in our lives, we co-create trouble, mishap and discord that trigger regressions, stir our emotions and expose our wounds.

You could say that this is how we dare ourselves and each other to grow, to complete what remains unfinished from our childhoods. The safest way forward is to embrace this unremitting inner urge for growth from a conscious and aware standpoint. Life and love are at their most vibrant when we don't merely give-in to the inevitable, but grab it with both hands.

In fact, all our relationships—and those with our children in particular—will on occasion poke us exactly where we are developmentally stuck—which means that the Inner Child Process can help you to work through impasses and conflicts that arise in all relationships, not just those with your children. Usually the triggering comes through conflict, but it can also come through the challenge of love—when the love and joy that our children evoke in us overflows the cup of our comfort zone. Love, joy, success and pleasure can also be powerful triggers for old, unresolved emotions.

This story of belated fulfilment is not bad news—far from it. Indeed it is intrinsic to the human condition. Much of what seems to go 'wrong' in our relationships—with our children, with each other—is traceable to one or more of our unfulfilled developmental needs. In other words, when we are triggered, our body-flashback is not merely a body-flashback; it also signals us about a vital need that remains unmet. Like a flare that helps rescuers locate a vessel in distress, the body-flashback points us to the unfinished business of our childhoods.

Conflicts are the markers that show us our wounds—those parts of ourselves that need our attention and a pathway of healing. Once we recognise that a developmental need has risen to the surface, we can respond to this need. In Chapter 13 we will look at creative ways to find adult-appropriate fulfilment for our unmet developmental needs as they come up, triggered in us via parenting.

Don't worry, you don't have to be a baby or a toddler all over again in order to nourish those developmental needs that hark to your early life. In Chapter 13 you will learn firstly how to distil the *themes* of any developmental needs that are exposed for you, and secondly, discover ways to address those needs in a manner that makes sense to your life as it is today.

When it comes to addressing our unfulfilled developmental needs, there is something else that I find reassuring. Meeting the need is not always what's required. Sometimes just listening compassionately to your emotions as they come up seems to be enough. Listen to the small voice of your Inner Child as you would listen to any child in your most empathic capacity. Simply telling your Inner Child that you understand might be enough to bring about some profound shifts. Self-compassion can work wonders if you say, 'I am here for you' or 'No wonder you feel that way' to the child that resides within.

But sometimes this need can be—or *must* be—met in actuality. Nothing less will do! How do we know when self-validation and self-empathy is enough, or when we need to find resolution through some kind of interaction with the world around us? The short answer is, your feelings will tell you; pay attention to your bodymind.

The idea that the agonies, woes and quandaries of parenting can be transformed into gifts is difficult to accept at first, it can even sound glib. A parent's pain and frustration can be overwhelming; sometimes all we can think of is how badly we want the problem to just go away. Turning inward for personal healing requires courage and effort, but also some assurance that the effort will be worthwhile. So, it is important to repeat and reaffirm the principle in a brief summary here.

The challenges and difficulties of the parenting journey are not for naught; they can shed light on a part of our Inner Child that has gone unheard. The purpose of the Inner Child Process is to locate the unmet developmental needs that have been triggered in us and then to give ourselves the corresponding healing and growth experience. The difficult emotions that come up—triggered via parenting—are the markers of these latent, buried needs. These body-flashbacks act as tracers that we can follow inward to find the wounded Inner Child, so we can give him or her a voice, and perhaps an answer.

As we mobilise to answer the call of the Inner Child this frees us to see our own children more clearly, and from that vantage point we discern more effective ways to respond to our children. Psychological healing is about continuing an unfinished developmental journey. That is why we refer to it as 'growth'. So when we finally begin to bring our unmet developmental needs to conscious awareness—to honour these needs and give them some response—we grow in wisdom. We deepen our capacity to love and be loved, and more powerfully align with our life's purpose.

You may be pleased to hear that you won't have to memorise the list of developmental needs to learn how these apply to you. Through your many interactions with your child, you will notice which of your core developmental needs have been well met and which still await fulfilment. Just by being themselves, your children help bring your emotional wounds to your attention. Hard times are the times of deepest learning, once we are willing to look inward. In times of despair and helplessness as parents, we can heed the demand to embark on an inward journey that uncovers the deeper meaning underlying our family troubles. It's not that the Inner Child Process can promise to resolve every impasse and tribulation. However, when parents choose to stop viewing the problem as being 'all about the child', and turn inwards for self-healing, some remarkable shifts become possible for both parent and child.

The Walkabout

During the early days of drafting this book, our 18-year-old daughter decided to fly the nest. Having saved her resources, she set off to travel the world solo. Just her, a backpack, a camera and a wide-open horizon. I was thrilled for her, proud of her courage and self-assurance. But I have to confess that fatherly delight was not the only thing I felt. A knot in my stomach periodically reminded me how afraid I was. And although I understood this anxiety to be natural, too often it overrode the possibility of trust. Could I have relaxed, let go and trusted in the emerging capacities of a self-reliant young woman? I find it difficult to conjure up more than a foretaste of such a trust. My bodymind did not then know how to generate that feeling.

On occasion my worrying may have, I suspect, made me intrusive. As I grappled with my gnawing disquiet, I was prompted to revisit my own youth. What was I doing and what was going on around me at the equivalent stage of my life? How well did I fulfil the developmental needs of adolescence, at the cusp of my own home-leaving?

As I peel back the layers, it's with no small chagrin that I acknowledge I was not entirely satisfied by my own rite of travel and adventure as a young man. In Australia we sometimes refer to this rite of passage as the 'walkabout'—based on the Indigenous cultural practice in which adolescents temporarily wander alone in the wilderness to master self-reliance and their personal intimacy with the vast wilderness. (Note: Although the term 'walkabout' has come to acquire a pejorative sense in some circles, I use it here in the spirit of its sacred significance.) My own walkabout felt unfinished. Granted, I have travelled alone extensively as an adult, and in many ways, I have managed to forge a worldview that is well differentiated from that of my ancestors and my cultures of origin. But compared to many of my peers, you could say that as an adolescent I was late to launch.

By contrast, my wife Linda travelled extensively when she left home, aged 18. She spent years exploring the world and has lived and worked in several countries. I think this has given her a formidable sense of self-reliance and inner security, and I believe she has fulfilled that developmental need quite richly. Her walkabout was done, in flying colours. It did not surprise me to discover that she felt far more relaxed than I did about our daughter's welfare; she naturally trusted her capabilities more readily than I seemed able to. Linda knew something I didn't know; she understood our daughter's potential, from the inside. How different one's vision can be when it is fed by a fulfilled developmental need.

Although I detected an incompletion in my own development, I preferred to think of that worrisome passage as one that pointed to a challenge I needed to give myself. I wondered what might happen if I were to adopt a greater sense of adventure, creativity and spontaneity in the way I live and work, in my political engagement, in all the things I do. Travel is not the only means of adventure (though I certainly have plans for more of that!) Challenging myself on that level broadened the scope and deepened the significance of my dilemma. As I dared myself to take more positive risks, I found that the fretting for my pathfinder daughter began to ease. Worry was gradually replaced by an excitement that grew in my belly as I felt the headwinds of my next step: into the mid-life version of my own walkabout.

I began to see that in order to trust my daughter a little more, I needed to trust myself a little more. Though separated by decades and an ocean, we were both embarking on our very different personal growth odysseys.

Grasshopper

Sometimes, drawing from a successfully attained developmental milestone can reinvigorate our capacity for parenting. I was finding it sad to deal with my daughter's diminishing communication as she moved deeper into her intercontinental walkabout. With messages fading to a trickle, I sometimes sensed that she was pushing us, her parents, away.

One night I asked for guidance as I went to sleep. I dreamed of a pair of bullhorns driving me back, telling me to keep my distance. I was stung by this message as I struggled to let go of the intimate parenting style that had been central to my life for nearly two decades. To assist me in letting go, I did some Inner Child Journeying; this time with the help of a psychotherapist friend.

The memory that came from my own youth took me by surprise. There I was, standing and facing my father. In my right hand was a length of dowel that I was planting spear-like into the floor beside me. We were toe-to-toe, entrenched in a clash of world-views. I was a young 20-something. Having just abandoned my studies in psychology, I had chosen to be a musician instead. To a father from an old European culture, a child of poverty, war and dictatorship, my life choices then must have looked frivolous—and I, perhaps, a fanciful itinerant. He launched an attack on my sudden vocational about-face. Today I feel compassion for my father and the fears he held for me, the outrages he saw implicit in my apparent abandonment of established pathways. To him my choices must have seemed so puzzling, foreign to any logic he could relate to. He was worried for me. But at the time, I felt so incensed, and so very shamed; as if my off-grid ways made me worthless to the core, destined to be relegated to the margins of society.

So there I stood, duelling with my father with dowel firmly stabbed into the carpet. I'm not sure exactly what I said—or rather, yelled—to him in that moment, but I do clearly remember stamping into the ground my flat refusal to deviate from my plan. My feet were rooted to the earth's core, and I would not be moved. Dad and I locked eyes. (Is that how Gandalf felt when he drove his staff into the rocky ground as he bellowed at the Balrog, 'You shall not pass'?)

Curiously, at that very moment, I saw something unexpected flash into my father's eyes. Just as my stance arrested him, for one brief moment, my father looked proud of me. Even without understanding my choices, nor a blessing for my undertakings, he saw in my gesture that I had snatched my own destiny out of his hand. From that day, I would carve my own way through life. It was a defining moment that, despite the conflict that raged on the surface, my father and I both instinctually understood.

Remembering how I felt that day when I burst out of my father's sphere of authority helped me come to terms with my own daughter's fierce grab for independence. Though at the time she was incommunicado, roving somewhere in the South American littoral, I felt more closely connected to her journey and its deeper significance. This helped soothe my heart, aiding me to let go of her a little more easily. I could see her wresting her own destiny from the hands of her elders.

This archetypal moment was so well symbolised in my favourite childhood TV series, 'Kung Fu'. When Grasshopper was finally able to snatch the stone from the hand of his blind master, only then was he finally ready to wander the world as an adult, to make his own path, to shape his own meaning. His freedom was not given him; he *took* it.

My Inner Child Journey helped me make peace with my daughter's turning her back to us—her turning forward to take-on the world. Fathering was metamorphosed into a new and unfamiliar phase—though I could no longer be happy *with* my daughter, I felt happy *about* her and *for* her. I returned from my Inner Child Journey with a message telling me that for the time being, what was being asked of me as a father was not about what to do or say, but rather about what *not* to say. Sometimes, love is a function of distance.

Now, to ease your mind, that length of dowel in my hand was material to build a box for my guitar effects. A spontaneous theatrical prop perhaps, that may have added some drama to the moment, but it was not brandished in anger. I did enjoy many wonderful years of live music performance, and occasionally, I still do. This enriches my heart far more than it does my bank balance.

The Developmental Nutrient

Every child is unique. That is why there is no substitute for listening and watching very carefully, and responding to the often-surprising challenges and gifts that each child brings.

But if you look at the deepest layers of the bodymind, all human beings develop according to universal pathways. As we saw earlier, this follows distinct stages, characterised by developmental needs that must be met. Specific nutrients meet those needs as they arise so the child can grow to his fullest potential. I am using this word 'nutrient' to represent a required *experience* that makes the next developmental step possible. Since such experiences stimulate the growth of new brain connections, the reference to a growth-promoting nutrient is more than metaphorical, it is grounded in biology.

We saw in Table 3 (page 108) how specialised the nutrients are for each distinct developmental stage. Sometimes a developmental nutrient must be provided by the child's environment. For instance, babies are entirely dependent on their carers to provide their developmental nutrients. The loving gazes, the touching and rocking, the nourishment and protection—these vital nutrients can only come from the baby's external world. At other times the developmental nutrient comes from inside the child herself, but the child must be given the support and the freedom to enact this experience. For a toddler, this might include the freedom to run, climb and explore the environment away from the parents, to be allowed to express her emotions, to assert her needs and to protest her frustrations. For the teenager, the developmental nutrients might involve support to find and develop his unique gifts and freedom to forge his own social identity. As the child matures, the nutrients increasingly emerge from within, as experiences to be seized, so long as the world that surrounds him does not block him and provides sufficient support and opportunity.

I like to think about developmental needs and nutrients *thematically*. In other words, they seem to fall into themes involving such things as holding, nourishment, safety, support, freedom, protection, boundaries, acknowledgement, belonging and more. Understanding the thematic character of developmental nutrients is very important if we are to address any unfulfilled childhood developmental needs later in life.

Here is an example of why understanding the *theme* of the developmental nutrient—and not just the *letter* of it—is so important. Imagine, for instance, a man who struggles with issues of co-dependence. Let's call him 'Adrian'. Adrian is controlling, possessive and jealous in his romantic partnerships, and this has cost him many relationships. Let's say that as a baby Adrian did not experience secure attachment; he was given insufficient or inconsistent parental nurturance. Clearly, Adrian will not be able to fill the unmet need in the same way as it first arose in childhood. I don't like his chances of finding someone willing to breastfeed him, or carry him around in a sling for much of the day, and so on. Most readers will be relieved to know that we don't have to go to those lengths to heal the wounds of childhood. And no, Adrian is not necessarily doomed forever to relive a cycle of co-dependency and rejection.

So, how does our friend restore the missing developmental nutrients so that he can grow and feel more internally secure? We cannot help him to feel more self-assured simply by instructing him to do so. As we learned earlier, our emotions are not at our command. Waving a finger at Adrian and telling him to grow up would accomplish nothing more than shaming him.

Of course, Adrian needs to take many steps for his own growth, including learning to be more mindful and respectful of his partner's personal boundaries.

But what will help him to gain the kind of emotional security that would prevent him being so grasping in the first place? We don't seem to fully move forward to our next developmental stage until the needs of the previous stage have been met. So the foundational step for Adrian is to find the developmental nutrient that addresses his core wounding.

Since Adrian had not experienced a secure attachment as an infant, his emotional deficit relates to the *theme* of nurturance, perhaps also the *theme* of holding. (Note: In psychotherapeutic terms, 'holding' is not necessarily meant in the physical sense, but in terms of empathic listening.)

If he can allow himself to receive a diverse range of emotionally nurturing and holding experiences in his life, it might be the precise developmental nutrient that frees him from his despair.

Thinking of nurturance as a *theme* helps us translate the infant attachment needs into a whole range of possible nurturing experiences that would be appropriate to this man's age. Adrian can build his inner sense of security and resilience without having to succumb to the life of a baby.

It is a beautiful thing for partners to be nurturing towards each other on occasion. But this is a far cry from saying that it is Adrian's lover's job to ensure that his deficit in nurturance is filled. A healthy adult relationship includes accepting limits to nurturance. It also includes the ability to connect in a host of other ways beyond nurturance. Without this limit, we overload our relationships with excessive or unrealistic demands, and this strain had cost Adrian a number of partnerships.

Looking beyond his pair-bonds, Adrian can avail himself of an abundance of options that involve consciously inviting and then accepting nurturance. There are so many potentially nurturing and pleasurable experiences that we can treat ourselves to. Adrian can seek to deepen the quality of his conversations with friends; to learn the art of heart-to-heart dialogue. He can reach out and learn to receive hugs, or book in for some massage therapy. He can take regular walks in the magnificence of Nature. He can read beautiful poetry or perhaps listen to exquisite or uplifting music.

There are few things as nurturing as rocking ourselves in hammocks, or better still, *being rocked*. In fact, I often include rocking as an integral part of my parenting groups. Each willing parent has a turn at being rocked gently in a hammock, while they simply lie back with eyes closed. Sometimes we might chant, hum or sing a lullaby to the person being rocked. It is awe-inspiring to see the transformation that takes place; their faces almost Buddha-like as they slip into a deep state of blissful release. Being rocked can feel utterly delicious, almost magical, with profound effects on our nervous system and brain chemistry. It is so moving to see how, after being nurtured in this way, people's behaviour changes—towards their children and towards each other. For a while at least, they naturally become more patient, better listeners. Receiving nurturance helps us to pass nurturance forward.

> *There are few things as nurturing as rocking ourselves in hammocks, or better still, being rocked … Receiving nurturance helps us to pass nurturance forward.*

When we commit to giving ourselves regular doses of nurturance, we begin to feel as if we have an internal 'friend' who watches over us, who affirms us and validates our deepest feelings. We are, in real terms, uploading new body-memories of wellbeing, connectedness and security—and this eventually begins to modify our behaviour. Adrian can be freed of his co-dependent reactivity as he begins to feel more secure at the core of his being; to believe that he can trust in a nourishing world.

Shall we look at one more example? A woman—let's call her Talia—finds herself getting angry when her children are demanding and needy for her attention. Talia was the daughter of authoritarian parents who cut her down harshly when she voiced her feelings assertively. Talia often felt emotionally crushed and had lost the self-confidence to say 'no' when she needed to. This left her feeling excessively exposed and vulnerable to external demands throughout her life. Now, Talia can't relive a childhood and have it unfold differently. But she can understand the *theme* of the missing developmental nutrient; which is about interpersonal boundaries. With help and support, Talia can learn to set boundaries in ways that she never has before, with her friends, co-workers and family. Little by little, she can practise saying 'no' when she is tired, when she has had enough, when too much is asked of her. Over time, Talia's world will begin to feel less overwhelming, and she will feel a new sense of her own strength. This would in turn fortify her resilience to her own children's push and pull.

Adrian and Talia are just two examples of how developmental nutrients remain *thematically* relevant throughout our lives, and it is never too late to give ourselves an adult-appropriate version of what we may have missed in childhood. As you saw in my personal anecdote, 'The Walkabout', I don't necessarily need to undertake the long solo journey I missed in adolescence to bring, with a little inventiveness, a new feeling of freedom and adventure into the way that I work and the way that I live.

We do not need to relive an entire childhood from scratch in order to heal. As you will see later, in the 'Third Movement' of the Inner Child Process, we learn how to distil the general *theme* of the developmental nutrient that would best meet a triggered developmental need. Sometimes all it takes is to acknowledge our need and give ourselves compassion, and already we start to experience some big shifts. But sometimes we might need to go a little further; to try to meet our developmental needs behaviourally, in some adult-appropriate way. Our Inner Child Process invites us to be as playful and creative as we can be in finding developmental nutrients for our developmental needs.

The Developmental Template

There is a final and important thing to say about our developmental needs. This may be one of my favourite principles of human psychology. Our bodyminds seem to know what they need—*even when we cannot yet imagine it.*

We all have inside us a template that can faithfully identify the right nutrient that fits our developmental need. Even if at first we cannot name or communicate what we need, we tend to recognise it once we finally receive it. Before we can give shape to—or find words for—the object of our longing, our bodies are programmed to welcome it when we find it, when Life offers it to us. The answer to our needs lies dormant, waiting to be awakened.

Our feelings tell us, via a sense of fulfilment, when we receive something we have needed all along. This developmental template is neurologically encoded, subconscious, visceral and instinctual, and it helps us navigate the winding path of needs-fulfilment; so we can develop and evolve.

If we pay attention to our breath, feelings and sensations, our bodies give us trustworthy guidance in our quest for healing. When we finally find what we seek, the body responds with pleasure, wellbeing, an outbreath and a new openness and vitality. With a feeling of expansion, we are moved forward to our next level of emotional and social intelligence.

This is heartening news for our healing journey. Though most of us retain some measure of unfulfilled—or incompletely met—developmental needs, it is never too late to address them. Even decades later, we are magnetised to the corresponding, stage-appropriate nourishing experience (developmental nutrient). The bodymind never stops sensing and searching. The Inner Child Process is an usher that helps us find direction and movement when we are stuck. When we are not sure about what we need in order to heal, we can begin by listening to our feelings. 'Which is the way forward? What do I need right now? Could it be this? Could it be that?'

Our bodies will resonate with the object that we long for, when it comes into view. We breathe a sigh of relief, our shoulders relax, perhaps we feel a tingle of excitement or a rush of energy. To know that we can trust this inner developmental template, and the validating signals that our bodies give us, is going to be important for the Third Movement in the Journey. Don't worry if this does not sound entirely clear just yet. The Process will become clearer with each of the following sections and chapters.

Here are two examples of what I mean by 'developmental template'. A baby is born with a 'rooting' reflex. She turns her head and reaches with her lips towards anything that touches her cheek. Her body knows how to search for her mother's breast long before she can form an idea about the object of her need. It is only after having found what—and who!—she longs for many, many times over that her reaching comes under voluntary control. You could say that the body knows before the head knows.

A toddler runs in the opposite direction to his mother automatically, before he can articulate his powerful yen for flight. He finds a new ecstasy as he explores his frontiers alone. He learns of this need by satisfying it when he can. An impulse codified deep inside him drove his legs to run, and he loved it! It is only by giving-in to this urge that he learned how to name his need for freedom. 'Let me go!' says the toddler.

As parents, we often find ourselves unable to guess what our children need when they complain or reach out. That is absolutely OK. Our task as parents is to offer our children a menu of options. Usually, though it may take several attempts, when they sense the object that would satisfy their need, they recognise it and they are fulfilled. This is how we can help our children to identify their needs and differentiate between their different needs. This is how we help them to answer the question, 'What is this new bodily sensation or bodily impulse actually asking for?'

First we help them know what they want, and as they develop language, we help them name what they want. As we offer the menu of options—Did you want more playtime? A cuddle? Are you cold? Do you need to sleep? Are you hungry?—children's inner developmental template lets them recognise the object of their need when it appears before them.

Their bodily pleasure, wellbeing or release lets them—and you—know when they have found their mark. Pleasure is the symptom of a need that has met what it longs for.

> *Pleasure is the symptom of a need that has met what it longs for.*

Our Inner Child responds in the same way, thanks to our own developmental template. If we are not sure what to reach for in our lives when we feel triggered, we can use our imagination to offer ourselves a menu of options. Just as our children do, our Inner Child orients us toward what we need through body signals. We will be exploring and clarifying this further in subsequent chapters.

As adults, our needs for security, for holding, for support, for belonging, for freedom, for pleasure, for passion (have I left anything out?) have not disappeared or diminished. Although the way we meet those needs has changed dramatically from our tender years—you won't see many 40-year-olds needing to sleep next to their parents or running around in a Spiderman suit—the themes of those same developmental needs remain with us.

When we are triggered and we feel stuck, helpless, frustrated or defeated, the key is to identify the right developmental nutrient that would free us. As we saw earlier, emotional development follows a set pathway, with corresponding developmental nutrients that are fitting for each stage.

A baby wants holding and responsiveness, a toddler wants healthy boundaries and freedom to express and explore, and so forth. We reach our fullest potential when we receive enough of the right nutrients for each distinct developmental stage.

And since most of us seem to be incomplete in one or another aspect of our emotional development, giving ourselves the right missing developmental nutrient—even late in life—helps us to evolve and take the next step in our expansion.

Our bodyminds are programmed to know how to grow and to know what the right nutrient is for each new step in our growth. Every wound contains cellular knowledge of what would heal it. Each aspect of our bodymind that has suffered a developmental arrest contains receptors for the experience that *wants* to happen. Our inner developmental template helps us to identify what this fitting nourishing experience is; we begin to feel relief or empowerment as soon as we sense it.

As you will see later, the Third and Fourth Movements in the Inner Child Process show you how to identify this 'experience that wants to happen', and then give yourself an age-appropriate version of this nutrient so you can disentangle from your impasse and move forward.

A Menu of Options

Baby Chao-xing kept crying inconsolably. Nothing her mother, Guan-yin, offered her seemed to reach her. Mum tried to offer her breast, but Chao-xing had recently fed and was ambivalent in suckling. She tried to lay baby down to sleep, but this only increased the crying. She tried singing to her but this made little difference. She tried to entertain her with a little soft toy, but this only distracted Chao-xing momentarily, and then her tears would return. But Guan-yin remained calm; she knew it was normal for a baby to cry for longer periods sometimes. Sometimes babies need to cry and simply be held, until all their stress is released. At other times, their cry asks for something that they have no words for. Guan-yin continued to speak to Chao-xing in soothing tones, all the while offering a menu of good things to her. If Guan-yin could not guess what Chao-xing needed, that was okay. She knew that her little baby's body would recognise what she needed once she felt it.

The next thing Guan-yin did was to lift Chao-xing and hold her against her chest, so she could spy the world over her mother's shoulder. Somehow, sitting vertically so she could view the world clearly, and being walked around the room in this position, really hit the spot. It's as if Chao-xing said, 'Ah ... perfect!' The developmental template in her little bodymind knew exactly how to recognise what she needed in that moment.

Living the Dream

Tarek had been depressed for over two years. His corporate middle-management job was supremely stressful. He tried every kind of self-help method he could lay his hands on. He took meditation classes. Though he barely had the time for it, he occasionally attended a yoga class. He had counselling sessions through the company's Employee Assistance Program. They threw their entire arsenal at him: cognitive behavioural therapy (CBT), neuro-linguistic programing (NLP), eye movement desensitisation and reprocessing (EMDR), narrative therapy and more. Tarek learned to think more positively; he learned how to communicate more effectively with his staff and how to speak more assertively with his superiors. Everything he attempted was helpful and for brief periods his mood would rally, but the improvements were short-lived and superficial. After months of mixed results Tarek eventually gave in and began taking medication, just to help him make it to the end of his workweek.

One day, a close friend of his family asked Tarek a simple but powerful question. Noticing that Tarek was most visibly grim when speaking about his work, his friend asked, 'If you could have your wildest dream come true and you didn't have to stay with your current employer, what would you be doing instead?' At first Tarek avoided the question, but with a little nudging from his friend he admitted that all his adult life he had been in love with artisanal furniture, homewares and design of north African, Middle Eastern and central Asian origins. He had often fantasised about being his own boss as an importer, with opportunities to travel and to surround himself with an aesthetic that deeply moved him.

But Tarek had always dismissed this as an idle fantasy—that is, until his friend dared him to take a risk. For as Tarek spoke about his beloved design styles, his eyes began to regain a sparkle that had not been there in a long time. Tarek's inner developmental template was showing all the signs that this conversation was right on target. His depression sprang from the fact that somehow, his life had not supported Tarek to pursue his natural passion, or to develop his most natural gifts. His vocational Self had not been allowed to bloom. And until Tarek could dare to be truer to his heart, all other therapies were merely tinkering around the edges.

Fast-forward several months. With some support from his wise friend, Tarek left his job and set up the import and retail business that he had long dreamed of. Something in him—his developmental template—knew exactly what he needed. His feelings clearly told him he was on the right track; he just needed a little encouragement to trust those feelings enough to act on them. Even though his income was now a little less predictable, and his work hours were no less than previously, Tarek now found new levels of fulfilment and self-actualisation. Like a child in a toyshop, he was infused with a joy that had eluded him for decades. Soon he was able to wean from his anti-depressant medication. Tarek's inner developmental template helped him, via the language of emotion, to recognise the developmental nutrient that was necessary for his liberation and growth.

A word of caution: on occasion, what we *think* we need isn't necessarily what's best for us. When we are doing our Inner Child work on our own, our self-healing efforts can be hindered by blind spots. That's why it is recommendable to work with a counsellor, or a wise elder sometimes—especially when we are working on big issues. It's okay—and in fact desirable—to be open to a second opinion regarding your best-fit developmental nutrients. An experienced therapist, or perhaps someone who has already passed through your current life stage—such people are sometimes able to see vistas that are beyond your viewfinder.

When it comes to identifying our next developmental nutrient, seldom is there just one right answer. Almost always, we can give ourselves a variety of helpful things that enable us to move forward and heal. So don't get hung-up on finding the perfect nutrient. Nonetheless at times another's perspective can help prevent us walking down blind alleys.

When it comes to identifying our developmental need, we sometimes struggle. The signal seems blurry; a clear sense seems to evade us. This is quite normal. An experienced coach, counsellor or therapist can help by asking a question that had not occurred to us, or by referring us to the Table of Developmental Needs (see Table 5 page 206).

Our bodymind's developmental template tends to resonate when somebody—ourselves or another person—finally utters the name of our deepest need. Our bodies signal this resonance in a variety of ways: our breathing changes, we sigh, we become flushed, perhaps some tears might well up or we might just feel a release of tension. A change in the pattern of our breathing, a bodily shift or an emotional release are all signs that we have pinpointed our need and lighted upon the nutrient that would feed it. It is as if our Inner Child has long been waiting for our attention, and appreciates finally being heard.

It is very common to feel uncertain about what our needs are sometimes. When our intuition falters, help is at hand. Table 5 explains how we can use our stage-by-stage developmental map as a guide for getting strong 'ah-ha's' about our developmental needs. An understanding of this unfolding sequence of core human needs is essential for our Inner Child Journey, whether we are undertaking the Journey for ourselves, or assisting someone else through theirs. Without a clear sense of the sequence of core developmental needs, we may choose a less-than-optimal nutrient and wander into a developmental blind alley.

There is an art to honing-in on the developmental need that is activated when we are triggered, as there is craft to recognising the developmental nutrient that would fit the bill. (Chapter 11 is devoted to this art-and-craft and it equips you with a map to aid your navigation.) As you move through the steps of the Inner Child Journey, your body tells you what would be nourishing and healing for you, and equally tells you what is not working for you—provided you pay very close attention to your body and its signals.

The Body Knows

Alyna sought the help of a counsellor when her promiscuous lifestyle began to create insurmountable problems in her life. Left to her own devices, whenever Alyna felt depressed she would compulsively seek new and fleeting relationships with men. Her counsellor was a sensitive and empathic man who offered an eclectic range of therapies. This included advising Alyna to take up a sport as a vigorous alternative way to channel her energies. These strategies were partially helpful, but they failed to bring long-term or transformational results.

When Alyna would undertake an Inner Child Journey, she would encounter deep but vague feelings of hollowness and loss. In one particularly powerful session, as she was recounting her childhood history, Alyna was surprised by the force of the grief that came up for her in relation to her mother. Alyna had become tragically estranged from her mother when her mother was struck by a debilitating illness that lasted throughout Alyna's adolescence. Alyna had missed out on the vital support of a strong and wise female elder during a critical stage of psychosocial and sexual maturation. She had consequently found herself unable to identify her own gender as a home base of security, guidance and support to turn to in times of uncertainty.

Alyna found a new counsellor, this time an older woman. She remained with her for some time as her new personal guide while also trying to spend more time among female friends—an effort to balance the energies in her social life. These new strategies bore fruit. When surrounded by female elders and confidants, Alyna felt herself blossom. Her internal developmental template clearly showed her, through warm sensations around her heart, bittersweet tears of relief and a pleasant hum at her core, that she had found what she needed for her healing and growth. Gradually Alyna came to feel more centred, calm and supported, which lifted her from depression and removed the compulsive extremes of her libido. The cognitive and behavioural therapies that she had tried certainly had their gifts, but they had not addressed a vital, unmet developmental need.

Just as well that Alyna persevered in sampling a broad menu of helpful interventions. She explored a range of nourishing experiences until her developmental template signalled that she was on the right track.

As with all our close relationships, the day-to-day acts of parenting or teaching recurringly expose our deepest emotional wounds. Learning to identify our incompletely met developmental needs is a vital step toward healing and growth. Equally, an Inner Child Journey can sometimes help us tap into a dormant strength, an attained but perhaps forgotten font of wisdom that dwells inside us. In both cases—whether we are drawing from a well of experience, or adding water where the well is dry—the Inner Child Process brings awareness and guides our steps. Coming home to our Inner Child—also our Inner Youth—and learning to hear his or her voice gives us ever deeper insights into our children's needs and how to address them.

Table 4: Glossary of Building-Block Concepts

Building-block Concept	Meaning
The bodymind	Body and mind are one. The body thinks. Mind is biological.
Neuroception	When our nervous system reacts—with emotion, perception and behaviour—to an environmental cue, in a manner that is beyond our immediate control.
Projection	We see others through a lens coloured by our own personal history. Memory distorts our perception of others. We see our own past superimposed on the present.
The trigger	When an interaction with something, or someone, in our immediate environment 'reminds' our bodymind of past experiences, feelings, thoughts and perceptions that may flood our consciousness.
Body-memory and the body-flashback	Our bodies can recall old feelings and sensations, even when there is no accompanying narrative memory. In a body-flashback, we are suddenly flooded with body-memory, in reaction to a trigger.
Emotions 'come up'	Triggered emotions seem to emerge from deep in our consciousness. They appear to arise from the gut and travel upwards for expression.
Regression	When our emotional responses and/or behavioural reactions spring from an earlier developmental stage, we have temporarily reverted back to a younger age, psychologically.
Taking ownership of emotions	You (not your child) are responsible for what you feel.
The developmental need	An essential emotional need that is critical for optimal psychological and emotional development.
The developmental nutrient	A lived experience that can satisfy the developmental need.
The developmental template	The bodymind's instinctive ability to recognise the developmental nutrient that would satisfy a developmental need.

'Ah, No Wonder!'

The human capacity for empathy has received a lot of attention from research scientists in recent years. This ability to somehow feel a little of what another person feels has enchanted neuroscientists since they discovered brain regions purpose-built for empathy.

Italian neurophysiologists started the conversation when, in the 1980s, they discovered 'mirror neurons'—those magical little radars in our brains that reproduce others' subjective experiences for us. With the help of modern brain-imaging technology we now know at least a dozen brain regions—including the amygdala, the ventromedial prefrontal cortex, the inferior frontal gyrus, etc—that comprise the engine of human empathy.[28] We are wired for shared experience and mutual understanding—should we wish to see the world through each others' eyes.

On some occasions, of course, empathic insight eludes us and no matter how we try, we can't seem to *get* where our child is coming from. But the more closely we tune-in to our Inner Child's world, the better we understand our children—as neuropsychiatrist Daniel Siegel puts it, 'from the inside'.[29] Although our Inner Child Journeys cannot promise this result every time; they can bring us a moment of revelation in which we can see how our children are feeling, what they are crying out for and why they behave as they do.

I like to call these sudden eureka moments the 'Ah, no wonder!' experience. What a relief when we can say, 'Ah, no wonder she's crying like that!', or 'Ah, no wonder he's been so angry!', and so on. The 'Ah, no wonder!' experience is a game-changing moment that clears the way for a new and more connected response to our children's needs.

Now that we have unpacked all the building blocks necessary for understanding the Inner Child Journey, let's see if we can put it all together.

The *Sequence* of a Personal Growth Cycle

A challenge arises in relationship with our child (or with someone else).

We are triggered, and emotions come up.

In other words, we experience a body-flashback.

In an *unconscious* situation, we blame the child for how we feel. We *project* our own past onto the child. We therefore respond in a way that is inappropriate to the situation, potentially exacerbating the situation.

In a *conscious* situation, firstly we become aware that we have *regressed* emotionally.

We *take ownership of our feelings* and thus we step away from blame.

Listening to our feelings, we then get in touch with an unmet developmental need.

We offer ourselves a menu of healing experiences as *developmental nutrients*. Our internal *developmental template* helps us recognise the most helpful experience.

We begin to feel a sense of emotional release, increased wellbeing and groundedness. We might even feel a sense of expansion around our hearts.

Our projections dissolve and we are free to respond more appropriately to our child. We more readily think empathically, '*Ah, no wonder* my child acts this way!'

The Process for Schoolteachers

Some years ago, I was invited to speak at an unusual progressive high school in regional Australia. Arriving early, I was guided to a staffroom to meet the teachers. As I walked the halls I'm sure I was immediately flooded with images and voices from my own high school days. Do footsteps echo the same way in all the world's school corridors? And is that the smell of linoleum taking me back? Looking ahead I imagined I'd be greeted by the familiar, casual rabble of teachers chatting irreverently at day's end, among untidy paper piles that speak of hustle and overwork. What I saw as the door opened was a total surprise.

Arranged on a circle of chairs, the entire teaching body was preparing to begin what I later learned was their regular weekly meeting. The collegial gathering was devoted to discussing any challenging situations involving their students, so they could support each other as a team.

As I was welcomed to sit among them and listen, I soon witnessed something atypical. In this school, the teachers did not discuss their day-to-day difficulties simply in terms of what was 'wrong' with the student, but also in terms of what the child was bringing up for them. I heard very little in the way of diagnosis or evaluation of their students. By agreement, the first emphasis was on the teacher's emotional and perceptual process. At times this included quite candid sharing about the teacher's childhood experiences; memories and emotions triggered by their students. Together, they examined how the feelings that came up might get in the way of their effectiveness as teachers, and they offered each other warmth, empathy and support. In this safe and confidential environment, every teacher prioritised looking at how their personal issues—the triggered body-flashbacks— might contribute to impedances or tensions in teacher-student relationships. Then, and only then, if appropriate or necessary, would they offer each other practical advice to address the student's need.

What they were diagnosing was the teacher-student relationship, rather than the student alone. It was astonishing, and deeply moving to see these teachers so willing to be emotionally vulnerable with each other, accepting such a level of responsibility for their students' progress. As I was to learn, soon afterwards, the teachers' own commitment to healing and growth was having remarkable flow-on effects on the students.

Later that afternoon, I had the privilege of speaking at the school's senior graduation ceremony, and I remained as a guest throughout the function. What I witnessed has stayed with me since. As they accepted their certificates one by one, graduates rose to the podium to address the community that crowded the auditorium. I have never before nor since seen a more impassioned and appreciative student body, so deeply respectful of their teachers. At times they addressed their teachers personally and directly; some telling their teachers they loved them. All the students expressed profound gratitude to their teachers for their dedication and mentorship. There was hardly a dry eye in the hall. I had never heard—nor did I imagine I would ever hear—the words 'I love you' uttered in this context. I had not heard the words 'thank you' spoken with such feeling, from a student to a teacher. I had not before seen students overcome with emotion, misty-eyed with voices trembling, as they delivered their homilies.

It felt to me that something revolutionary had been achieved at this school. A *volte-face* vision for the teacher-student relationship enabled a new kind of intimacy that underscored the success of this community.

Here the child was not an island to be mapped from a distance. A learning problem or a behavioural issue was no longer to be framed simplistically as being about the child, and only about the child. The teachers maintained a stance of asking, 'What might *I* be doing that fails to evoke the best from this child?' or 'What might it be about my lesson, or my teaching style today, that is calling forth less than this child's best?' or 'Could something about my presentation, or about this child's environment, be triggering this child's challenging behaviour?'

At the heart of this orientation is the recognition that a child's responses cannot be seen as wholly separate from their environment. The ocean shapes the island. And in the crucible of the classroom, the teachers' inevitable Inner Child presence forms part of the sum of influences on each child, if only indirectly. In this regard, the classroom is no different to the home. No adult is free of neuroception and body-memory.

When the Inner Child perspective is included in the supportive dialogue among staff, this adds a new dimension of healing to the teacher's life, making professional development inseparable from personal growth. Classroom hindrances are more likely to be turned into growth opportunities when there is a shared map for how to do so. In this school, the safe space provided for emotionally authentic dialogue among the staff engendered a warm and vibrant camaraderie that radiated welcome and enveloped the students. No wonder this smallish school was such a success, and such a pleasure to be in.

Introducing inner-child-informed dialogue in a school's staff meetings might represent a considerable cultural leap that requires leadership as well as consensus.

The group space needs to be made emotionally safe and confidential. Not all schools are ready for such a leap, and departmental pressures and regulations might limit the freedom to delve into a more open interpersonal space.

But even if teachers and school principals do not find a way to include some inner child work as a team, I believe it is, at the least, an invaluable tool for teachers to use in private. The more closely we get to know our Inner Child, the more clearly we come to understand the children we work with—their motives, their baffling behaviours, their fears and longings—from the inside.

What kinds of Inner Child issues might come up for teachers in the classroom? They might encounter relational dilemmas and challenges particular to the classroom, and somewhat different to issues in the home. For instance, a teacher might be confronted with a child's reactions to a non-familial authority. There might be a gap between the style of authority that you aspire to—or perhaps the style of authority promoted by your school—and your actual reactions under stress.

In times of overwhelming pressure or insufficient support, teachers are not necessarily less prone than parents to triggered, body-memory based responses; we can all lapse into being either over-controlling or dismissive at those times. Under pressure, we all tend to reproduce automatic ways of speaking and interacting that spring from our own childhood libretto.

As a teacher, it is relevant and valuable for you to explore the styles of authority that you experienced when you were a student. How did your own teachers affect you as a child? How did you feel when you were in their class? Which teachers most inspired you to *want* to work? Which teachers helped you feel safe? Did any of your teachers make you feel ashamed? Were you ever scared of a teacher? What exactly did these teachers do or say that made you feel in these ways? How did the manner in which your teachers treated you affect your capacity for learning? How do those experiences continue to affect you today?

The challenges in your classroom offer you an opportunity to deeply examine and re-evaluate your deepest assumptions about how teaching and learning work.

Some assumptions are indeed gained through your study and experience, but some might spring from your subconscious—from the way you were once taught as a child and how that made you feel at the time.

Some of your philosophies on the nature of the educational relationship might be helpful, some may be hindering you.

It takes courage to re-examine where our convictions and our impulses come from; to be willing to re-evaluate our approaches and to learn new ways. Here are just a few of the kinds of questions you might consider as teachers (and I am sure you will think of many more):

About Motivation

What are your beliefs about children's motivation to learn? What drives children to commit themselves to study, to practise and rehearse, to sustain effort? Is motivation most effectively driven by the joy of learning? Or is it via the coercion of an authority figure? How important is pleasure in learning? How important is it for children to endure the onerous, repetitive and mundane in the course of education?

About Attention and Focus

What best helps a child to pay attention? What facilitates the human ability to focus attention in a sustained way?

About Authority

Do your students have the right to question your knowledge and your methods? How do you feel and react when they do so? How do you feel and react when your students disagree with you?

About Work and Play

When you think about words like 'work' and 'effort', what associations and images come up for you? What associations and images come up when you think about 'play'? What are your beliefs about the roles of work, effort and play in the course of learning? Where, when and from whom did you learn the ideas you currently hold about these things? How do you see yourself transmitting these ideas and faculties to your students?

About Discipline and Boundaries

Regarding the management of behaviour in a group of children, what are your beliefs about the value of punishment and rewards? What about the value and efficacy of restorative justice? What are your beliefs about 'discipline' in the classroom—your sense of the best methods for encouraging considerate, respectful and collaborative behaviour? What about the role of shame and guilt as motivators in education and socialisation? The role of love and empathy?

Get to know the personal life experiences that inclined you towards the convictions and beliefs you currently hold about the above questions. How did your own teachers 'manage' your behaviour as a child, how were you 'disciplined'? Most importantly, how did that feel for you? How do you feel these experiences have influenced the person—and teacher—you are today?

When a child appears disinterested in the classroom, often the child is singularly characterised, as perhaps lazy, or as if he has an attentional 'disorder', etc. Parents, teachers and psychologists tend to conceptualise behavioural challenges as springing from inside the child, as if there is no systemic or relational base. Unfortunately, this tendency is quite predominant and has taken on a hazardously diagnostic tone in modern times.

Before assigning pathology or blame too soon, a revolutionary move for teachers would be to self-examine, to openly explore the inner landscape of emotion. Take the time to make things about *you* momentarily, and not merely about the student in your care. Your internal psychological processes may affect your relationship with your students more than you realise. A child's entire environment influences his progress, and you are a major part of that environment.

How do you feel when a student is not listening to you? Do you feel rejected, offended, worthless, frustrated, powerless, worried for the child? Any of these reactions, and more besides, are quintessentially normal and human. Pay close attention to what is triggered for you when students seem to spurn the lesson you had prepared. These feelings can be painful, nobody likes feeling ignored or devalued; especially if you have worked hard to prepare a lesson.

Firstly you need to acknowledge the emotions that have been triggered in you. Honour and validate these emotions. See if you can then separate your own needs from the needs of your student. Though your fervent wish might be for your lesson to proceed according to a plan, might your plan not be the right fit for your student?

In Parts B and C, you'll get the opportunity to look at how you were taught at the same age (as your student), paying special attention to how this caused you to feel at the time. Recall what helped you feel safe in the classroom and what most awakened your own desire for learning; even if your personal interests were quite different from those of the student who sits in front of you today. Recall also what might have blocked you, frustrated you, caused you to feel diminished, intimidated or ashamed. It can be easy to lose sight of how powerfully an authority figure can affect a young person.

Alternatively, think about that young part of you that most closely resembled your student; an aspect of your behaviour or attitude that bore a similarity, even if only slight. What about your teachers—or your learning environment—was most helpful to that part of you? What most hindered that same part of you? Finally, think carefully about what you would have wished to be done differently for that same part of you. How would you have liked to be spoken to, what would you have wished to be allowed to do at the time? This might offer you some clues on how to help your student grow past her current impasse.

Inner Child work for teachers can bring a trove of new insights that indirectly benefit the student, while offering healing and growth for the teacher. The wielding of authority is a fine art, thorny and devilishly difficult at times. I'm sure if we had many lifetimes to hone it, there would still be more to fine tune at the end. This seems especially true when the simple certitudes of yesteryear, 'Do as you're told, or else' and 'Because I am older', no longer have traction—the emperor's undress is obvious to all. Social evolution, for all its fits and starts, has steered away from authoritarianism; and a new model of authority is emerging. Some like to call the new model 'authoritative' as opposed to 'authoritarian'. Others call it a shift from a dominator to a partnership model.[30]

How do we strike that fine balance between the overbearing and the *laissez-faire*? How do we inspire and how do we assert boundaries of behaviour, without disempowering the child? As with any art that deserves continual perfecting, we should consider this quest for mastery of loving authority to be perpetual.

Our own childhood experiences with authority figures, the good the bad and the ugly, are all equally worthy sources of wisdom that can shed light on what to pass on, and what not to pass on to the next generation. Our emotional memory carries the messages we need, when we are willing to listen inwardly.

Self-enquiry of this kind is no substitute, of course, for the palette of practical skills that any teacher must amass. But a model of mentorship that deeply investigates how the mentor's psychological processes influence the outcomes is far more flexible, fair and effective than a diagnostic model that objectifies the student. This ultimately liberates teachers to be more helpful to the students in their care, as I witnessed in the unorthodox school I described earlier.

Having the grace to continually re-evaluate our style of authority averts a great deal of unnecessary conflict with the child; it prevents us from going against her natural flow. When we choose to take ownership of our triggered emotions, we free the child from blame. We begin to see past our projections and find the true needs and gifts that each child brings. Teaching and mentorship can acquire the quality of a dance, in which the learning environment can be adapted and re-adapted to enliven the emerging proclivities of each child.

If a student appears to lose his way, how could we change the style of delivery or the content itself? How can the child shape her own inquiry more compatibly with her interests? A rapidly growing international educational movement is moving toward decentralised, student-led curricula and play-based learning (the 'emergent' or 'negotiated curricula', and inquiry-based learning).

The trends produced are consistent internationally. They include a much more collaborative atmosphere, significantly lower friction between students and teachers, a remarkable reduction in bullying and other problem behaviours, and children achieving excellent academic results.[31]

Throughout the ages, mystics of every tradition have told us that our seeing is distorted by our past, until we learn to distinguish actuality from projection. In this matter, modern neuropsychology has awarded the mystics plenty of scientific street-cred. Since it's universal for us to blur our vision with our history, some Inner Child work could benefit us in all professions and in all endeavours, not just as parents and teachers.

We don't need to erase our past; our history is a formidable internal reference library. We simply need to distinguish it from the present, so that we can break free from old patterns, create new, more life-affirming ones.

The Inner Child perspective as a tool for teachers can transform and expand your capacities and keep your teaching style dynamic. It brings you and your students closer and reinforces the friendship between you. Teams of teachers can create a working culture that welcomes compassionate and respectful self-examination by instituting regular, safe and confidential environments in which to hold Inner Child conversations. Every teacher was once a student who felt empowered, inspired, fascinated; or belittled, punished, shamed, even abused. Your greatest gift to your students is to keep consciously learning from all of those experiences.

Before We Go On

'*Medice, cura te ipsum*'—'Physician, heal thyself'—the ancient edict reverberates through the ages. It makes sense across so many fields of human endeavour. In the spirit of that timeless caveat, our Inner Child Process says to us, 'Parents, parent yourselves!' and 'Teachers, study yourselves!'

We've looked at the building blocks that underpin this Process, and now we can learn each step in detail, one at a time. In Parts B and C we will be discovering how to use the Inner Child Process for ourselves and as a tool for helping others. The process is a conversation, a question-and-answer practice.

The Process contains enough flexibility and informality so that even without taking all its steps, you can dip in and out of a mindful state, attentive to your Inner Child feelings and perceptions. You can take a deep-sea dive, or merely a snorkel. You can do it alone, with a therapist guiding you, paired with a friend or colleague, or in a group.

You need to consider a number of safety measures first, so you can enjoy learning more about yourself without fear of being engulfed or overwhelmed by your emotions. Whatever your way of applying it, I hope that you deeply enjoy this Process, and that all your relationships will be nourished as a result.

PART B: Steps in the Journey

CHAPTER 4

Overview: What's in a Journey?

The building blocks we looked at in Part A give our Inner Child Journey its meaning and life. With a good working understanding of these phenomena, we can now begin to explore the nitty-gritty of the Process.

The Process is made up of five distinct and essential movements. If you like, you can think of them as the movements in a symphony, acts in a play or moves in a dance. Each of these five movements is a line of inquiry, tracing a five-point arc that begins from our relationship with our actual child, to our inner world, back to our past, through to a renewed present and finally back to our relationship with our actual child.

Each of the five movements is comprised of a number of optional steps that offer alternative pathways of inquiry. In turn, each of these steps (numbering 20 overall) can be accomplished via one or more possible questions. In other words, the Process offers an abundant choice of tools. You choose the tools that seem to work best for you—you certainly won't have to use them all.

Every step in our Inner Child Process has its own purpose, its own inherent value; so something of value can be gained even if all you do is take one or two of the steps. However, the ultimate benefit would of course come from travelling mindfully through all five movements in the Journey.

Since many of the steps in the Process are optional, think of these as alternative doorways into a comfortable room where your Inner Child awaits, to voice her feelings and needs to you. On some days, she prefers that you enter from one particular door, on other days from quite a different door. We rarely know in advance which door will be best. Your Inner Child appreciates your willingness to keep trying new doors, knocking gently as you do. We have an abundance of possible doorways, and they seem to vary with each quest according to the nature of the memories and emotions involved.

Many doors to the room where your Inner Child awaits

If each of the optional steps is a possible doorway to where your Inner Child awaits, then you can think of each of the optional questions (within the steps) as keys on a keychain. If one question does not seem to open the door in front of you, that is fine. Drop that key and try the next. Soon enough you will find the right door for your particular inquiry, and the right key to unlock it.

Each question is another possible key

Part B explains the rationale and purpose for each step, helping you see how it fits into the whole. Please note that this Part contains only explanatory notes, it's not designed to guide you through an Inner Child Journey. When you think you've understood how each step works and you are ready to begin your guided Journeys, you can use the applicable steps in Appendix 2. A shorter and simpler form of the Journey—the Inner Child Journey 'Light'—appears in Appendix 3. And finally, Appendix 4 offers a 'Super-Light' way to check in with your Inner Child that only requires a few moments. (You can find printable versions of the Appendices here: robingrille.com/ inner-child-journeys/.)

You certainly don't need to memorise all the steps in the Process; it's perfectly fine to read the steps from the page as you take your Journey. Appendix 2 is designed for this purpose. Chapters 6–10 will give you a firm understanding about the meaning and purpose of the steps so that when you finally embark on your Journey every step will make sense to you.

Perhaps you'll be tempted to skip to the Appendices ahead of time, to begin dabbling in the Process. Peeking is irresistible—has your Inner Child taken you to the Appendices already? I would encourage you to explore this workbook in whatever order pleases you, according to your shifting interests.

However, before using this for yourself, and *especially* before guiding another person through it, you need to read the safety measures in Chapter 5 (see pages 145). Although this Process is essentially conversational, since we are touching upon childhood emotions it's vital that we provide a safe environment to contact our emotions. It's equally important to know an easy way to wind the Process down if we feel like it's all too much. We are all more comfortable in a room when the exits are clearly marked. Ultimately, you gain the most from the Process once you've digested all the explanatory notes in this Part.

The Inner Child Process is about having a conversation with a child, only this time you are conversing with the child that is always there, dwelling inside you. The child is *you*.

Each step in the Journey is a question—or rather, a number of related, possible questions. It's really quite straightforward—obvious perhaps. At its heart, the Process simply asks the Inner Child, 'How did you feel, when that happened to you?', and then, 'What do you need right now?'

If You Encounter Roadblocks

When you begin asking your Inner Child what she *feels*, you might be amazed at how readily she speaks to you, that is, once she really gets that you are interested, and that you will welcome whatever she has to say to you.

Your Inner Child appreciates your open curiosity, and the more you do the Process, the more readily your body yields useful and important messages. However, don't be too surprised if your Inner Child seems to be hiding from you on some occasions. You may encounter static on the line, and feelings and thoughts may seem hazy. That's just one of the common roadblocks we encounter in our Journeys. Help is at hand, that's what Part C is all about. When you encounter resistance along the way, there's an art to finding a way through, and you will find simple and empowering travel tips throughout Part C.

At the point in the Journey when you come to ask your Inner Child what he *needs*, sometimes things can get a little more complicated. There are times when he will know exactly what he wants; he will whisper it to you, perhaps even shout it. But at other times, your Inner Child will have no idea about what might help make things feel better.

Don't be discouraged at that moment, as it happens quite commonly. As you will see when you arrive at the 'developmental needs' part of the Journey, it's not unusual to get stuck there temporarily.

As we saw earlier, children cannot picture what they need until they are shown the object of their need at least once. They don't yet know what's next, until they directly experience it. The body feels the need, but the object of the need does not yet have an image or a name. That is why evolution has equipped our bodies with a developmental template; enabling us to recognise the object of our need once we sense it for the first time. Again, help is at hand. In Part C, you'll learn how to ask the kind of questions that help your Inner Child identify what he wishes for.

Part C shows you a developmental map and teaches you how to use it. This map is essentially a more in-depth and detailed version of Table 3 (page 108). The map will guide you as you strive to interpret what your Inner Child might require in order to grow.

By now you may have begun to wonder what happens when you are unable to recall a relevant narrative from a key formative time in your childhood. Most people think they cannot remember anything before the ages of two or three. For others, large chunks of childhood seem to be blank, out of recall's reach. When body-memory is all that is available, that gives us more than enough to work with. In Part C you will find a number of alternate routes for your Journey. Even without any access to narrative memory, as you will see, there are other powerful ways to reach your destination.

The most creative and playful part of the Process lies in devising ways to meet the developmental need of your Inner Child, in a way that might be appropriate to your present-day reality. Remember, it's not necessarily the *letter* of the need, but the *theme* of the need, that needs to be met for healing and growth. Part C assists you with the imaginative craft of conceiving fitting developmental nutrients appropriate to your current age and circumstances. The Inner Child Journey should be an adventure, and this part of it can be particularly exciting.

Although the resources in Part C will definitely deepen the quality of your Journeys, you don't necessarily have to read it before you start. You might choose to leapfrog over it straight to Appendix 2 and begin your first Journey (or two!)

after you read the explanatory notes in Part B. However, I'm sure you'll want to come back to Part C as you encounter challenges or impasses along your travels.

One thing for sure, getting to know Part C well is a must *before* you set out to help others through their Journeys—should you decide to be a guide one day.

So, to recap: please remember that you won't need all the questions in all the steps on every Journey. When one door doesn't seem to work for you, that's okay; you are offered others. And when one key doesn't turn the lock, simply try the next. The best way to avoid feeling overwhelmed by the number of possible steps and questions is to remind yourself that *you don't need to memorise it all.* The Appendices can help you, and the explanatory chapters that follow will give you confidence and clarity about each of the Journey's steps.

Although each of your Journeys will take you through different terrain, and you are likely to skip some of the suggested steps, try to follow the *movements* in the suggested order. Once you have grasped the objective of each of the five key movements in the Journey, following the steps inside each movement will then flow easily for you.

Here is a brief summary of the five movements and what they mean.

First Movement: Looking Inwards

You begin your Journey by turning your sights inward, away from the external 'problem' that prompted your inquiry. Essentially, this is a decision not to act, but to reflect. This movement is about scanning your inner landscape to identify the thoughts and emotions that come up—triggered by the 'problem' you currently face.

Second Movement: Tracing Back

You then allow the emotions, bodily sensations and inner voices you encounter to take you back to their origins in your youth or early life, when many of your habitual reactions were learned. You'll connect with originating experiences or source events that may have conditioned your responses, and name how it felt to be in those experiences.

Third Movement: The Wishing Question

This is where you will help your Inner Child connect with what he or she would have wished to happen differently, when faced with the originating experience or source event. You'll move from naming your feelings towards identifying your developmental need.

Fourth Movement: Healing You

Now you will find a way to translate the theme of your Inner Child's developmental need (wish), into an adult form that will make sense for your life as it is today. Relying on your inner developmental template, you will search for and identify a fitting developmental nutrient and then devise realistic steps to meet this need for yourself.

Fifth Movement: connecting with Your child

Finally, you'll return to your actual child, and the 'problem' situation that you began with. You'll examine what you may have come to understand more deeply about your child, and your child's behaviour, as a result of your dialogue with your Inner Child. What new ways of responding to your child have been shown to you as you moved through your Journey?

Although you won't need to learn all the steps by rote, I would advise you to learn the five movements, their meaning and purpose, in their right order. This will help orient you, like an inbuilt navigation system, over the changing terrain of your Journeys. Consult the guide-map below when you need to locate your location in your Journey and understand what comes next. In no time at all you'll probably find you can easily remember all five movements and how they work together.

So, let's begin by setting the stage for a most safe and rewarding Inner Child Journey.

The Inner Child Journey
~ In Five Movements ~
First Movement: Looking Inwards.
Second Movement: Tracing Back.
Third Movement: Wishing Question.
Fourth Movement: Healing You.
Fifth Movement: Connecting With
                    Your Child.

CHAPTER 5

Essential Preparation

With any process that taps into childhood memories and emotions that flow beneath the surface, we need to look at safety measures first.

Create a Safe Experience

To begin with, I'd like you to consider these agreements to create a space safe enough to conduct your Process.

Ensure confidentiality

If you are working with another person, agree to a strict code of confidentiality before you begin. Make a verbal agreement that the *details* of the stories you share with each other will not be revealed to anyone else. Revealing our most intimate personal experiences requires privacy and strict confidentiality for engendering trust.

Choose a safe space

Select an environment where your absolute privacy and freedom from interruptions or intrusive noises can be assured. Whether you are indoors or out in Nature, make sure you are physically comfortable, that your body is well supported. Your surroundings should feel friendly to you. Create a space that is emotionally safe enough for your Inner Child—or the Inner Child of the person you are working with—to come forth. Avoid environments that might carry negative associations or triggers. The more sensitive you can be to the needs of the Inner Child, the more fruitful the Process. The Inner Child responds when he or she feels safe.

Choose your moment

Choosing a *time* when you can count on freedom from interruptions is as important as a safe *space*. Clearly, when you have to keep your eye on small children, that won't be the most conducive moment. Remember also that the Process is not appropriate for use in parenting or teaching situations that demand a quick response from you. It's not a substitute for intervention and engagement with your children. Set aside some moments to take the Journey and consider it as a sacred time-out that you are awarding yourself.

Listen without judgement

Make a commitment to yourself—or to the person you are working with—that you will listen to the voice of the Inner Child without judgement or opinion. The purpose is to get in touch with how it felt to be a child. Like all children, the Inner Child needs to trust that all emotions are permissible, meaningful and valid.

No emotion is better or more desirable than another. All emotions arise for a good reason. Remember to think of behaviour separately from emotion. Whereas none of us want to accept behaviours that are destructive, emotions themselves are never harmful.

Be prepared to welcome even those emotions that are culturally frowned upon; including, for instance fear, hatred, lust, jealousy and envy. Lay aside the assumption that some emotions are 'positive' and others are 'negative'.

Greet each Inner Child response with empathy, whether you are working with yourself or with another person.

Listen without expectation

Make a commitment not to rush the Journey. A child does not open up and voice her deepest feelings if she is *expected* to. Allow, rather than push. In a welcoming tone invite the Inner Child to speak, and then wait … leave a space.

Let it be

Agree also to listen to the Inner Child without offering advice. The temptation to fix things for the Inner Child will undoubtedly arise, and when it does, please lay that gently aside.

The goal is to help the Inner Child find his own voice, his needs and wishes; you provide the holding, the curiosity, and the acceptance.

(The only time to offer suggestions—as opposed to prescriptions!—to the Inner Child is if he feels unable to imagine what he wishes for in the Third Movement in the Journey. Instructions for the careful offering of a relevant menu of options will be given in Step 13.)

Ensure the right to self-regulate

Remembering our childhood feelings does not mean re-experiencing childhood trauma in its full force.

Just to touch down for a brief visit, to catch a glimpse from a safe distance is usually more than enough to reconnect us with the sensitivity, fragility and exuberance that were once ours. A light recapturing of childhood can sometimes be all that is needed to renew our self-empathy and self-compassion.

Rather than *reliving* our past, the aim is simply to get close enough to it that we can be moved in our hearts—that is, until we can genuinely say to our Inner Child, 'Ah, no wonder you feel this way!'

If at any stage the Process feels too scary or overwhelming, if emotions come up that feel too difficult to bear, give yourself permission to ease back, or stop altogether.

Many have memories that are forbiddingly traumatic, and we don't necessarily know when such memories might come up. It's therefore essential to proceed slowly and gently, always knowing where the exit is.

Remember that body-memory is state-dependent; you can step out of your Inner Child state by standing up and moving about in an adult way; such as making a cup of tea.

Remember that body-memory is state-dependent; you can step out of your Inner Child state by standing up and moving about in an adult way; such as making a cup of tea.

If it's all too much, move as an adult and soon enough you begin to feel and think like an adult again. If you find yourself still feeling fragile, try the following:

Exercise 10: Grounding and Self-settling

Here is a simple and effective bodymind approach to releasing yourself from anxiety or panic.

Begin by placing the soles of both feet firmly on the ground, roughly shoulder width apart. Choose whether to sit on a chair or stand, whichever feels most comfortable for you right now. Wiggle your feet a little, or rub them on the ground to bring sensation to them. This will help you feel grounded.

> Now place the palms of your hands on your lower belly, warmly supporting the area beneath your navel. Allow your shoulders to relax downward and take a few longer breaths, all the way to your lower belly, until you feel your hands being pushed outward. Emphasise the exhalation with a few long and audible sighs, 'Aaaaaahhhhhh …' With every outbreath, let go of the muscles around your neck and shoulders, relaxing them a little more each time.

It's okay to stop the Process at any point if it seems too scary. Your hands are on the wheel, your foot is on the brakes; apply those brakes if you need to. You can resume the Process later when you feel safer, and if feelings and memories come up that are too difficult, please consider continuing your Inner Child Journey in the presence of a trained counsellor or psychotherapist. The safer you feel, the more comfortable you will be to go deeper and to remain present with all the emotions that come up.

Note the importance of feeling held

It's hard to overstate the importance of holding when we contact our deeper layers of emotional vulnerability. Holding can be physical, but doesn't always need to be. Sometimes we can feel beautifully held when someone listens to us with empathy. If you are good at holding yourself, at giving yourself supportive inner dialogue when you feel tender, then this might be all you need.

And of course, sometimes it can be especially wonderful to ask someone you trust to hold you, just as you'd like to be held. Before you begin your Journey, consider how you might feel during and afterwards. Is there are trusted person who is a good listener nearby, and can they be on stand-by for you? If you are alone, is there a safe and nurturing place for you to rest after your Journey?

Your tone matters

When you converse with your Inner Child it's good to use the same tone as if you were speaking to a real child, asking her how she feels or what has happened to her. Ask with the same kind of interest and care that you would take in speaking to a child that means the world to you. If you really want to get to know this child, then when you ask how she feels, leave her plenty of space to answer you. Listen patiently and without judgement. Don't rush to give advice. And when you ask what she needs from you, don't necessarily rush to the rescue. First give her a chance to speak for herself and tell you what she needs in her own words. That is the attitude with which you would address the Child Within.

A safe space to feel deeply

Keep a Record of your Journey

Consider keeping a pen and writing pad by your side as you settle into your Journey. Make notes about your discoveries and the new insights you have along the way. Whether you prefer to write some notes at the end of the Process, or to record your discoveries as you move through the steps—that's entirely up to you.

Combine your note taking with your inward forays in your own way, according to what best helps you stay connected to the Process. Writing is a powerful way to process emotions, hone your insights and crystallise your thoughts. And since it can be easy to forget what we learn, the notes you keep can help you keep track of new realisations while evidencing how far you have travelled on your personal growth path.

How Long Does the Journey Take?

Both the length and the depth of each Journey you undertake are entirely up to you. Recall that sometimes all you need to do is pause for a moment before you react towards your child and quietly ask yourself what feelings are coming up for you, what has been triggered. It's surprising how often this simple recess is enough to bring you a game-changing 'aha'. In just a few seconds, your Inner Child can help to open your eyes in a new way.

It's not always necessary to travel along the entire, five-movement Journey. Once we've become fluent with this kind of inquiry we can weave questions like, 'What comes up for you when that happens?' or 'How was that for you as a child?' gracefully in and out of conversations with trusted friends. So many new insights can be gained in this way, and this kind of dialogue adds a wonderful intimacy to our friendships. You could say that this kind of Inner-Child-aware conversation takes up no time at all.

If you want to take the whole Journey with some depth, ideally put aside an hour or so. The Inner Child Process tends to fit comfortably into a standard psychotherapy session. But feel free to regulate the depth to which you dive into the Process; we have much to gain, even in the space of an ordinary, 20-minute meditation.

Choose a 'Problem' Situation

In Chapter 1 we talked about what constitutes appropriate uses for the Process. The Inner Child Process is best for addressing the pattern-like, recurring situations that arise in relation to your child, the ongoing impasses, when as a parent or teacher you find yourself feeling stuck. From this point on, I'll be referring to the issue you choose to work on as the '*situation*'.

To prepare for the Inner Child Journey, give your *situation* a name; you might even like to write it down. Define your *situation* as simply as possible in terms of what actually happens. Give a factual description that avoids any judgement, or any attempt to analyse the 'whys and wherefores' of what happens.

It might sound something like this, 'That thing that happens when we go to the mall, and my toddler has a tantrum', or 'When my toddler won't stop asking for something even though I've said "no" many times.'

Some other examples might include, 'When my baby cries and nothing I do seems to help', or 'When my teenager rolls her eyes at me and walks off.'

Alternatively, you might prefer to describe something that happens inside *you*, such as 'Those times when my toddler wants me to play and I feel incredibly reluctant', or 'When my kids argue and I feel like screaming', or perhaps 'When my teenager scowls at me and I feel hurt.'

Once you have devised a simple definition of your *situation*, you'll be ready to move into the steps of Process. But for now, let's begin with an in-depth look at how the Journey works, by unpacking and explaining each of the 20 steps, one at a time. Chapters 6–10 cover the steps in each of the Journey's five movements.

About the Wording

If the instructions that follow seem too copious, please don't worry. Don't forget: you don't need to learn it all by rote. The notes in the coming chapters are there to help you gain a solid understanding of how each step works. Your grasp of each step's purpose will determine the success of your Journey. When you are ready to embark on your Journey, you will be referring to the user-friendly, summarised steps in the Appendices.

One last thing. If you don't like the wording of the questions as they appear in this text, feel free to tweak them so they sound more like *you*. As long as the intent of the questions remain unchanged, it's important that your language feels natural to you. For instance, do you prefer to address your Inner Child in the first person, as in 'How do *I* feel today?' or in the second person, as in 'How do *you* feel today?' You might find other instances where you'll be tempted to modify my wording. You're in charge, so please adapt the phrasing to what helps you feel connected.

CHAPTER 6

First Movement: Looking Inwards

This movement is about turning your attention inward and noticing what is going on inside, so you can learn more about yourself, instead of reacting to your child and the challenging *situation*. You are opening with a self-awareness exercise to find and validate the emotions, sensations and thoughts that move through your inner landscape.

Before you step into your Journey, let's prepare the ground by looking at what it means to pause, reflect and self-regulate emotionally.

Your entry into a reflective, self-inquiring state begins when you stop; take a few moments to pause and become still. Make a space for attending to yourself.

If you are feeling strong impulses to react to your *situation*, take a few longer, deeper breaths into your lower belly; it helps to place your hand supportively on the area below your navel.

Ground yourself by bringing your awareness to your legs and feet, wiggle your feet on the ground to bring sensation there.

If you are feeling an overwhelmingly strong emotional charge, you may need to remove yourself from your child's presence for now (of course, checking first that your child will be okay).

Sometimes it's just too difficult to pause and reflect when you're flooded with emotion. If you're feeling a strong agitation around your arms or shoulders, give that some movement to begin with. 'Listen' to your arms and hands: how do they want to move? It may help for instance, to shake your hands vigorously, stretch and extend your fingers and alternatively squeeze them into a fist.

If you know how to discharge emotion safely, do this as you need to. So, for instance—away from your child—scream into a pillow, punch a mattress, take a towel in both hands and twist it as hard as you can while growling, run on the spot or dance vigorously. If you allow your body to express that build-up of energy in a safe way, this will ease your entry into quiet, inward attunement. Let's call this *managing your emotional charge*.[32]

At times pausing, reflecting and managing your emotional charge is enough to clear a space for you to reconnect with your child helpfully.

Pausing to reflect, if only for a few seconds, engages the 'stop-and-think' region of the brain: the frontal lobes. The frontal lobes act as a transformer that eases your emotional voltage, filtering it down from 240 volts (or in the US 120 volts) to a more manageable 12 volts. This pause to breathe, reflect and manage your emotional charge is how you save yourself from doing or saying what you may later regret. The object is never to suppress your emotions, but to contain yourself so you can bring more awareness and choice into your actions; moving from *reaction* to *response*.

Once you have cleared some space and time to further your self-awareness, you can begin your Journey. Let's look at the steps of the Inner Child Process.

Step 1

To begin your Journey, find a quiet enough place to sit where you won't be interrupted or distracted—a space you can devote to yourself. You can lie down if you prefer, but sitting upright is generally ideal for maintaining an alert state. Take a few moments to make your body comfortable, support your back with a pillow if that feels good. If you are a meditator, your usual meditation position might be just right for you. Wiggle around until you find yourself comfortable and supported enough to invite your attention inwards. Close your eyes gently, allow two or three longer and slightly deeper breaths, and with each exhalation, release your shoulders down. For the time being, slowly let go of attending to the world that surrounds you. Begin by simply allowing your attention to scan your body, just noticing what is happening inside you now. Notice any sensations that take place in your belly, around your chest, in your throat or anywhere else that draws your attention. Ask yourself:

⊛ How does it feel to be here right now?

⊛ What emotions accompany the body sensations that I am noticing?

Be an inner observer; taking note of the feelings you encounter without doing anything to change them.

Step 2

Now let's define the challenging *situation* you have been experiencing with your child. If you haven't done so already, give your *situation* a name, or describe it in one sentence.

Listen closely to the words that come up inside you to describe what you are going through. Don't censor these words as they arise in your mind. Don't bother to make your description sound reasonable or to sanitise it in any way. This is not the moment to attempt a mature 'I statement', not just yet. Let yourself be spontaneous, giving permission to your own words as they appear. For now, these are your words, so let them be. Some examples: 'My baby cries too much', 'My child whinges and whines', 'My toddler is too demanding', 'My teenager is rude', 'I have a terrible temper', 'I can't take this anymore', 'I am a terrible parent'. You'll notice these phrases tend to be faultfinding; either exteriorising the blame or blaming yourself. Those types of fleeting thoughts are extremely common. If you find that your inner voices sound like blaming or shaming, just let them be so for now. You are listening to your thoughts silently and in private. This is how you prevent yourself from acting them out; for now it is safe to allow these thoughts to come just as they are. It's precisely these unedited thoughts that will later lead you to your Inner Child.

Alternatively, you might hear yourself thinking in phrases such as 'That thing that happens when my baby wakes me at night', or 'When my child refuses to eat', or perhaps, 'When he refuses to get up in time for school'. Of course, you might have an entirely different and unique way of describing your *situation*. Most importantly, you need to listen faithfully to your own words—the way they naturally come to you—and to give your bodymind the time to speak.

For the time being, don't look at your *situation* as a problem to be solved. The time for seeking solutions will come later. In this stage of the Journey, you are exploring your thoughts and perceptions without trying to change them in any way. Like threads, these thoughts can later be traced down to an originating spool of body-memory.

If you are feeling disturbed by the nature of the thoughts and feelings you encounter, remind yourself that these feelings arise because you have been *triggered*. These thoughts and feelings are not entirely about your present-moment reality; you are in fact closely monitoring a *body-flashback*. Acknowledge that what you think you see about you—or about your child—may be at least in part due to *projection*. And remember that this is an entirely normal and ordinary bodymind phenomenon.

Step 3

Now repeat the description of your *situation* a few times in your mind, this time paying attention to how you *feel* as you do. We are now beginning to 'listen' for body-memory. Ask yourself:

❀ How does my belly feel when this happens with my child?

❀ What do I notice going on around my chest? In my throat perhaps, or in my jaw?

Bring your attention to your arms, your hands, your legs and feet.

❀ Is there something my arms and my hands want to do?

❀ Is there something my legs and my feet want to do?

Remembering to listen inwardly without judgement or expectation, take note of any emotion that comes up. Even if you appear to feel nothing, validate that; feelings of nothingness, emptiness, blankness or numbness are just as valid as any other. Give your body time to speak its mind.

Sometimes emotions can be like mist, and it takes time to focus-in and find adequate words for them. Honing-in to our emotions does not always lead to immediate clarity. Sometimes, identifying our feelings can seem like trying to tune-in to a distant radio signal. It really does take a little patience and, since emotions are a bodily phenomenon, body awareness is the key. I strongly recommend the book *Focusing* by psychologist Eugene Gendlin;[33] it is the best guide I know to help you locate and name your deepest feelings through awareness of your body.

As your emotions become clearer to you in this step, let them be exactly as they are. Avoid filtering them or giving them a positive spin. Don't look for how you *think* you *should* feel right now. Just welcome your emotions unconditionally. Don't feel you need to go too deeply into these emotions either. Just observe, acknowledge and honour each emotion as it comes up.

Little by little you are writing your Inner Child narrative as it relates to your *situation*, and now you have a longer sentence. It might be something along the lines of: 'When my child does <u>these things</u>, I feel <u>this emotion</u>, or <u>these emotions</u>'.

Step 4

Now bring your attention to your self-talk; the 'voices' you hear inside. Ask yourself:

✳ What do I 'hear' myself thinking about my child when this *situation* arises?

✳ What do I tell myself about myself, as a parent (or carer, or teacher, etc)?

Again, try not to censor anything about your self-talk; it holds vital clues about things you have witnessed in your life, or ways in which you were once treated. Allow the good, the bad and the ugly. You can keep this as confidential as you need to. Some of your inner dialogue is likely to be unkind, critical or shaming—perhaps even vicious. We all possess a realm of our minds known as 'the shadow'; that part we'd prefer to disavow. If you've suffered any moments of controlling, abusive or neglectful treatment as a child, it won't be unusual for you to carry hostile-sounding, shaming or even hateful inner voices from time to time, particularly in times of stress. It takes quite a bit of courage and honesty to acknowledge these 'voices'. The good news is that the more mindful we become about our self-talk, the less influence these 'voices' have on our behaviour.

As you listen to your mental chatter related to your *situation*, know that these 'voices' show you the *projections* you have about yourself as a parent, and about your child. We all create projections about ourselves, and about others. Take stock of your projections, they are doorways into your subconscious, screenshots from body-memory. (You might like to review 'Projection', for particular examples of commonly held projections on page 69.)

Remind yourself that all of us are subject to *neuroception* (see pages 61) when we are triggered. Projection is the mental verbalisation of our body's neuroception. We cannot switch off our projections, but we can recognise them for what they are. How often do we hear that children are 'misbehaving', that babies are 'fussy' or that they are 'good' babies, that toddlers are 'brats', that they are 'spoiled', that they are 'angels' and so on. Sometimes our own thoughts add to the chorus of projections around us.

chronicling your Journey

So, let's look at what you have so far. The narrative from your Inner Child Process might now sound something like this: 'When my child does <u>these things</u>, I feel <u>this emotion</u>, or <u>these emotions</u>; I have <u>these thoughts</u> about myself, and <u>these thoughts</u> about my child.' (You fill-in the underlined text in your own way).

You have completed the first movement in your Inner Child Journey. Thank yourself for acknowledging what might be difficult thoughts and feelings. Anchor the work you have done so far by appreciating your honesty; this will help to fuel your further treks along the Journey. If you are assisting someone else through their Process, offer them the same appreciation. And now you are ready to proceed to the Second Movement in your Journey.

CHAPTER 7

Second Movement: Tracing Back

From here, you can take many possible paths to finding the Inner Child connection beneath your emotional reactions and projections. In this movement, we look at a number of optional routes for tracing your present-day reactions to any origins they may have among your earlier life experiences. If one avenue does not work, or yields a blank, let that be okay. Try another path. Different paths find their destinations at different times. Overall, I commonly use one of six optional paths (listed here as steps 5–10 of the Process). You can try some or all of them, in any order or combination, if the first path you choose doesn't seem to bring you answers.

Remember, the purpose here is to arrive at an 'aha', to better understand yourself. The goal is to be able to genuinely feel, 'Ah, no wonder I sometimes react this way'—in other words: to generate self-compassion. This involves touching on how you felt when you were a youth, or when you were a child or baby. It means feeling your way into the memory just enough so you can know it from the inside; from the perspective of your Inner Child. It does not mean that you need to relive that experience.

This movement—'tracing back'—tries to distil the most significant elements of the memory that has been brought forward for you. This level of attention to your memory will later help you get to the bottom of what drives your reactions. In other words, study these memories now, and soon you unearth the developmental need that was driving your triggered reactions.

Let's begin with Step 5; the first of several *optional* doorways to getting in touch with an originating experience. (Remember: you can think of each of the questions within the steps as a possible keys; if one does not open the door, then try another.)

Step 5

Keeping your eyes closed, bring your attention to the body sensations, feelings and emotions that came up for you in Step 3, letting yourself be aware of *all of that*—its general 'felt sense'. Take a few moments and let yourself be with the totality, the combination of all those feelings. Now choose any, or all, of the following questions to ask, whichever seems to work best for you. Remember that these questions are options. As before, if the first question does not resonate or yield a response, simply move to the next. Ask yourself:

⊛   Is this feeling-state in any way familiar to me?

⊛   Do I have any sense that somehow, I have been in this position before?

⊛   When have I felt something just like this before?

Wait, make a space and allow your bodymind time to respond. Pay attention to any images or sounds that come to you. Some of these images may be clear representations of your past, or perhaps the images that come are symbolic, representing the *feeling* of something you have lived.

If the images or memories that come to you are clearly and directly about a specific moment in your past, then ask:

⊛   When did I feel this way?

⊛   How old was I at the time?

⊛   Who was I with?

⊛   What was going on around me?

⊛   In this original situation, were things happening to me—or was I witnessing things happening to somebody else?

⊛   How was I reacting at the time?

You might be recalling one or more situations from an earlier time in your life. Perhaps from your childhood, adolescence, or simply from younger days—either way, the memory carries a message for you, as will become clear later.

The memory might relate to a single event, such as childbirth, a time you cried for your mother and she would not come, a time you got lost in a shopping mall, a fight with a sibling or parent, or an embarrassing moment in class. It could equally be about an ongoing circumstance: such as an authoritarian parent, a punishing teacher, a period of great loneliness or entrenched conflict between your parents. Whether it happened in a moment, or over several years, for the purpose of our Journey let's call your memory the *source event.*

At this point, are you are satisfied that you've connected with a *source event* that resonates well for you? If yes, you have the option of skipping the rest of the steps in this movement and starting on the Third Movement right away. But there is no rush. If you wish, you could explore the further steps—and don't be too surprised if you gain additional valuable insights.

If Step 5 did not help you connect with your source event, don't worry. There is always another door: let's try Step 6.

Step 6

Sometimes the Process does not lead you to a clear sense of a *source event.* Some things are beyond your narrative recall, and that's perfectly fine. Instead of receiving a particular memory, as you hold your triggered feelings you might be struck by a vague sense of familiarity—a kind of fuzzy deja vu; you have felt something like this before but you have no idea when. If this is the case and Step 5 drew a blank for you, then just pay attention to any images or sounds that come to your mind naturally as you ask the following questions:

- What do I *imagine* might have been happening around me as a child (or younger person) to make me feel this way?

  Validate whatever images come to you. Your fantasies are not random; they are symbolic characterisations of something that felt real to you. Trust the *theme* of your imaginings, rather than the detail.
- What is my imagined story *about*? For instance, is it about loss, oppression, helplessness, injustice, humiliation, or something else altogether?
- Though no detail might be available to me, do I get a sense of the *theme* of my *source event*?

You've now well and truly begun to explore the origins of your feeling-states. To get a more rounded picture, you might also like to look at how your self-talk may have originated. That's what Step 7 is for.

Step 7

Thinking about your self-talk—the 'voices' you hear inside in relation to your *situation*, the things you say in your mind about yourself as a parent (or carer, or teacher), and about your child—ask this:

⊛ Where did I first hear this kind of thing being said?

⊛ Who first said these kinds of things in my life?

⊛ How did I first learn this way of describing a person?

⊛ How did I feel when I first heard someone speak this way about me or about another person?

⊛ What kinds of emotions or bodily sensations do I feel when I remember these voices now?

If, for example, you hear yourself thinking, 'That child is a brat!', think about where you might have first heard this said in your life; who was saying it to whom, and how hearing these words—and the tone with which they were spoken—made you feel at the time. Perhaps you hear yourself thinking, 'I am a hopeless parent'. Again, ask yourself where you first heard someone—yourself, or someone else—characterised as 'hopeless'. And then, most importantly, how did it feel for you at the time?

If the feeling-states, and the inner voices you are working with do not seem familiar in any way—if you appear to be getting nowhere in trying to find a *source event*—that is absolutely fine. One possibility is that, quite genuinely, you have never in your life experienced anything that makes you feel remotely as you do today when faced by this *situation* with your child.

You could choose to let go of your Inner Child Journey at this point and deem it unnecessary for this particular circumstance. However, further possible paths to an Inner Child connection are worth exploring. Here they are:

Step 8

Think of a time when you might have behaved somewhat similarly to the way your child behaves in your current *situation*. Even if you feel you are very different from your child, just think of a time in which your behaviour came at least a little bit close to that of your child today—whether you were the same age or a different age at the time. And then explore the following questions:

⊛ When I behaved comparatively to the way my child does today, how was I treated by my carers (or other people around me)?

⊛ How did that make me feel?

⊛ When I showed emotions similar to those of my child today, how was I responded to?

⊛ How did that make me feel?

If, for instance, today you are triggered by your baby's crying, think about how your tears, or simply your sadness, were treated when you were a child. Did anyone listen to you, validate you, hold you? If it is your child's defiance that you feel embattled with, think about how your own, child-like dabbling with personal power or self-assertion was once treated. Were you supported to have a voice? Most importantly, try to recall how this made you feel at the time. Here it is vital that you focus on your own experience—as you felt it *from the inside*. It can be too easy to remember ourselves through the lens of what our elders would say about us. Their voices can heavily distort our sense of ourselves. Be particularly focused on the *emotional* quality of your internal experience. Did you feel scared? Ashamed? Angry? Hurt?

Step 9

Still unsure about your *source event*? That's fine: here is yet another possible path you could explore. Ask yourself any or all of the following questions:

⊛ When I was about the same age as my child is now, what do I recall about my life then?

⊛ What have I heard from other members of my family about what was going on for me at that age?

⊛ What are some of my most significant memories of that time?

⊛ How were significant people treating me at the time?

⊛ And how did all this make me feel?

⊛ What feelings come up for me now as I contemplate that period of my life?

Step 10

And here is one final possible approach to help you connect with your *source event*:

⊛ What about the part of me that *is* my child (you might like to refer to your actual child by name in this step)?

⊛ How well acquainted am I with the part of me that *is* my child?

✸ How do I feel about that part of myself that is most like my child? That part of me that shares similar attributes, even if I rarely express those attributes?

✸ What has the world said to me about that part of myself?

(Refer to 'The part of you that is your child'—page 43.)

Some Immediate Rewards

It can feel scary at times to become more intimate with our Inner Child's story. The perspective of our Inner Child is often very different to the way our childhood story has been painted for us by others. Inner Child work reclaims an emotional vulnerability that we had, at some time or another, hoped to leave behind. Moreover, in many cultures today it is considered subversive to acknowledge our real feelings instead of the feelings we have been told we should feel. This is no romp in the park, and therefore don't be surprised if at times you feel some resistance to the Process. It takes a measure of courage to do Inner Child work, but the rewards really do make it worthwhile.

So by now you're likely to have gained a fairly good sense of the *source event* that gave rise to the feelings and projections triggered by your present-day *situation*. It will either be an original *source event*, or a more recent and more accessible one that may have reinforced your proneness to being triggered.

Sometimes, merely to recall how you felt during the passage of your *source event* is enough to nourish your heart and renew your bond of understanding with your child. The cascade of insights that follow can almost feel magical, when you come home to your Inner Child. You might experience a welcome release of emotion that liberates you and lets you see your own child through more compassionate eyes, untrammelled by projection. So, even if you only do these first two movements, you may gain something of great value.

Remember that you won't necessarily want to take all the steps in the Second Movement. You are simply trying to understand the *source event* that relates best to your *situation*, so choose the step—or the combination of steps—that seems to bring you the clearest insights. If one step in the Second Movement seems to lead nowhere, then simply try the next one, and so forth. You are visiting your Inner Child by entering into his or her story for a few moments, just long enough to feel 'Ah, no wonder I react this way today!' That is the sole purpose of this port of call on your Journey. In this Second Movement you'll find that different steps work best at different times, depending on the content of your Journey.

caring for Emotions that come up

Let's briefly revisit the importance of emotional safety. At this point in the Journey, you might like to pause and ask:

⊛ How am I going emotionally?

⊛ Is there anything I need for support or comforting right now?

If you are feeling fine, centred and able to stay with your emotional process, then go straight on to the Third Movement.

If a lot of emotions are coming up, it's fine to interrupt your Journey at this point—to get off the train at this station and take a look around for a while. It's entirely up to you; you can make this your terminus, or resume your Journey later.

If you are feeling tender or fragile in any way, I invite you to place your hands on that part of your body where those feelings are centred (it might be around your heart, or perhaps your solar plexus). Let the warmth of your hands permeate that part of you, and breathe in the holding and support that you are giving yourself.

If you are feeling small, vulnerable and shaky, you might like to curl up, wrap your arms around yourself, perhaps even cover yourself with a blanket and rest for a while.

If instead you are feeling charged with frustration or restlessness, you may need to stand up and do something physically vigorous to release the emotional charge: perhaps a jog, some strenuous exercise, or a workout with a punching bag.[34] Listen to what your body wants; trust your body's message and respond to it in the best way that you can.

Would you like to reach out and talk to a trusted person at this point? Talking to a friend can sometimes be the salve that our hearts need. We feel less alone, and the intense phase of emotion passes.

Alternatively, you might be feeling the sense of peace, bliss and fulfilment that can come from deeply connecting with your Inner Child. If so, give yourself time to let these feelings flow through you, soak them up and be nourished by the experience.

You can do much to self-regulate so that you feel in charge of how much emotion you will be dealing with. Recall that if feeling like a child becomes too much for you, you can feel like an adult again. Just place yourself in an adult-like body posture, engage in an adult-like activity, and this will trigger the feeling and body state of being an adult again: in control. Get up, make a cup of coffee, check your emails, perhaps do a little work in your garden. The more you learn to trust your ability to resurface from the Process whenever you need to, the more confident you will feel to sustain longer and deeper dives. Your commitment to self-regulation will help you to stay present, even when your most intense emotions come up. (Re-read the principles of state-dependent body-memory on page 92 if you need to revise.)

Do you keep a journal? Taking the time to write down your experiences is a wonderful way to digest what you are discovering about yourself. Journaling can often unlock deeper seams of insight as you write, and again during subsequent re-readings. Writing can lighten your heart by transmuting your emotions onto the page. The same is true for drawing, painting or any other art form. One of the best things you can do to continue this conversation with your subconscious is to give some expression to the feelings, thoughts and images that this Process has brought up for you.

Taking this Journey alone can be quite different to the experience of being guided and held through it by a qualified practitioner. Both ways have their advantages. Please remember that if at any time you encounter a block in the Process, or you get in touch with memories that are too painful or scary to bear alone, your best course of action is to ask a trained counsellor or psychotherapist to work with you. They don't necessarily need to use this particular Process with you, in fact, your counsellor might prefer not to. Either way, show your counsellor this book, or the steps in the Process as they appear in the Appendices, so your counsellor can understand what you have been working with.

chronicling your Journey

Now the narrative emerging from your Inner Child Journey has grown a little further. You could tell it along these lines, 'When my child does these things, I feel this emotion, or these emotions; I have these thoughts about myself, and these thoughts about my child, and much of this springs from a time when this *source event* was going on for me.' It's getting kind of long isn't it? It might be a good idea for you to write it all down—after you complete your Journey, if you prefer.

The next two movements in the Journey are devoted to bringing you personal healing, release and empowerment for the Inner Child reality that you have connected with through your Journey so far.

CHAPTER 8

Third Movement: The Wishing Question

So far you have asked your Inner Child about *feelings* in relation to the circumstances of the *source event*. This Third Movement in the Process is about asking your Inner Child about *needs*.

The first of two approaches to eliciting your Inner Child's needs will invoke the power of his imagination to give shape to his dearest and deepest wish. Giving a voice to your Inner Child's most tenderly held wishes can be both a painful and a sweet experience. Moreover, once the wish is named, a stream of creative potential is released that will have far-reaching effects in your life.

Your Inner Child's fantasy contains vital clues as to the developmental need that seeks completion. Decode the theme of this core need, and the need can be addressed in real time. Once you have given wings to your Inner Child's secret wish, a path forward is opened and new energies are made available for your mobilisation.

Our Inner Child's longing to complete a developmental quest is never ending, though at first we might be deaf to his voice. If the Second Movement was all about listening to the Child Within, the Third Movement is our way to begin answering his call.

In the 'developmental template' section (page 118) we saw that the knowledge of what might fulfil our core developmental needs is encoded in our neurobiology. Even when we don't appear to know what we need, we tend to recognise it once we have seen or felt it. Our imagination can play a key role here. If we allow ourselves to daydream a little, the fantasies that spring from our subconscious mind offer us clues about what we need in order to grow.

Our fantasies speak for the developmental template that uses the language of symbol and metaphor. The child who imagines a magical saviour, for example, longs for the protection that is her birthright. The child who sees herself flying on a magic carpet may be longing for more freedom. The themes of protection and freedom are just two of several core developmental essentials that we all need at critical moments of our development, if we are to reach our fullest potential.

When we understand a developmental need in terms of its *theme*, this enables us to translate the need into a form that we can appropriately receive as adults. Then we need to do a little deciphering.

Table 5 (page 206) lays out the developmental *themes* belonging to each stage of infancy, childhood and adolescence. This table is an interpretive map designed to help you understand even the most cryptically expressed desires of your Inner Child.

Table 5 also helps you identify adult-appropriate developmental nutrients that can fulfil each childhood developmental need. When we reach out and receive the longed-for developmental nutrients, our hearts expand; we grow in confidence and compassion, and we become more capacious parents, teachers and mentors for others.

As parents or teachers, the pattern-like challenging *situations* that we find ourselves in with our children tend to be related to our own psychological wounding (the developmental needs incompletely met in our early lives). This Third Movement helps your Inner Child define the developmental needs that were not met in your *source event*. Your challenging *situation* may contain a gift; helping you become aware of a long-buried and unmet need.

Remember, some of our developmental needs are about *doing*—there is something we wish we could have done or said, in the occasion of the *source event*. Other needs are about *receiving*—there is something we wish someone else might have given us, or done for us.

Returning to your Inner Child, let's continue the Journey.

Step 11

Let's go back to the *source event*. If you have taken a break from the Journey, it may be helpful to repeat the steps of settling-in (see Step 1). When you feel settled in and attentive, take time to contemplate the *source event* you had come to, and connect again with how it felt to be there as a child. Begin by repeating to yourself your description of the *source event* in simple terms, such as: 'When <u>this</u> was going on around me, and I was feeling like <u>that</u>.'

Now, here are some new questions to ask, in any order or combination that feels right for you. After each of these questions, make sure you wait patiently and give your Inner Child the time she needs to respond. She might reply with words, with imagery or with fantasy. Ask yourself:

✸ When <u>this</u> was going on around me, and I was feeling like <u>that</u>, what do I wish might have happened differently?

✸ What do I imagine would have helped me feel better?

✸ Is there something I wish I could have said or done that would have helped me feel better?

✸ Is there anything I wish someone else might have given me that might have helped me feel better?

✸ Is there anything I wish someone else might have done for me that might have helped me feel better?

Do you see what you are doing here? You are using the power of your imagination to begin giving a definition to the unmet (or incompletely fulfilled) developmental need.

Sometimes when you arrive at this point of the Inner Child Journey, the Inner Child's response is clear and immediate. He knows exactly what he needed for the *source event* to resolve. He tells you his need in no uncertain terms. It might sound as simple as 'I wish Mum would have picked me up and comforted me!' or 'I wish I could have fought back against the school bully!' or 'I wish my dad would have played with me!' or 'I wish my school had stopped forcing me to study maths!'

On some occasions, however, your Inner Child will simply be unable to imagine what she wants. Perhaps the need lies buried under heavy layers of shame or fear. Many of us carry limiting beliefs that prevent us from telling ourselves, even silently and in secret, what we really wish for. On the threshold of a wish, a harsh inner voice tells us, 'I don't think I would be allowed that', or 'That would be too embarrassing for me to do that', or 'Surely I don't deserve that'. The invitation to wish has triggered a new body-flashback; a signal arises from body-memory to warn us that asking for more could land us in hot water. Should our deepest wishes slip our defences momentarily, we might quickly rein them back in. There is audacity in wishing; it can feel dangerous.

Sometimes the power to wish does not even get off the ground. Our Inner Child seems utterly stumped; unable to conjure the faintest idea of what would meet his need. This impasse is not always due to body-memories of fear or shame. As we discussed earlier, sometimes we can't think of our need until we are shown for the first time what would fulfil it. This is especially true in childhood.

But every child wishes to be free to wish; and here is the moment to give the faculty of fantasy its freest possible rein. If this is a difficult stage in your Journey, please know that it's more than worth it. Acknowledge your Inner Child's wish and validate it; and you release a formidable force for healing and personal growth. The wish provides fuel as well as a compass to set the direction of your unfoldment.

The next two steps in the Journey are only necessary when your Inner Child feels stuck or uncertain about what she needs.

Step 12

If your Inner Child is unable to name her need or make a wish in Step 11, you might need to give her a helping hand. If you are working with another person, you may find yourself needing to offer their Inner Child some encouragement. If your Inner Child seems afraid to acknowledge her wish, begin by validating her hesitation. Let her know that it's perfectly okay for her not to be able to articulate her wishes. If she is afraid or ashamed to confess her dearest longing, she has good reason to feel this way, based on her past experience. Let her know that help is at hand and assure her that there is no pressure to produce. Ask your Inner Child what might help her feel safe enough to voice her wishes right now. Perhaps she needs your promise that she can confide in you because you will keep her wishes a secret. You might need to let her know that she is protected, that you will keep her from danger. Perhaps she simply needs reassurance that you will not judge her.

Getting the ball rolling can be difficult, but often just one helpful nudge is enough to bring the imagination to life. When the power of fantasy is somnolent, following are some helpful questions that can rouse it.

Begin by taking a few moments to think about the *source event*, and how you felt as it was all happening…

⊛ If I could wave a magic wand that would make it totally okay for me to have exactly what I would have wished for, then what would this wish be? Or,

⊛ If by magic I could have had whatever I wished for at that moment, with absolutely no retribution, then what would that have been?

In this part of the Process the logical or rational can be a hindrance; it's very important to encourage free flights of fancy. Perhaps your Inner Child wishes she could have sprouted wings and flown away—welcome every kind of playful and symbolic thought. Give yourself permission to fantasise. Ask:

⊛ In my wildest dreams, what would have made it all feel okay?

Begin to distil the theme inherent in the fantasy. A dream of being held and comforted might be, you could say, about nourishment, or perhaps about nurturance. A dream about a heroic rescuer might be about the longing for protection. Perhaps a fantasy about your own magical heroism could be about the need for recognition or acknowledgement—or maybe the need to disinhibit your personal power. Do you find yourself craving a windfall of money? What if at its heart, this yearning is about security? Or could it be about the need for more playfulness in your life?

Our castles-in-the-air are not random. In symbolic form, they reveal our primal needs for belonging, safety, support or connectedness. Read your flights of fancy and therein you will discover your unmet longings for freedom of self-expression, freedom from burdens, from shame, guilt or enmeshment. Violent or vengeful fantasies often bespeak an urgent need to better assert one's interpersonal boundaries. If the developmental needs that are being stirred hark back to your adolescence, you might find yourself fantasising about sexual vitality, about a truer expression of your vocational gifts, about social belonging. Perhaps you can think of even more examples of core developmental needs that might animate your Inner Child's wishes.

As you can see, it's not the substance of the wish or fantasy so much as its theme that matters for our purposes. The theme of your Inner Child's wish represents the developmental nutrient that would promote your next step in healing and growth. When we reconnect with a painful *source event*, the wishing that emerges is a faithful tip-off about our unmet developmental needs.

The wish holds a most powerful evolutionary function; it's our prime mobilising agency. Springing from a neuropsychological script—a record of our unfinished business—the wish is a password that unlocks the door of change. If you struggle to deduce a meaningful developmental theme from your Inner Child's wish, review Table 5 (page 206). You will find clues there. And you will discover that the theme—rather than the letter—of your wish (and the developmental nutrient it represents) can readily be met in the real world. Make sure you keep careful interpretive notes about the theme of your Inner Child's wish, as later in the Journey we will explore how you can creatively fulfil this need in your life as it is today.

Now, what happens when your Inner Child has wish-paralysis? No matter how you ask, she hasn't the foggiest idea of what she can wish for. This is where the Inner Child Process can get a little tricky. Now we need a second, more interventional approach to help your Inner Child locate and identify her need.

Remember that even if your Inner Child is stumped and cannot conjure up any idea about what she needs, your body will respond noticeably when someone suggests a nutrient that resonates well with your current need. Hear someone else articulate a need you did not know you had, or see this need exemplified in your environment, and your body offers a pulse of recognition. You might spontaneously sigh, feel a tingle of excitation, a sudden tension or some other kind of somatic signal. That's why it's so important to pay attention to the subtle shifts that take place in your body as you move through this step in the Journey.

So, perhaps your Inner Child was befuddled in the face of his source event. Offer him a judiciously-selected menu of possible wishes and his developmental template kicks-in. Your Inner Child tugs on your sleeve as if to say, 'Yes, that's the one!' when he recognises the nutrient that would help him take his next developmental step. Think of yourself as the broker of this Process; your role is to bring your lost Inner Child to the place of need fulfilment. When you have helped your Inner Child locate his need on the inside, then he will know what to reach out for in the outside world.

So, if Steps 11 or 12 have already helped you name your Inner Child's wish, then skip to the next movement (next chapter). Otherwise, try Step 13.

Step 13

This is the point in the Journey where you will need to reach into your pocket, pull out your developmental map (Table 5 on page 206) and unfold it. This map will help you to orient your Inner Child towards the need that she was unable to articulate or imagine for herself. We will take a deeper look at the sequence of core, developmental needs in Chapter 11.[35]

Our developmental map offers a range of key developmental nutrients that we all depend on in order to move through each psycho-emotional rite of passage. But in offering options—'Would you like this? Or perhaps that?'—we need to be cautious about how we ask to avoid being invasive or overly prescriptive. A tentative style of questioning is important if we are to avoid interrupting the Inner Child's capacity to tune in to the sometimes faint signals from her inner developmental template.

In Part C we will be looking in close detail at the art of helping your Inner Child identify her wish. In the meantime, here are a few examples of questions by which you can bring wishing-options to your Inner Child:

✳ Imagine: when I was in the middle of this (name the *source event*), what if I was offered this outcome, or that possibility? How might I have felt then?

✳ How might I have felt at the time of my *source event*, if by some magic, this had happened instead? Or if, by some magic, that different outcome was offered to me?

✳ Imagine: what if, at the time of this *source event*, I was somehow given the freedom, with no retribution, to express exactly what I was feeling inside. What would I have really wanted to express? As I imagine myself saying this, or perhaps shouting that—how might that have felt?

✳ Imagine: what if, at the time of this *source event*, I was somehow given the freedom, with no retribution, to allow my impulses to come through and to let my body do whatever it needed to do. What would I have really wanted to do? Imagining myself doing this, or perhaps doing that, how might that have felt?

An attitude of playfulness helps to unlock the power of imagination, and to bring your Inner Child to her undiscovered longing. For the time being, allow yourself to suspend your sense of what is probable. One by one, imagine a range of different outcomes—or happier endings, if you like—for your *source event*, and tune in closely to your body as you visualise each one. Which imagined new ending gives you the greatest feeling of ease, of empowerment, of inner peace or inner pleasure?

The wishing question is really a power question. The permission to wish can propel you forward in unexpected and amazing ways. Don't be surprised if at first this step in the Journey exposes some of your most self-limiting beliefs and assumptions about what is impossible, what you are not allowed to have or what you do not deserve. These beliefs; formed in early-life moments of trauma, shame or emotional pain, may have seemed perfectly true given the circumstances of the time. But our negative beliefs are often projections; they reflect our past but are not necessarily true about the larger world we inhabit now. These limiting beliefs have blocked our vision and with this step we are giving ourselves an opportunity to see beyond them. Permission to wish lifts a veil from our eyes and fills our lungs with fresh air. I often find the release brought by this movement to be profound.

Checking in on Emotional Safety

If, in the course of your Journey, feelings come up that seem too overwhelming, or if you find yourself emotionally fragile afterwards, remember to consider seeking the support of an experienced therapist. You might also like to review 'Create a safe experience' (page 145).

Chronicling your Journey: The Narrative Grows

Now you have even more to say about your Inner Child's learning. Let's review what you have discovered so far. 'When my child does these things, I feel this emotion, or these emotions, I have these thoughts about myself, and these thoughts about my child. Much of this springs from a time when this *source event* was going on for me. When the *source event* was happening, I wish I could have done this, or said that.' Alternatively, you might want to conclude your growing narrative with, 'I wish someone would have given me this, or done that for me.'

Now, remember that you don't have to be a child again to fulfil the *theme* of the developmental need—or needs—that you have now identified. Let's see what you can do about having at least a little of this need met in your life today!

The wishing question

CHAPTER 9

Fourth Movement: Healing the Parent

The Third Movement helped you to name the developmental needs that were triggered to awareness through the challenges of parenting. The Fourth Movement is about answering those needs and completing a developmental sequence that was once arrested.

The biggest shifts happen when we give ourselves the developmental nutrients that meet our unsatisfied developmental needs. But how can we do this without having to fully relive our births, without having to hop onto our mother's breast or onto our father's lap all over again, hoping for a happier ending? How can we meet our developmental needs creatively, in ways that are appropriate to our current life circumstances?

In this movement you'll begin by taking the *theme* of your developmental need—rather than the *literal* presentation of the need—and artfully adapting its meaning so a realistic and attainable nutrient can be found for you today. That's what your Inner Child has been pushing and prodding you for, for as long as you can remember, and possibly earlier. Your actual child's behaviour, that you find irking, is now compelling you to listen to that inner voice, to validate its message and to act upon it. In the Fourth Movement, you'll attend to your Inner Child's need by offering her a material response.

I realise that at first, this might seem like a daunting prospect. A number of unsettling questions tend to arise at this point. Isn't the thirst of a wounded Inner Child virtually unquenchable? Is it even possible to erase, with any finality, the pain of our childhood wounds? Aren't we better off turning from our past and facing forward? To answer these questions we need to take a very short detour.

Your Inner Child wants assurance that you will respond to her simple needs. This doesn't mean she needs you to make up for every moment of suffering she may have lived. Sometimes simply a loving validation of your Inner Child's voice is enough. She needs to hear you say, 'Ah, no wonder you feel this way!' and to mean it from the bottom of your heart.

Your Inner Child's needs are not bottomless, nor are they incompatible with your needs as an adult. Responding to these needs can only enrich your life, empower you in all you do and deepen your capacity for compassion towards others. I have no way of predicting for how long or how deeply you need to address these needs before you feel 'healed' because there is no final destination in healing. You are not repairing something broken—just learning to become kinder and more responsive to yourself—a more empathic parent to yourself.

Your Inner Child's needs may ease, but they will continue to re-emerge in novel ways as unexpected triggers occur. With every rite of passage through adulthood, we newly revisit our issues of childhood and adolescence. Our emotional age elevator keeps going up and down. But it's good to know that the simplest gestures to heed the call of the Inner Child can often produce the most profound shifts.

If healing and growth have a final objective, I am not sure what it is. And if they have a final destination, I have no idea where it is. I don't expect that our body-memory of pain or trauma is ever completely erased once and for all. Some vulnerability to triggering seems to remain with us, albeit in more moderate form as we grow. However, we can always deepen our understanding of the emotional needs that the triggering has exposed, as well as our capacity to meet these needs dependably. To put it another way, we can learn to defuse our triggered states more readily. But that's not all. With every act of loyalty to our Inner Child, our self-compassion grows, as does our compassion towards others. We gain energy and vitality and our way forward is made clear.

Family conflicts are not riddles to be solved; they are portals to a deeper intimacy—with self and others—if we are willing to step through. We don't need to close the book on our history; nor wipe clean the slate of our past. The past does not resolve, but when we embrace all that our experience can teach us, a circle is completed. With this acceptance, our capacity for love and joy expands and our children benefit from our clarified vision.

Try as we might to turn from our past, the Inner Child never ceases to call. Through our dreams, through our over-reactions and under-reactions, our body-flashbacks and at times through disease, our wounded Inner Child continues to claim our attention. Each time we consciously survey our past we are released a little further into a future less likely to repeat its themes.

I am amazed at the boundless variety of inventive ways in which the theme of any developmental need can be met. Meeting our core emotional needs does not have to be difficult and it certainly needn't be costly. Just saying 'yes' to your Inner Child's need is a watershed moment that opens your heart and brings you into closer coherence with life's natural rhythms. Don't worry if at first the idea of finding your developmental nutrient seems complicated, I will be offering illustrative anecdotes in Part C that I hope will help clarify your way.

Step 14

Thinking about the *source event* at the centre of your current Journey, take a few moments to contemplate what your Inner Child wished could have happened differently. Knowing your Inner Child's dearest fantasy, consider now the central motif of this fantasy by asking yourself:

- What does my Inner Child's wish tell me about the *theme* of my developmental need?

What is meant by the *theme* of a need? Let's take a look. For example, does the wish carry a theme of protection? Is it about asserting new boundaries? Is it about receiving more support? Perhaps the wish speaks of the right to pleasure—the right to play perhaps? Or is it about nourishment? About the right to express your feelings? Something else altogether? You might like to consult Table 5 (page 206) for help in distilling a theme. Give a name to the theme of your Inner Child's developmental need. It might be, for instance, self-assertion, reassurance, nourishment, asking-for-help, escape, belonging, etc.

Now that you have identified the *theme* of your developmental need, let's try to understand how this need might apply to your life as it is today. In other words, how does this wound manifest in your relationships, generally? When our children push our buttons, the wound they expose in us is likely to have already been impacting other areas of our lives for some time.

For obvious reasons, the parenting relationship is not an appropriate forum for us to work on our own childhood issues. Though our children shed light on our wounds, we must momentarily turn away from them—towards ourselves, towards other adults and towards Nature—to reach for our developmental nutrients.

Simply by being themselves, our children serve as mirrors for us, but theirs is not the job of healing us. This step in the Journey requires us to explore other arenas in our lives in which the same issue might similarly manifest. Use any or all of the following questions to answer the question: Where else in your life does the same unmet developmental need rise to the surface?

⊛ Besides the challenges my child brings me, do any other situations in my life cause me to feel similar feelings?

⊛ Do other people in my life trigger similar feelings in me, as my child's vexing behaviour does?

⊛ Is there a situation affecting me currently in which I feel similar to the way I felt, as a child, during my *source event*? Is there a situation in which I currently *need* something similar—or of a similar *theme*—to what I needed back then, as a child?

⊛ Thinking about significant people in my life today, with whom do I sometimes feel similarly to how I felt as a child, in my *source event*?

⊛ Thinking about my life as it is today, to what aspect of my life might the theme of this developmental need apply most closely?

Step 15

Now let's move from the need, towards what would address it. The aim is to identify an appropriate *nutrient* that you can realistically work towards or reach out for.

⊛ Can I give myself the essence of my Inner Child's wish, simply by *imagining* it being fulfilled?

Take all the time you need to immerse yourself in an elaborate fantasy about your need being fulfilled, adding as much detail as you can. Pay attention to how you feel as you imagine receiving your wish coming to fruition. What happens to the way your body breathes? What new sensations arise in your body?

There might also be a way to fulfil your Inner Child's wish in *real time*. Consider the questions:

- Can I think of ways to give myself the *essence* of what my Inner Child desires? How might I do this practically and realistically?

If you feel stuck at this point, consult Table 5 (page 206). Look under the 'Restorative, healing developmental nutrients (for the adults)' column. This will help you identify the nutrient(s) to match your Inner Child's need. Then ask yourself:

- What changes would I like to experience in my life in relation to the developmental need my Journey has highlighted? Is there something new that I need from the world around me? Is there something I need to ask for, from significant people in my life?

Consider a new course of action that you can practise. Here are some examples, and you might be able to think of more:

- Do I need to reach out for help from others in a new way?
- Do I need to take more time to engage in my favourite, self-nourishing activity?
- Do I need to practise being a little more up-front about my feelings to others?
- Do I need to let go of some burdensome responsibility that is no longer relevant in my life?

Make sure that the new behaviours you are attempting remain consistent with the theme of your need. Now ask:

- Can I now make a commitment to myself to take steps—even if these need to be baby steps—towards my chosen course of action (my developmental nutrient)? Can I make this promise to my Inner Child?

Effort—even the smallest—is the embodiment of commitment. A palpable movement—whether it succeeds or fails—helps your Inner Child feel validated. Pay close attention to how you feel when you commit to giving yourself your developmental nutrient. In particular, notice what happens throughout your body—how your breathing changes, the sensations that move through you.

This Fourth Movement is particularly powerful and life affirming because now you are offering your Inner Child more than just your attention; you are offering her a *response*. This could be a watershed moment in your personal growth; there are some key points to understand in relation to finding your developmental nutrient. Let's take a little detour for a closer look at what developmental nutrients can be.

Concocting a Good Developmental Nutrient

The right developmental nutrient might be obvious and easy to find sometimes; but at other times it might take a little ingenuity. Allow yourself to experiment and be playful. Your imagination can help you find an abundance of ways and means.

Let's say, for instance, you uncover a need to be heard or to receive empathy. Ask yourself who in your life (not your actual child, but another adult) you would like to receive this attention from. Can you dare speak to that very person about your need? Or perhaps is it better to seek the company of an individual whom you already know to be a good listener? Are you a good listener to yourself? Might you need to practise making 'I' statements so that others might more clearly understand your feelings and needs?[36] For example, an 'I' statement might sound something like this, 'When I share my feelings with you, I just need to be heard.' Or like this, 'I don't really need advice right now. I'd just like to know if you can relate to how I feel.'

If your wish bore a theme of escape, does your life contain an onerous burden that you need to offload? Might you need to be more mindful of limits in your work rhythms? Should you be taking time off sooner, more frequently? What if you give yourself permission to lie on your couch and watch a sci-fi movie? Think about the many ways, large or small, that you could get 'away from it all'.

If 'boundary' was your theme, do you need to say 'no' to a certain person in your life more often? Like many parents, your child might be the first person you think of in this context, but that might be a little too easy. Who is the adult in your life to whom you need to say 'no' a little more? This can sometimes feel quite challenging, so how could you do this in a way that feels as safe as possible?

And what if your theme was about nurturance or comforting? What kinds of comforting or nurturing experiences best resonate with you? Maybe you need to curl up with a good book, slide into a warm bath, ask someone you trust for a warm hug or schedule a massage. Perhaps you might take yourself for a beautiful Nature walk, or listen to a sublime piece of music.

The theme of freedom is another one that often comes up. Is there something a little wild that you have dreamt of doing but have not yet dared to do? Go out wearing something a little 'crazy', dance with more abandon than usual, sing in public for the first time—or, what the hell—go bungee-jumping! Get the picture? What little step can you dare take into an experience that is just breath-taking enough to make your heart say, 'yippee!'

Sometimes the developmental nutrient might need to be something momentous that involves macro changes in your life, such as starting an entirely new career, travelling overseas or leaving a relationship that has run its course. Often, it might involve no more than a simple act of self-care, voicing your feelings to someone you love, or just a moment of mindful attending to your own internal space. Your nutrient might be as humble as placing a hand on your belly, on your heart or another place on your body that craves warmth and support. Honour your developmental need with a meaningful gesture and as a result, you develop.

Whatever your developmental nutrient, you will probably need to give it to yourself more than once; perhaps even to install it as a new and regular feature in your life. Begin as soon as you can. Your commitment to yourself eases the urgency felt by your Inner Child—and this in turn takes the heat out of your reactivity; you become less easily triggered. Sometimes, your Inner Child simply wants to hear that it is all right to wish what she wishes for, and your validation suffices to bring release and inner peace. Some needs require action, while others are quenched simply with compassionate inner dialogue.

Recall what we learned earlier about your 'developmental template' and how this internal compass helps you navigate towards the right developmental nutrient. If you take the time to experiment, your body soon tells you when you have found the nutrient that most appropriately fits your developmental need. If your first idea doesn't work as you would like, that is okay. Give yourself room to explore, to try one thing and then another. Remember that you don't have to be alone; if necessary, seek the counsel of a trusted friend, perhaps a trained therapist. There is always some way to say 'yes' to your Inner Child. We will be revisiting the wonders of our developmental template, and how to consult it, when we are searching for a nutrient that is 'just right' in Part C. You will find plenty of helpful tips in Chapter 13 to make your nutrient taking as easy and enjoyable as can be.

Lastly, when we bring our Inner Child home, he does not arrive empty handed. He lends us his genius, his vitality, spontaneity, playfulness, warmth, humour, irreverence and the boundless creativity that a healthy child can never lose. As we reclaim our lost Inner Child, we are renewed; even our bodies and immune systems receive a boost.

Your Actual child, Before Your Inner child

What happens when your child needs a prompt response from you and you don't at first have the time to start giving yourself your developmental nutrient? In fact, that might be the case more often than not. As we will see in Chapters 13 and 14, to create enduring change we usually need to reinforce our nourishing and re-empowering experiences many times over. Our children can't wait that long. Fortunately, they don't have to. If all you have time for is to validate your Inner Child's needs—to offer yourself a moment of compassion—just the time it takes to get the 'Ah, no wonder!' experience—that is likely enough for now. Already, your perceptions about your child will have started to alter.

Clearly it is a priority to interact with your child, to attend to her needs as your situation calls for it. When you are satisfied that you have connected with your child appropriately—the fifth and next movement in the Process—then you can apply yourself to the more ongoing commitment to self-care and development. In other words, you don't have to stick rigidly to the order of the steps in the Process.

When you have heard your Inner Child's wishes (Third Movement, Steps 11–13), you can skip to the Fifth Movement (Steps 16–20) if you need to, and then come back to engage with the Fourth Movement (Steps 14–15) when you have the space and time later. Over time, as you continue to nourish and liberate yourself, your capacity for connection with your child grows ever more. With each repeat of the Fourth Movement, you become more present as a parent, and your passage through the next movement is made easier. Your healing heals others.

chronicling your Journey: The Narrative Grows Further

We have added a new twist to the tale now. It might sound something like this, 'When my child does these things, I feel this emotion, or these emotions—and I have these thoughts about myself and these thoughts about my child.

'Much of this springs from a time when this *source event* was going on for me. When the *source event* was happening, I wish I could have done this, or said that; or I wish someone would have given me this, or done that for me.

But today I can receive the *theme* of this wish in the shape of an appropriate developmental nutrient. I can make a commitment to respond to the needs of my Inner Child. This will help me to heal and grow.'

Segue Towards the Fifth Movement

The Fourth Movement in the Journey has paved a pathway for you the parent, carer or teacher to grow, to heal and thus to gain from the provocation that your child has brought to you. Even without a further step, once you have taken ownership of your emotional reactions you have loosened any projections that might have clouded your perception of your child.

Your commitment to self-care is highly likely to ease the dynamic between you and your child, even before you begin to enact and absorb your chosen nutrient.

As you begin to shift your attention from yourself back towards your child, you may discover your feelings towards him, as well as your perceptions about him, have transformed. Your capacity to understand your child's struggles has expanded in leaps and bounds. Judgement gives way to epiphanies as we foster our Inner Child connection.

When you choose to see that each parenting dilemma is at least as much about you as it is about your child, this does more than improve your vision; it also amplifies your patience and strengthens your resolve. Ultimately, taking ownership of your emotional cargo and answering your emotional needs enlarges your reservoir of calm, compassion and warmth. You find yourself responding with added playfulness, as well as clearer self-assertion. Your capacity for presence grows organically with every growth step that you take.

Have you noticed how often your child's needs seem to coincide with yours, and have you wondered why? When you are triggered by your child in a way that blocks your responsiveness or muddies your vision, that's how you know that one of your own wounds has been activated. Triggers happen through similarity; so the issue that has been triggered for you is thematically related to the issue that your child is struggling with. We are not triggered randomly; there is order in evolution. Heal yourself and you can heal your child. Give to yourself, and it becomes so much easier—and more enjoyable—to give to your children, as well as to decode their most baffling and quirky behaviours.

So, now that you have at least initiated a new, validating conversation with your Inner Child, it's time to return your attention towards your actual child.

CHAPTER 10

Fifth Movement: Connecting with your Actual Child

Having answered the call of your Inner Child, it is time to use that wisdom for the benefit of your own child. Let's bring the focus back to your actual child, the partner in your challenging *situation*, the one who triggered you and prompted you to embark on this Journey. These are the final steps in your Inner Child Journey.

Step 16

Now that you have validated your Inner Child's voice, think about your actual child and pay close attention to how you feel. Ask yourself:

⊛ Do I still see my child in the same way, or have my perceptions changed since I began this Journey?

Take careful note of how your perceptions about your child have shifted—whether the change is subtle or a profound transformation. Then ask:

- Has my Journey given me an 'Ah, no wonder!' experience, in relation to my child's challenging behaviour?

Think about what first triggered you, and then look further at how your Journey has changed your experience. Ask:

- Does the trigger still seem to affect me in the same way?
- How has the Process affected my feelings towards my child, and how I feel about her behaviour?
- Which of my feelings have intensified, which have softened and which have disappeared altogether?
- Have any new feelings about my child come up for me?

Step 17

Your intimate conversation with your Inner Child may have already given you new clues about what your actual child needs—the inside story. The following questions can help to shape your enquiry. Choose any or all the questions that seem to fit best for you:

- What might my child be feeling inside when: he cries that way, acts that way, looks that way, or speaks that way, etc?
- What might my child be asking for when she behaves that way?
- When I once felt or behaved similarly to how my child does now, what would have helped me? What would have best connected with my heart?
- If I were in my child's shoes right now, what would meet my emotional needs?

Step 18

If your Journey so far has moved you—brought you some emotional release, clarified your thoughts, sharpened your resolve or allowed your heart to be a little more open—then your body language, your eyes and the tone of your voice are likely to reflect that. Even when you are not aware of these shifts, your child detects the changes in the quality of your presence, albeit unconsciously. Ask yourself:

- Have the changes in my state affected my child's mood, perhaps even my child's behaviour?

It is not unusual for this transference to happen even before a verbal exchange occurs between you. Having sensed the energetic changes in you, your child can be changed in synch with you.

Step 19

Over and above the subtle and beneficial changes in your energy, your behavioural follow-through is now all-important. Make a commitment to a new response set, a new course of action designed to better connect with your actual child. In all likelihood, you are already feeling more open-hearted as a result of your Journey, and a natural tendency to want to act differently has already surged naturally within you. Make a clear statement to yourself:

- ❊ What can I commit to doing differently for my child, or saying differently from now on?
- ❊ How do I feel when I make this agreement with myself?

Think about the developmental nutrient you chose for yourself in the Fourth Movement, then ask:

- ❊ As I think about receiving my developmental nutrient—or as I begin to actually receive it—how does this affect my feelings towards my actual child?
- ❊ How does receiving my nutrient affect my ability to respond to my actual child's needs?

Step 20

Thank your Inner Child for voicing her feelings and sharing her wisdom, and let her know you will visit her again. If you like, visualise yourself giving your Inner Child a hug, and allow yourself to voice any parting words that come to you. Make a pledge to your Inner Child that you will be there again to hear and respond to his needs, when you can. The more secure your Inner Child feels, the less susceptible you are to being triggered. To finish, acknowledge yourself for having had the courage to take this Journey.

Pause, take a breath and perhaps have a stretch. You've now finished reading the explanatory notes for all the steps in the Process. Congratulations for arriving to this point, I'm sure there has been quite a lot to digest. Let's now look at what your completed Journey has shown you.

chronicling Your Journey: Back to Your child

'When my child does <u>these things</u>, I feel <u>this emotion</u> or <u>these emotions</u>; I have <u>these thoughts</u> about myself, and <u>these thoughts</u> about my child.

'Much of this springs from a time when <u>this</u> *source event* was going on for me. When the *source event* was happening, I wish I could have <u>done this</u>, or <u>said that</u> or, I wish someone would have <u>given me this</u>, or <u>done that for me</u>.

'But today, I can receive the *theme* of this wish, in the shape of an appropriate developmental nutrient. I can make a commitment to respond to the needs of my Inner Child. This will help me to heal and grow.

'My Inner Journey has also helped me to understand what my child needs when he or she does <u>these things</u>, and it has given me <u>these new insights</u> about how I can respond most helpfully to my child.'

Final notes

Your Inner Child connection may have already given you a strong intuitive sense of what your child is struggling with and what your child longs for. Even when your child cannot directly tell you what she needs—as is often the case—your Inner Child offers you a kind of subsoil, intuitive connection that can orient your responses. As you return to your child with a new vision, the way she receives you—or doesn't receive you—gives you some indication as to how close you have come to understanding her.

Take the time to reflect on the new insights and compassion you've gained along the paths of your Journey. If you are still uncertain how to respond, bring your questions to your child; that is, if he is old enough and willing to talk with you openly and frankly. Alternatively, offer your child a menu of options and let him choose what he would like from you.

Finally, remember that the wisdom you gain through Inner Child Journeys is not a substitute for up-to-date parenting information. Inner Child work is a vitally important supplement, but not a replacement for what the science of child development tells us. On occasion, you might still need professional consultation.[37]

Your Inner Child Journeys will most likely help make you a better listener towards your child (as you become a better listener of yourself). You naturally become more patient, more spacious towards your child's unique ways. This shift in your presence will not go unrewarded. Good listening encourages good communication. Your child will learn to articulate her needs more clearly and directly as she feels increasingly heard and validated.

You have reached deeply into your heart, felt the tenderness, innocence and yearnings that were once yours. This cannot but move you, alter your energy and modify the way you speak. In turn, your child learns to be more open to you. With their immediate feedback, our children are our best teachers.

But at times you may want more. You may want a toolkit for active listening. You may also want tips on how to speak to your child simply, non-threateningly and assertively so she will be more likely to listen to you, to be interested in you and to accept your guidance. You'll find a helpful source of communication and conflict resolution skills in my books *Heart-to-Heart Parenting*, Chapters 13–14 and *Parenting for a Peaceful World*, Chapter 20.

As much as you can, enjoy and even celebrate your growth and the insights you gain during your Journey. You may experience pain as you uncover distressing memories. Nevertheless, if you pay close attention, you will note that growth brings an intrinsic pleasure; the satisfaction of 'aha's' gained, the exhilaration of Eureka moments. When you have an 'Ah, no wonder!' experience about yourself, it feels like you're coming home to yourself—something that had been torn asunder inside you finally reintegrates. Be sure to bask in that moment for at least a few breaths.

The same is true when you feel 'Ah, no wonder!' about your child. Relief envelops your heart, coupled with a sense that an unforgeable divide has been bridged. By making sure that you pause to notice the fulfilment you feel after a good Journey, you anchor it in your bodymind. Revel in your success and you lay new tracks in body memory that can more readily be accessed again in future.

Doing the Process—without the Notes

When you start using the handy and portable versions of the Process in the Appendices, don't worry if you lose your way. You can always revisit the more in-depth explanatory notes in Chapters 6–10 and review the meaning and purpose of the steps.

Appendix 1 is a condensed account of the five movements, and the 20 possible steps within them. It lets you review all the possible questions in order, with only brief supplementary notes. I suggest you review the steps in Appendix 1 before proceeding.

You can then use Appendix 2 to guide yourself, or another, through the Process, simply by reading each step as you go, skipping any questions that seem redundant. There are points along the Journey where travellers occasionally get stuck. Impasses are common and in chapters to follow you will find plenty of tools, travellers' aides and coaching to help you move through them.

When you are short of time, or not inclined to dive in too deeply, Appendices 3 and 4 offer much abbreviated versions of the Process. It might surprise you how a couple of brief but powerful questions can suffice to transform your perspective and deliver a new flash of insight.

Now we move on to Part C, which offers you a developmental map, helpful instructions for finding your nutrients and moving through resistance, and tips on how to share Inner Child Journeying with others.

PART c: Pathways of Development

CHAPTER 11

The Stages of Emotional Development

'My Inner Child doesn't know what to wish for!' A common refrain, when Journeyers arrive at the Third Movement. If you—like countless others before you—get stuck at the wishing question, you need a roadmap. This chapter offers you a developmental map, with instructions on how to use it.

Why Emotional Needs Hide

Your Inner Child Journeys will grant you a clear body-sense of what you need to help you grow, but this will not always happen immediately.

Sometimes you'll find yourself knowing exactly what you would have wished for in the original situation (*source event*) that you are exploring. Once recognised and named, that wish will help you to move; to satisfy your developmental needs sooner. Equally, when you facilitate someone else's journey—a friend, a colleague or a counselling client—sometimes you will see them nailing their developmental need promptly, boldly and with certainty.

But on some occasions you will draw a blank: 'I have no idea what to wish for!' Sometimes you come to the wishing questions (in the Third Movement) and feel bogged down, struggling to conjure up a wish that makes sense. You might suspect that you would wish for something if you weren't so afraid, or so ashamed to admit it to yourself. The same impasse can occur when facilitating someone else's Process and you feel uncertain as to what would have helped them at the time of their *source event*.

We sometimes seem to hit a dead end at the point of the wishing question. This is where a map comes in handy—one that reveals the stage-by-stage sequence of core developmental needs. (You'll find the map in Table 5 on page 206.)

To recap, Step 13 (page 172) of the Journey is intended for those instances in which, recalling how it felt to be a child in your *source event*, you are unable to imagine what would have helped you to escape, overcome or feel better. This is the point at which you would unfold your developmental map. Table 5 helps you recognise the developmental need that has been activated in you.

If you pay attention to your body's feelings as you peruse the table, your inner developmental template will signal you; giving a noticeable pulse of recognition when you sight the developmental need that your Journey has uncovered for you.

You will recall that your bodymind not only retains a felt sense of all you have lived, it also possesses a developmental template that 'knows' what *needed* to happen differently when things went wrong for you.

If the right developmental nutrient was not available at your time of crisis, your bodymind waits on, maintaining a vigil. For every challenge that Life presents you—from how it felt to be in your mother's womb, through the drama of childbirth, the vulnerability of babyhood, onto the search for autonomy in toddlerhood, competency in childhood and belonging in adolescence—a corresponding developmental nutrient exists to help you move forward. We all possess a programmed inner longing for this nutrient; let's call it the *experience that wants to happen.*

Our developmental needs are distinct for every stage of childhood and adolescence, following a universally shared sequence. At our depths, we all travel the same developmental path. But as children, we often struggled to articulate what we needed—beside a vague and nagging sense that something was missing for us, that something did not feel quite right. We relied on our carers and elders to help us understand and vocalise our needs. Sometimes they could give us this help, and sometimes they couldn't.

Our needs can be hard to pinpoint. This is why carrying a developmental map as we re-enter the realm of the Inner Child can be so helpful.

Keep this map handy. But don't treat it like a gospel of developmental needs. First and foremost, trust your bodily impulses; trust what you feel. Consult Table 5 if what you feel is unclear. Within it you are likely to find strong hints about the nature of your emotional needs. You can also use Table 5 to assist someone else; a friend who is discussing their Inner Child experiences with you, or perhaps a client whom you are counselling (if they get stuck at the 'wishing question').

Do you recall our anecdote about baby Chao-xing, when her mother Guan-yin had to offer her all kinds of things, by trial and error, before she finally found an answer that felt just right ('A Menu of Options', pages 121)? On another day, something quite different might have comforted Chao-xing—perhaps some rocking, a lullaby, her mother's breast, or simply to be held lovingly while she cried out the stress of her day. What Guan-yin did on this day was to keep gently offering a menu of comforters until Chao-xing's little body responded. As little babies, we often did not know what we needed, until *after* it was offered.

The same can sometimes be true for toddlers and children. At those ages, on the one hand, sometimes we knew exactly what we longed for. We were quite clear, for example, that we wanted someone to leave a night-light on for us. We were adamant that we wanted to run outside and play in the backyard with our best buddy. We knew in every detail the game that we wanted our dads to play with us, or the exact story that we wanted our mothers to read us. And sometimes our bodies gave us strong messages when we wanted to push away, or to run away.

But on the other hand, there were plenty of times when our language and imagination failed us. We knew we were unhappy; that something was not okay, but we could not say how. Though we were sure that something needed to be different, we could not name or picture the change we needed. Shrouded beneath conscious awareness, our unmet and wordless needs lay undetected manifesting through our irritability, our unpleasant behaviour or even through illness. In situation after awkward situation, we were stumped for words, befuddled or frozen to the spot.

The disturbing feeling that something undefinable is bothering us can be one of life's most frustrating experiences. Perhaps someone in our family hugged us too tight; it felt confusingly nice, yet icky and creepy at the same time. What to say? How to escape without offending or causing a ruckus?

Perhaps we froze in fear, becoming mute and invisible when we witnessed a fiery conflict between our parents. In high school, did we stare speechlessly at someone attractive, perhaps even reacting in a hostile manner to conceal our desire? Through sheer luck, or hit-and-miss experimentation, on occasion we found our own way to put our formless need or desire into words. But as children, we tended to benefit most from role models who would intervene on our behalf, showing us how to find and express our needs assertively and respectfully. Once we have been shown some choices—preferably more than just once—we become more adept at knowing and saying what we need. This remains as true for us as adults as it was when we were children.

Taking a Stand

Teresa was being repeatedly bullied by a group of girls at her primary school playground. Her teacher, Ximena, had a few ideas about what might help or empower a girl of this age. Not being entirely sure what would work best, she resolved to try a few different tactics.

To Ximena's surprise, Teresa did not seem to appreciate being rescued; her body-language was a graphic display of embarrassment. Speaking sternly to the ring-leader of the bullies only resulted in modest gains.

The bullying continued, albeit more subtly. With each attempt to help, Ximena was turned back to the drawing board.

Finally, it occurred to Ximena to use a role-play game to show Teresa how to exert a boundary; how to say 'Go away!' in a strong voice. Thus far, Teresa had been voiceless before her tormentors, entirely lost as to what to do or say. But when she was shown a clear framework for assertion and given opportunities to practise it, it was a game changer for Teresa. She found her voice, managed to ward off her antagonists and she flourished in both class and playground. Putting the power directly into Teresa's hands seemed to press all the right buttons.

Sometimes a rescue is exactly what is called for. But Teresa's developmental template was making it clear that something else was needed at this time. She needed help to connect to her own personal power. Luckily, her teacher was willing to try every tool in her kit until she hit the developmental nail on the head.

Ximena's search for ideas was facilitated by her understanding of the developmental needs that likely corresponded to Teresa's age. Armed with this developmental map, Ximena rolled with Teresa's cues about what worked best. It was easy to see how Teresa came alive when Ximena's intervention hit the spot. The 'map' narrowed Ximena's search, but Teresa's developmental template did the rest.

Children are not the only ones who struggle to recognise their needs; as adults we often fail to read our bodies' signals. For example, you might not know that your body craves massage until you've received it a few times, until you have directly experienced the wellbeing that it can bring you. Once you have felt the spiritual sustenance a long walk in Nature gives you, you may begin to realise this is a need, and not a luxury. Free your body to dance with full abandon for the first time, and you might discover that you've been craving this all along. Take more time out to be in your own company, and you might realise, in the bliss of aloneness, that you had been needing your own silent company all along.

Pleasurable touch, connection with Nature, rhythmic movement and personal space—science affirms these as fundamental human needs. And yet we so often overlook these fundamental needs, unaware that we are living with the symptoms of their deprivation. It can be a blessing when someone helps us identify and validate a psychological need that we had played down. In the labyrinth of human psychology, a needs map is an invaluable tool.

Why is it so hard, from time to time, to figure out what we need? Some of our needs are so deeply buried that we feel astonished when we finally uncover them. This blocking-out of our needs makes sense when you consider how many of us had our needs invalidated or trivialised in childhood. Some of us were shamed or punished merely for expressing our needs. For others, our voices were ignored or disregarded until self-denial became the only way to survive. Modern culture remains unfriendly to human vulnerability; it applauds stoic self-reliance and emotional imperviousness. Under a lifetime of pressure to minimise or repudiate our needs, we lose track of what we deserve, and we lose sight of what would nourish us. Is it any wonder we sequester our needs where they won't be found?

Today there is a growing gusto for diagnosing human frailty, as if we existed in a social vacuum, disconnected from other people and void of personal histories. We treat psychological suffering as if it springs from inside, like a genetically-delivered curse—as if our pain has nothing to do with our relationships.

If you are afraid, you have an anxiety 'disorder'. If you feel depressed, then you *have* depression. Language is as powerful in shaping our choices as it is in revealing our underlying assumptions. Frame emotional suffering in terms of disease, and the answer looks like a pill. To what extent are commercial interests biasing our current way of thinking? The psychopharmaceutical industry is a giant. It is worth tens of billions and is able to deploy further billions for marketing campaigns and guided research. A pill may temporarily ease our pain. But it does not address the issue that caused it.

So many of us have no idea what we need—from inside ourselves, from our relationships and from the world around us—in order to feel happier. The more we use diagnostic labels, the further we get from knowing and validating our needs.

I see this in my private practice every week. People describe some of the most unsatisfying life situations and some of the most harrowing childhood histories—not once having wondered whether the latter might be at the root of the former. It is as if their emotional needs are of no relevance to their dilemma. It might be, for instance, a gifted individual who is depressed. Every day he works at a job he does not love, a job that has nothing to do with his true vocation. But he has never considered that pursuing his personal passion might be central to his wellbeing.

It might be someone who no longer feels desire towards her partner of many years. She wonders if something is wrong with her sexually: is she becoming 'frigid'? As a couple, they have never communicated their deep and tender feelings to each other. She is bereft of emotional intimacy yet oblivious that her heart's need for connection is a vital condition for arousal.

Someone else comes in asking for anger management; he considers himself to have a problem controlling his temper. He recounts how his parents would punish him physically, harshly and often, all the while telling him that he deserved it. In his current workplace, his managers speak to him with disdain and contempt.

And yet he draws no links between his outbursts and the way he has been treated all his life. His need for respect all but forgotten, he has been left without a context for his chronic temper issues. He shoulders the blame as if his relationships past and present have no part to play in his excessive reactivity.

How chronically we downplay, or even entirely overlook, some of our most important emotional needs. Without this essential validation, we are left to wonder what's wrong with us instead of what would help us. When we diagnose individuals instead of relationships, we are committing a fundamental error. Human beings are not separate entities floating in space.

Instead of labelling what we *are*, we should label what we *need*, or rather: what our hearts need. Name the need, and fulfilment becomes possible. And so, though we learned early to bury those needs that were unacceptable to people around us, every Inner Child Journey we take restores the voice of our hearts a little more.

> *When we diagnose individuals instead of relationships, we are committing a fundamental error. Human beings are not separate entities floating in space.*

> *Instead of labelling what we are, we should label what we need, or rather: what our hearts need.*

Though there is little mention of this (yet) in international human rights conventions, our basic psychological needs should absolutely be thought of as 'human rights'. They are no less important to our general health and wellbeing than any of our other recognised human rights (clean food and water, education, freedom from violence, etc). A number of developmental psychologists have accordingly framed our universal, stage-specific developmental needs as 'rights'.[38]

We suffer greatly, both psychologically and physiologically, when these needs—or rights—are not met. One of the largest investigations ever conducted on the long-term outcomes of childhood trauma—the Adverse Childhood Experiences study (ACEs), and its follow-up studies [39]—showed that early psychological wounds, if left unhealed, dramatically multiply the risk of heart disease, stroke, respiratory disease, depression and substance abuse.

Childhood experiences matter enormously.

Healing the wounds of the heart is the greatest preventive medicine there is.

*Healing the wounds of the heart is the greatest
preventive medicine there is.*

The simple needs of the heart should therefore be considered no less a human right than the quality of air we breathe. As you will see below, I have accordingly tabled our core, psycho-emotional developmental needs as a sequence of rights.

What does it take for us to become conscious of our needs when they seem hidden from us, blurry or indecipherable? First and foremost, we need to give ourselves time. We need to pay careful attention to our bodily sensations, as these comprise the bodymind's lexicon of feeling and need. For this we need an emotionally safe space where we can be certain we won't be judged or shamed and where our needs, should we speak them out loud, won't be trivialised by others. Sometimes our Inner Child's need will only make itself known in the presence of a sensitive friend or experienced counsellor who can hold us in their empathy.

On some days you know with crystal clarity what you want in order to feel happy again. You need a hug, a hand on your shoulder, someone's acknowledgement or someone's helpful guidance. Perhaps you want to tell someone you love them. Perhaps you long to express something from your depths that has never emerged before.

Similarly, some of your Inner Child Journeys will reveal your wishes straightforwardly, without the need for any map. When that is the case, simply skip Steps 12 and 13, and move straight onto the Fourth Movement.

But for those times when all you have is a shapeless longing, a vague dissatisfaction, perhaps even an emotional paralysis; that's when you can refer to the map for directions (whether alone, with a trusted friend, or with the assistance of a trained counsellor).

Once you have consulted the map, check back with your body to see what resonates. Your bodymind's developmental template signals when you are hearing about something that truly resembles what you need.

Locating your needs and learning to speak them takes a little time and practice, and requires a back-and-forth dialogue with your body.

Begin by looking at examples of stage-specific needs and their corresponding nutrients in Table 5 (page 206). See that each row in the 'Psycho-emotional developmental needs (for the child)' column has its corresponding, adult-appropriate nutrients in the adjacent 'Restorative, healing developmental nutrients (for the adult)' column.

Once you think you have found your nutrient, check in with your gut and your heart. 'Does this one feel right for me, in this situation? Does that one feel right for me?' Often, when we are shown the thing we want most deeply, our bodies recognise it: something stirs in our bellies, or in our chests. We might become excited or agitated. We might want to spontaneously call out, 'Yes, that is it!' Or alternatively, we might experience an upwelling of sadness as we weep with relief. So, taking your time, peruse the needs in Table 5 below, and your body will tell you when you have identified a need that feels just right, relating to your source situation.

When you are satisfied that you have identified your need for now, your next challenge, as laid out in the Fourth Movement, is to find an appropriate way of answering that need for yourself in real time. Your own healing and growth soon translate to your child's growth, enriching your relationship.

Consulting Table 5

Bertrand was often irritable when he came home from work. It was not unusual for him to greet his family half-heartedly, retire with his laptop to play computer games and then remain grouchy for the rest of the evening. From the moment he arrived, he seemed prickly and allergic to interaction; increasingly his family felt rejected. Bertrand was not conscious of the fact that his way of claiming personal space felt hostile and insensitive to his loved ones—a fact that led to mounting complaints at home.

When Bertrand decided to explore this issue via Inner Child work, he got in touch with a long-held sense of invasion—a sense that as a child, his personal boundaries were not respected. His mother tended to be intrusive and emotionally demanding, his older siblings would burst into his room without knocking and even help themselves to his belongings without asking. Since his protests fell on deaf ears, Bertrand had gradually lost any awareness of his need for a personal buffer zone. He had adapted to his family environment by ignoring his body's signal of overwhelm and the need for sanctuary. He had learned not to trust that the world would respect his need for space, and that if he wanted time to himself in this life, he would have to fight for it. No wonder Bertrand sounded defensive when his family asked for his attention at the end of his workday.

At first, Bertrand was unsure what exactly was missing for him. All he knew was that he resented others' demands on his time—to the point of excessive reactivity and a tendency to be reclusive. But as he began to browse through the Table of Developmental Needs, the 'right to a personal boundary'—and the personal space that this implied—seemed to ring the loudest bell. The developmental map affirmed Bertrand's vital need for a little space and time alone. This need was no less valid in his adulthood than in his formative years. The body-memory of having had to fight for this need in an unsupportive world made him so abrasive. When we know our needs are valid, we tend to ask with grace.

Thinking about how to offer himself the corresponding developmental nutrient, Bertrand resolved that every weeknight, upon arriving home, he would take 15 minutes of solitude to meditate or read. Just as importantly, he agreed to explain his need more thoughtfully and to ask his family's support for this plan. In this way, his partner and children would be included in his healing and no longer targets for his irritability.

As Bertrand began to get used to this new routine, he found that this precious time-out fed his capacity to enjoy his family time afterwards, and he had more warmth to offer them.

Surprisingly, sometimes just identifying our need can be satisfying enough. That 'aha!' moment can, by itself, feel empowering. When our need finally gets a name, this is a powerful act of self-validation that helps us to feel grounded and at peace with ourselves. We sigh with relief, and that will do.

But sometimes a newly recognised need calls for a follow-up: we must give ourselves the corresponding developmental nutrient experientially. The more we commit to nourishing ourselves, the more we blossom as individuals, accrue wisdom, gain in patience and empathy towards our children. That is the purpose of the Fourth Movement; you devise an adult-appropriate way to fulfil your developmental need in real terms.

Let's recap. For each of your unresolved *source events*, your Inner Child needs a specific experience to evolve—the *experience that wants to happen*.

Specific developmental themes belong to each stage in the sequence of psycho-emotional development. Each stage builds on the strengths of the previous one, so that when we receive the nutrient that meets the needs of one stage, it helps us expand into later stages more fully.

Understanding the thematic nature of these developmental needs enables you to creatively fulfil them in ways relevant to your life situation. For example, if you weren't held enough as a baby, you can be held in different but equally powerful ways that can bring profound healing as an adult, and it is never too late. If you missed out on playfulness as a child, you can be playful as an adult in myriad ways. If you struggle to find what your needs are, the developmental map below will help you with directions.

A Developmental Map

Table of Developmental Needs

Like a cake built one layer at a time, we all develop psychologically according to a universally shared plan—one childhood stage at a time.[40]

As we enter each new developmental stage, a new set of needs arises. But rarely do we see neat and tidy boundaries in Nature. The age ranges delineating each developmental stage are not strict cut-offs, you'll find quite a bit of overlap. Each stage is known for the needs that predominate within it, but none of these needs entirely disappear as we advance to the next stage. Albeit in ever-changing form, our developmental needs remain with us—dormant perhaps, but often reactivated.

Though similar to Table 3 (page 108), Table 5 below has a few additional features.

Firstly, it presents developmental themes as *rights*.

Then, by offering hints as to the developmental nutrients that might address these needs, the table provides steppingstones towards fulfilling them in adulthood.

Finally, a further column shows the faculties of emotional intelligence that are gained when each of these needs are met. It is encouraging to see the various ways in which we blossom as individuals with each answer given to the needs of the heart.

Table 5: Table of Developmental Needs

Age range	Developmental theme	Psycho-emotional developmental needs (for the child)	Restorative, healing developmental nutrients (for the adult)	Resulting emotional intelligences
In-utero, birth, the perinatal period until 3 months	The Right to Exist (Connectedness)	To feel wanted. To be held, *sensitively*. To feel safe. To feel *seen*. To feel affirmed.	Being warmly received. Making our presence known. Saying 'I am here'. Feeling safe with others. Comforting touch, holding and eye contact. Inhabiting our body. Connecting with the Earth.	Trusting in Life. Groundedness. A strong reality principle. A feeling of inter-connectedness with all Life. *I am here, I am worthy and I belong.*
Birth to 18 months	The Right to Need (Inter-Dependence)	To trust others. To feel secure. To have bodily and emotional needs met promptly. To have needs met on our own terms. To be held and comforted. To have pleasurable nourishment.	Reaching out for help, support, connection. Allowing ourselves to receive. Allowing the expression of grief.	Emotional security. Self-assertion. Ability to tolerate alone-ness. A feeling of Life's abundance. Balance of giving and receiving. Healthy trust and healthy scepticism. Tolerance of delayed gratification. *It's okay to have needs.*

Age range	Developmental theme	Psycho-emotional developmental needs (for the child)	Restorative, healing developmental nutrients (for the adult)	Resulting emotional intelligences
18 months to 3 years	The Right to Have Support (Autonomy)	To receive support for vulnerability—without demand or expectation. To receive protection in times of fear. To be allowed to learn and grow without pressure—at our own rate, on our own terms. To be shown boundaries without shaming or manipulation. To be *heard*.	Receiving acceptance for vulnerability. Learning to reach out for—and to accept—support. Learning to accept limitation, and embrace failure. Learning to enjoy instead of trying to impress.	Humility. Honesty and realness, authenticity (instead of seduction and manipulation). Loving and respecting vulnerability, in self and others. Freedom from toxic shame or pride. Trusting essence rather than investing in 'image'. *It's okay to be vulnerable.*

Age range	Developmental theme	Psycho-emotional developmental needs (for the child)	Restorative, healing developmental nutrients (for the adult)	Resulting emotional intelligences
3–5 years	The Right to Freedom (Spirit/ Creativity)	To explore the world. To freely express emotion. To express negativity. To say 'no!' To say 'I don't want.' To say 'go away!' To assert our boundaries. To have space. To be shown interpersonal boundaries without shaming or punishment. To be protected without smothering. To play. To be *enjoyed*.	To expand outward in creative self-expression. To voice feelings. To assert boundaries. To repel shame and guilt. To separate what is others' experience from what is our own (healthy differentiation).	Healthy self-containment (instead of suppression). Healthy boundaries: knowing when to say 'no'. Strong self-assertion without violence. Strong self-expression. Spirit, creativity: a balance between the practical and the aesthetic. True empathy instead of *enmeshment or obligation.* *I am free to be me. I am free to play and create.*

Age range	Developmental theme	Psycho-emotional developmental needs (for the child)	Restorative, healing developmental nutrients (for the adult)	Resulting emotional intelligences
5–7 years	The Right to Love (Passion)	To express passion and sensuality. To give and receive affection physically, without invasion, judgement or exploitation. To explore and discover the pleasure of the body. To be free from moralisation or shaming.	To give and receive tenderness. To accept the softer feelings. To honour the body. To honour the right to privacy. To respect and set limits against unwanted intimacy. To give flight to the imagination. To trust feelings, rather than rigid or abstract rules.	Sexuality as an expression of love. Open-heartedness. Open-mindedness. Flexibility of mind. Freedom from conformism. Embracing paradox, nuance and relativity. *Pleasure is healthy.* *Sex is not separate from love.*

Age range	Developmental theme	Psycho-emotional developmental needs (for the child)	Restorative, healing developmental nutrients (for the adult)	Resulting emotional intelligences
7–12 years	The Right to Playful Learning (Competence)	To receive instruction without shaming. To receive patient mentorship. Peer-group belonging. Playful learning. To be allowed bodily integrity, privacy.	To learn playfully, without coercion or shaming. Freedom to pursue our interests and affinities. Support to develop competencies without imposed expectations. Bonding with like-minded others.	Competence. The courage to try new things. The ability to focus attention on a task. Acceptance of failure. Persistence. *Learning is exciting. I can be good at some things, and not so good at other things. Both are okay. I am a valued friend.*

Age range	Developmental theme	Psycho-emotional developmental needs (for the child)	Restorative, healing developmental nutrients (for the adult)	Resulting emotional intelligences
12 to early 20s	The Right to an Opinion The Right to a Vocation The Right to Sexual Autonomy	To form and voice opinions. To enjoy social-group identity and belonging. To receive support for pursuing our passion(s). To receive vocational mentorship and opportunity. Freedom of sexual expression and discovery. Questioning authority. Questioning culture.	Joining a 'shared-values' tribe. Following our bliss. Vocational development and enhancement. Flow-state immersion. Expressing and sharing our unique gifts. Respectful exploration of our sexual identity and desire. Learning about love and ecstatic sexuality. Voicing our opinions, learning to listen to and respect those of others. Contributing to community. Connecting to something greater than ourselves.	Heart-centred sexuality. Vocational fulfilment. Self-motivation. Self-responsibility. A sense of our place in the world. A sense of our value. Social and political awareness, and a commitment to democratic engagement. Healthy scepticism and self-assurance. *My voice is important.* *I have unique gifts to share.* *I can take responsibility for my actions and for my destiny.* *I am connected to a larger world, and I have a role to play in it.*

Limits of the Map

Our map is not one-size-fits-all; it does not deal in absolutes for every situation. Flexibility is key; you can respond in more than one way to your Inner Child's need. So, use this map as a prompter of ideas if you feel stuck at the wishing question, but give your bodymind the final say. Your internal developmental template will tickle you or tug at your ear when you spot the developmental nutrient—or nutrients, sometimes more than one—that best answers your Inner Child's call.

One of the most common questions that arises at this point is, 'When should I meet this need for myself, from the inside and when I should seek to have it met from outside?' Again, it is okay to try one thing and then another if the first strategy did not seem to help. In other words, it's okay to accept uncertainty and to be willing to experiment, to risk making mistakes in the service of our personal development. Just as our parents sometimes had to learn what we as little children needed through trial and error, finding the right nutrient for our Inner Child can involve a little hit and miss at first.

On some occasions, the most empowering nutrient involves treating yourself in a new way—perhaps voicing your feelings more or asserting new interpersonal boundaries. At other times, the nutrient involves interaction with others. This might be about reaching out for help and support, or demanding a new kind of respect from people in your life. The nutrient that any given Journey points to depends largely on where in the sequence of development your Inner Child has been feeling stuck. Developmental arrests that take place in earlier stages of childhood tend to involve the themes of receiving nurturance and protection, whereas wounds that take place in later stages are more likely to be about self-assertion and self-responsibility. And of course, remember that we never grow alone; when your Inner Child undergoes a shift, your actual child will shift along with you.

Our developmental map makes us well informed explorers; good safari guides for Inner Child Journeying. But it does not give us certainty about what's best for the Inner Child at every turn. That's why, when the Inner Child falters at the wishing question, we need to offer her a menu of possibilities in the form of a question, rather than make a statement about what she *should* wish for, or what would be *right* for her. So, instead of saying, 'This is surely what you need!' we need to ask 'Is *this* perhaps what you need? Or could it be <u>that</u>?' and then patiently allow time for the Inner Child to feel her way to the choice that strikes the right note for her.

Bringing attention to our bodies is essential to this part of the Journey. A warmth in the belly, a tingling in the chest, a sigh of relief, a lump in our throats or stinging in the eyes, are common examples of the body's way of saying 'Yes, I want that'. The recognition of a previously unacknowledged need can bring excitement or pleasure, but it can also bring out the pain of having waited too long. Either way, the innate wisdom of our bodies helps us recognise our next developmental nutrient—if we pay attention.

How to Use the Map

If you feel stuck at the wishing question, take a break from your Inner Child Journey for a while. And just as if you had stepped off your train at a station where you wished to explore the territory further, you can resume your Journey later from that same station.

Peruse the map; simply begin by looking down the column of developmental needs and the one with corresponding developmental nutrients. As you read through the list of needs and nutrients, notice if something jumps out at you; a nutrient that addresses the feelings that came up for you as you recalled your *source event*. Which of these nutrients would have best helped you feel happier at the time of your *source event*? Which nutrients listed might have brought you the greatest satisfaction, had it been possible at the time? Each of your needs has a specific object; each longing has an essential answer that would bring fulfilment. So, as you read through the range of nutrients, ask yourself, 'How would I have felt if this was done for me?' or 'How would I have felt if I could have done this?'

So that you don't have to read through the entire list of developmental nutrients each time you take a Journey, give yourself permission to go straight to the developmental stage that your intuition points to. With time and experience, you will find that you can more easily hone in directly on the developmental stage that pertains to the emotions your child has triggered in you.

Some issues may seem to have the flavour of a struggle from your adolescence, for instance, while other issues might have the feel of a battle from your toddler stage. And at other times yet, your child stirs up your baby-like feelings.

If you have a sense of the life stage that has been triggered for you, then go straight to the corresponding part of the table and start your search there. Even though this is not always necessarily the case, the emotions that come up for you as a parent or teacher tend to arise from a life stage similar to that of your child. Knowing this can help to narrow your search for the right nutrient.

As you become increasingly familiarised with the Table of Developmental Needs, you will be able to identify your needs more rapidly—at times almost automatically—without having to consult the table. And of course, our map is only necessary when you get stuck at the wishing question. In some of your Inner Child Journeys, you will know exactly what you would have wished for in your *source event*. In those Journeys, you won't need the map at all.

Guiding Others

Whether you are a counsellor or psychotherapist, or you are assisting a friend through their Inner Child Journey, you will often find that those you guide— let's call them your 'clients'—will stumble at the wishing question, as we all sometimes do.

One of the first questions to determine is whether your client's need is to move from within (to reach out, to push away, to fight, to speak out, to run away, to play freely, etc), or to receive help or support from others. Needs that emerge from the earliest developmental stages tend to rely on outside input. To put it another way, the lower the floor that your client's 'emotional age elevator' has descended to, the more likely they are to be contacting needs that involve feeling protected, helped, nurtured—perhaps even rescued—by others. Deeper regressions are more likely to evoke more fragile emotional states and a greater sense of dependency. Later developmental stages are more often associated with the need to self-assert, self-express and expand outwards as individuals.

So it is useful to get a general sense of the emotional age that your client is tapping into. That's why, as you move through the Second Movement of the Journey, an important question to ask (see Step 5) is 'How old were you at the time (when this *source event* was happening)?'

Having a sense of the emotional age that has been triggered for your client is a major source of clues about the developmental needs that may have been awakened. But your own emotional responses towards your client can offer you further valuable clues. As you guide your client deeper into their Journey and their story begins to unfold, what do you feel your client's Inner Child might need next?

It is helpful to imagine your client as a youth, child or infant, at whatever age they have regressed to emotionally. Let yourself visualise what he might have looked like, imagine what she might have sounded like, and allow yourself to sense what he or she might have felt during their *source event*.

As you move into an empathic connection with your client, pay attention to what begins to happen in your own heart. If your client does not know what to wish for, then what do *you* find yourself wishing for your client's Inner Child? To help you gain a sense of your own most caring desire on behalf of your client, you can ask yourself the following questions:

- ✤ What do I wish might have happened differently for my client?
- ✤ If I was magically transported back in time to my client's *source event*, what would I have liked to do for her as a child?
- ✤ What would I have wished for, had I been in my client's shoes?

Voicing your own wish for your client's Inner Child might be, on some occasions, the very thing that helps them find a way through. When your client sees how you have been stirred by their plight, this can be both affirming and encouraging.

But there is a caveat. When someone is immersed in their Journey, it's vitally important that they recognise their needs—and the nutrients that would fulfil them—*from the inside*. Only when they have this organic 'thumbs up'—the signals from their inner developmental template—can they fully take ownership of their path to fulfilment.

So how do we, as Journey guides, make suggestions without being prescriptive, without tampering with our client's capacity for inner vision? It is one thing to offer a suggestion, quite another to impose our view. Perhaps the best way to offer our insights non-intrusively is by *asking*, rather than *telling*.

How to Propose a Wish without Invading

When your client's Inner Child does not know what kinds of change or new outcomes to wish for, but you have a wish on their behalf, offer your wish in the form of a question. This helps you test its appropriateness to their situation. If you are selecting probable nutrients from the Table of Developmental Needs, offer a menu of options and allow your client time to feel for the one that resonates with him. Here are some sample approaches to offering your client a range of new possibilities.

- ✤ What if, at the time of your *source event*, this (new occurrence) had happened for you instead? What might that have felt like for you?
- ✤ What if someone had done this (helpful thing) for you? What might that have felt like for you?

❀ What if somehow, magically perhaps, it was made entirely safe for you to have said <u>this</u> or done <u>that</u> as you were experiencing your *source event*? What might that have felt like for you?

You might also choose to share with your client the wish that came up for you as you heard her story. Of course, this would involve stretching your and your client's imaginations a little further.

❀ 'If I was there with you—in my current adult form—at the time of your *source event*, I would have wanted to offer you <u>this</u>—would that have felt okay for you?'

❀ '<u>This</u> is what I find myself wishing for you: how do you feel about that?'

A third and equally fruitful path of assistance involves your willingness to enter the world of your client's Inner Child, and for a few moments attempting to feel his world through his skin.

❀ 'If I were in your shoes, I think <u>this</u> is what I would have liked to receive' or '<u>That</u> is what I would have wanted to do, or to say. How do you feel about that?'

The questions above are intended as suggestions; you might like to think up your own questions and ask them in your own manner.

As you propose each wish, give your client time to reflect and pay attention to all the feelings that come up for her in response. Remind your client, if necessary, to bring attention to her body and to notice any sensations, emotions or impulses that arise as she weighs up your idea. You can give a helping hand with follow-up questions such as 'How does my suggestion feel to you? How does it feel when you imagine yourself receiving this? What happens for you as you imagine yourself acting this out?'

Suggestion is delicate territory, and as guides we need to take measures to safeguard our clients' sense of autonomy. Consider how easy it might be for your client to feel obligated to accept your ideas about his developmental needs. Shield your clients from pressure by assuring them that if they don't relate to the wish you have for them, you will accept their instruction. Don't worry, we can often miss the mark with our clients; none of us are above the occasional projection. So, if your client does not like your first suggestion or two, keep offering a menu of wishes until your client, in consultation with his bodymind's developmental template, recognises one that feels just right.

'See Me Where I Truly Am'

A common and easily committed mistake we can make as guides or therapists is to over-infantilise our client; to overprotect or mollycoddle her. Just as some of us can err on the side of smothering our children when, as parents, our own fears are triggered, the same can happen for us as Journey guides, counsellors and therapists. If we overestimate our client's emotional fragility or underestimate her strength, we risk dampening her emergence.

The other common mistake is to expect something from our client that is beyond the emotional stage that he has been triggered into. This unfair expectation is evident when we spur someone to: 'Get over it', 'Stand up and fight', 'Let go of the past', 'Forget that person' and so on—when they are abjectly unable to do any of these things due the psycho-emotional stage to which they have regressed.

Let's say for instance that your client has been triggered into an emotional state that puts him on the third floor of his emotional age elevator. Push your client for a response that belongs on the 18th floor, and he is likely to feel crushed, ashamed about his helplessness, perhaps even alienated from you. Since most of us mask our emotional fragility all too well, it's easy to overlook the depths of another's vulnerability. That's why it's advisable to ask rather than tell; to allow your client to refer your suggestions to his own inner developmental template.

We all want to be seen *where we truly are*. We find ways, often unconsciously, to resist other's expectations to be bigger and better than we're feeling in the moment. In equal measure, we're repelled by unwanted protection or disproportionate nurturance. I never cease to be fascinated by this marvellous paradox of developmental healing; see me *where I truly am*, and I become a new me.

Misreading our client's emotional age is easy to do, and it happens often, but it's not the end of the world. As long as we keep checking in with our client, ensuring that she only accepts ideas that feel aligned with her sense of herself, it prevents our projections from contaminating her Journey. Remember that some developmental needs are *outside needs* (requiring input from other people) and some are *inside needs* (involving self-expression or self-assertion). *Outside needs* can arise at any stage of life, but they're more common at the earlier developmental stages of childhood, while later stages tend to involve more *inside needs*.

The human capacity for healthy self-reliance develops naturally to the degree that our dependency needs have been met. The baby who is consistently picked up and held when he cries is more likely to grow to be autonomous and independent. This is entirely different to the defensive self-reliance we adopt if, in early childhood, we were not allowed to reach out. As a shield that covers our vulnerability, defensive self-reliance becomes a block to intimacy. But when our *outside needs* are validated, this helps us grow organically into self-actualised, autonomous individuals; *inter*dependent as opposed to clingy and co-dependent. Feed the need at the emotional stage from which it arises and we organically move forward in our growth, returning to our adult consciousness renewed, empowered, at peace.

With a Little Help from my Friends

These days the idea of 'rescuing' gets a bad rap. How often do we withhold help lest our children be 'wrapped in cotton wool', or in fear that our friends might feel belittled if we toss them a life raft in times of need? To be sure, both these concerns can be valid, sometimes. But our distaste for giving or receiving help can equally be, at times, a question of pride. What if instead of asking, 'Is rescuing "good" or "bad"?' we asked, 'Under what conditions is rescuing appropriate?' When might rescuing be exactly what the doctor ordered, and when is it smothering or interfering? And how do we tell the difference?

Let's think about our children and the trials and tribulations they ordinarily face. Sooner or later, as a routine part of life, they all find themselves entangled in the kind of trouble from which only outside help will save them. A child's wish to be rescued is as valid as any other wish. And yet we all suspect that over-rescuing robs the child of opportunities to practise using their own power and to speak with their own voice. So, how do we decide when to intervene and when to sit back and allow our children to deploy their own resources? Are there guidelines that tell us when it is okay to let go? We may never know with absolute certainty how to make a call on this vexed question, but the following formula might help.

I believe that children generally learn to master new relating skills along a sequence of predictable steps. Four steps take children from unskilled helplessness in which they depend on our intervention, to skilled self-empowerment in which they can take over from us. Here are those four steps:

1. First, you do it *for* the child.
2. Then, you do it *with* the child.
3. Then, you step aside and supervise while the child does it.
4. Finally, you step away and the child takes over.

You could say that every act of role modelling, protection or nurturance is an act of intervention. Children gradually learn how to take care of themselves by drawing from the behavioural repertoire of their elders. For instance, the way we step in to protect them from an invasive older sibling becomes a standard for how they will one day set their own boundaries. In further examples, our style of nurturance and self-care sets a pattern that they will one day mimic, and our way of expressing needs and feelings becomes the scaffold on which they build their own emotional intelligence. To a considerable degree, the elder's voice becomes the child's voice—how he speaks to himself—how she speaks to others.

And so, just as children's learning begins with outside input until they can take over for themselves, the same can be true for us as adults when we do Inner Child work. We all carry unfinished stories that strive for completion, unfulfilled longings and stifled impulses that seek instruction, guidance and support; so that we can find release and expansion. When Life presses on those lower-floor buttons of our *emotional age elevator*, we can feel as vulnerable, helpless or lost as a little child. Early body-memory can involve helplessness; we find ourselves not knowing what to say or do. If the wish that arises in your Journey involves an *outside need*—to feel rescued, protected, nurtured or supported by others—please know that this is okay. Validate this wish. In Chapter 13 we will look at creative ways to respond to our own and each other's needs for nurturance or protection, in adult-appropriate ways. Validating our *outside needs* does not infantilise us; it nourishes us so that we can organically attain greater states of autonomy, self-empowerment and generosity. Sometimes, our growth requires us at first to accept 'a little help from our friends'.

But first, we'll look at what to do when our narrative memory fails us, and that is what we cover in Chapter 12.

CHAPTER 12

When Narrative Memory Fails

When I lead group Journeys, there are always a few individuals whose furrowed brows seem to be saying, 'Nnnnn … nope. Not getting anything.' In your own Inner Child Journeys, you'll occasionally struggle to retrieve childhood memories. The good news is that this apparent impasse need not halt the Inner Child Journey. You can tap into the wisdom of the Inner Child in many ways, even without access to an originating *source event*.

This chapter looks at a number of ways we can connect with our Inner Child's voice, even when we cannot remember a relevant *source event* or circumstance.

The Problem with Narrative Memory

Let's begin by looking at why our memories so often seem to be lost to us. There are two main reasons. The first involves the ordinary neurobiology of story-telling memory. Most people are unlikely to be able to retrieve clear and orderly recollections from before 2–4 years of age. The hippocampus, central to the brain's archival system, does not mature until that age. As brain scientists tell it, 'Thus, in the first few years of life only the quality of events, but not their context, can be remembered.'[41]

Although we still don't understand how, on rare occasions individuals have retrieved verifiable memories dating back to their birth experience—even earlier. These unusually early glimpses tend to be confined to occasions when we are very powerfully triggered into a regression, or under a hypnotic trance.

Narrative memory is famously rubbery and therefore not always reliable. Although it can be accurate sometimes, it can also be highly subjective and distorted over time. However, for the purposes of our Inner Child Journey, the malleability of narrative memory is not at all a problem. You will see why later.

The second reason why narrative memory is sometimes barred from our view relates to functional amnesia in response to severe stress or psychological trauma.

When we experience something overwhelmingly scary or painful, our brains generate opiate-like chemicals that numb the pain and blank out the explicit memory of the experience. Say our brain scientists 'Severe or prolonged stress can disrupt hippocampal functioning, creating context-free, fearful associations, which are hard to locate in space and time. This results in amnesia for the specifics of the traumatic experiences, but not the feelings associated with them.'[42]

Modern science has made sense of why we so keenly feel a past that we can no longer see. We are given a sense of *how* it was, even if we don't get a sense of *what* it was. The blurring of traumatic memory is surely beneficial to our survival, permitting us to process our most nightmarish experiences in gradual, tolerable portions.

When do our buried tales emerge from the deep? Usually, not until we feel safely held in an empathic and non-judgemental environment, strong enough to face them and resourced enough to digest their meaning.

When feelings come up without a historical narrative, we cannot know what lies beneath. A curtain is drawn over an experience for good reason. And that is why, whether we are taking our Journey or assisting someone through theirs, we should tread carefully. Never push. Don't *dredge* stuff up; observe the intelligence of the body. Resistance to content recall has its own inherent wisdom and timing, and above all this must be respected.

Begin each Journey from the feelings that have been triggered in the present situation, and trust the body to choose the *source event* it wants to go back to. You might be surprised by the memory road your bodymind travels into. Respect for yourself, or for your client, means accepting the confounding of your expectations. Our Inner Child Journey never begins with a preconceived invitation to explore a specific moment of life. We don't launch a Journey by pre-selecting the outcome, such as, 'Let's look at what happened for you at birth, or at 3 years of age, etc.' Allow the body to tell you to where—and when—it needs to go.

The Power of Imagination

The good news is that we can work with the feelings that come up, even if the historical context is unclear. For the purpose of our Inner Child Journey, body-memory (see page 82) is enough. That's because the emotions triggered through the challenges of parenting are clear representations of lived experience, whether or not we have a narrative that affixes our experience to its original space and time.

One of the options offered in the Second Movement invites us to use our imagination, to pay attention to the images that might surround our triggered emotional state. In the absence of narrative memory, symbolic memory will do. Here's why: a major reason for delving into memory as part of this Journey is to help us locate the theme of our developmental need. Though our childhood experiences have passed, our unfulfilled developmental needs remain in the here-and-now. Once our needs are made conscious, we can move forward towards fulfilment. Symbolic representations of memory can reflect the emotional issue being grappled with. Just as clearly as a true narrative memory, the imagination can shine a light on our developmental need. Even imagining what *might have* happened to us can be useful. The fleeting images and sensations that spring up around an emotional state hint strongly at the needs that sit beneath. Your core emotional needs are on the mark, even when your memory is not.

If you recall my personal story in which I overcame a claustrophobic reaction to driving through a tunnel, I had only a vague sense that this irrational fear was traceable to birth trauma. To this day, I cannot tell you whether this is true or a figment of my imagination. Notwithstanding, the symbolic memory showed me what I needed and pointed to a nutrient that was just right for me, enabling me to overcome my fear.

The Second Movement contains several optional steps (Steps 5–10). Some are alternate pathways to insight—useful if narrative memory is unobtainable. You don't need to ask all the questions in the Second Movement; they are simply alternative entry points. Use the steps that work best for you in any given Journey, in any combination. If your narrative memory comes to you readily, then you don't necessarily need to visit the other questions in this movement; and if you like, you can then skip through to the Third Movement. But if you cannot find a response for Step 5—in which you ask about earlier experiences of similar flavour—try the subsequent steps, thinking of each as another possible doorway into the bodymind.

Step 6 invites you to fantasise about what *might* have happened, sometime earlier in your life, to cause you to feel as you do in your present-day, challenging situation. 'What do you imagine might have been happening for you, and around you, when you first felt these kinds of feelings and had these kinds of thoughts?' Encourage yourself—or the person you are working with—to allow the mind to wander, to invent a story uncensored.

For example, someone who arrives at this point in the Journey might say, 'I'm not sure exactly what was happening for me in my *source event*, but it feels *as if* I were a baby and someone was angry with me for crying too much.' Someone else might say, 'It feels *as if* I were made to feel stupid in front my entire primary school class.' Whether or not these stories reflect something exactly as it happened, the feelings involved are entirely valid, and they point clearly towards what the person needs next in order to develop.

In the first example above—the person who saw himself as a scorned baby— the journey-taker might grow by reclaiming the right to reach out for nurturance of comforting without fear or shame. The developmental nutrient might involve facing the discomfort of asking others for help, support or empathy, and learning to receive these without shame. This journey-taker might have also noticed impulses rising from his gut and moving into his arms and his jaw; perhaps his first need is to express anger at having felt judged and abandoned.

In the second example—the person who saw herself embarrassed before her school class—the journey-taker might benefit from working on her interpersonal boundaries; by learning to say 'no' when she really needs to and learning to confront her critics vocally, so she can feel safer to express her individuality. There are so many playful ways to fortify our outer edges. Perhaps a few sessions with an assertiveness coach might be a perfect developmental nutrient. Again, for this journey-taker a symbolic rather than literal memory has guided her recognition of her needs, clearing a path forward.

Your imaging and free-association offer a window to your unconscious mind, like a radar that helps you find your buried needs. The *theme* of the fantasy, rather than its literal sense, points to the developmental need that has been activated.

In exploring fantasy, look at the spontaneous, unscripted imagery that arises from your emotional state and the self-talk that accompanies it. The first audio-visual your mind produces is the one most likely to be faithful to your body-memory. At this point in the Journey, the focus is not on your wishful thinking; your fantasies about how things should have been or how you would prefer things to be. That very different emphasis comes later in the 'wishing question' of the Third Movement. In the Second Movement we are not yet moving towards what we want; we are tuning-in to how things *are*.

Using Recent Life Experiences

If Steps 5–7 have not led you to a *source event*, that's absolutely okay; you have not reached a dead end in your Journey. You can try a different avenue for exploration in Step 8, which asks how your world has treated you when you've behaved similarly to the way your child behaves today. You did not necessarily have to be the same age as your child is now. Similarity of behaviour, rather than similarity of age, is the spyglass you are peering through now. This alternative line of self-inquiry can yield profound 'aha's' about your unheard needs and thus make sense of the needs that drive your child's most vexing or baffling behaviours.

Feelings in common with your child

Steps 9 and 10 offer two final alternatives for tuning-in, in the absence of a specific, recalled *source event*.

In Step 9 we try to get a general feel for what life might have been like for you when you were a similar age to your child, instead of narrowing the focus onto a single event. That approach can often bring interesting revelations, but if it fails to, all is not lost; you can navigate another passage to an empathic bridge.

Step 10 asks you to acknowledge that part of you that, as an adult today, most closely resembles the aspect of your child you are having difficulty with. Here you can draw from moments in your recent past that are perfectly accessible to narrative memory. You might be taken back to when you were a youngster, or you might be taken back to last week. Either way, what you learn about yourself paves the road to learning more about your child.

Still having trouble connecting with relevant internal experiences? Then let's review the goal of this Second Movement. Somewhere along the line you have felt feelings similar to those of your child, felt comparable longings or behaved in similar ways. Connect with that experience and you have stepped a little closer to your child; your child will seem less strange to you now.

Your own body holds clues about your child's inner world. When at first you struggle to understand your child, turn your attention towards yourself. Begin by trying to understand what blocks you; what drives your resistance or aversion to your child's behaviour. If at first you cannot say, 'Ah, no wonder!' about your child's behaviour, do not give up. Another way to gain understanding is around the corner. Seek the 'Ah, no wonder!' experience in relation to your own reactions first. Begin with self-compassion and compassion towards others will soon follow.

In the quest to deepen our empathic perceptivity, our visceral sense of self is the medium. When one door of introspection does not seem to open, we can try another, then another if needed. If we keep trying, we are rewarded soon enough.

Below are a few more inroads to finding a connection to your child's inner world, *from the inside*. It's not an exhaustive list (feel free to explore other fruitful modes of inquiry):

Your Adult Mirror

How have others treated you when you've behaved as an older version of your child's current behaviour? For example, let's say your toddler is having intractable tantrums; how has Life responded to you as an adult when you've openly displayed frustration? Or let's say your baby clings desperately to you and screams when separated from you. How have others responded to you as an adult when you have felt lonely, needy or insecure? How do you treat those aspects of yourself? Pay close attention to your self-talk about those parts of who you are.

Other People as Mirrors

Instead of thinking about how you have been treated, consider how you have witnessed other people treating one another. What happened to others in your life—friends, colleagues, siblings, etc—when they expressed what your child is expressing today, or when they behaved similarly to how your child is behaving now? When you witnessed these exchanges, how did you feel? What we see happening to others can affect us as powerfully—and sometimes even more powerfully—as the things that happen directly to us.

Trust your Imagination

Imagine yourself as a child, behaving exactly as your own child does today. Based on your experience of how people cared for you and educated you, what do you *imagine* your elders—or your siblings, or your peers—might have said or done if you'd behaved as your child does today? What is the first image that comes to your mind about how others might have responded to you? What emotions come up for you as you let yourself imagine all of this?

Body Mirroring

Find a safe and private space. For a few minutes, try to imitate your child's voice, your child's manner, posture and bodily movements. To the best of your ability, allow yourself to momentarily adopt your child's physical reality. Pay close attention to the feelings and longings that arise within you as you do this.

Each one of these investigations can bring you new and vital clues; casting light on your reactions as well as on your child's behaviour.

Our Emotions Show Us What We Need

Table 5 (page 206), offers you a guideline for pairing your developmental needs with corresponding nutrients; fulfilling experiences that nourish your growth. It aims to help you figure out what you can reach for, to heal and move forward.

Even if you cannot access a backstory that explains the complex feelings that have been brought up for you, you can still seek to have your needs met. If you feel stuck, browse the second column (Developmental Needs) and the third column (Developmental Nutrients) until you identify what resonates most strongly with how you feel.

Trust your body sense as you read through. Bringing your attention to your body, scan for the signals from your inner developmental template—the sigh, the gasp, the excitation in your belly, the tingling in your solar plexus, the upwelling of tears—that tell you 'Aha, that's the one! That is what I need!' So, even without knowing exactly *why* you feel something, you might still discover *what* you need. Your body holds the answers.

When you are unable to access any conscious memory of childhood, just think of the childhood developmental stages figuratively; with each stage being a metaphor for your present-day feelings and needs. You might, for example, say to yourself, 'I feel small and helpless … it's *as if* I was a baby', or 'I feel like screaming … *like* a misunderstood toddler', or 'I feel embarrassed, *it's like* being at school again', or perhaps, 'I'm feeling rebellious, *like* a teenager'.

Look for the row in the table that corresponds to the age group that you have tentatively identified with, and see if any of the needs and nutrients suggested there resonate with you. Once again, when you see a nutrient that attracts your attention, run it past yourself to see if your body says 'yes'.

Once you understand the stages of emotional development, your feelings alone—even without a story to go with them—can show you what you need. Let's take the example of a situation that brings up helpless fear. When a person is feeling helpless, in great fear or terror, their needs are likely to have something to do with *being held*, or *being protected*. Even if the person is a fully functioning adult, you could say, figuratively, that this is a baby-like situation. The baby stage of development represents the nadir of helplessness in our lives.

The needed holding might be physical, or it might simply involve empathic listening (holding can feel invasive when it is the wrong kind). Sometimes the best kind of holding might involve another person's reassurance, at other times another person's protection. Perhaps we might need to give ourselves permission to escape an oppressive or perilous situation (to take flight). Alternatively, we might need support to push back, to say 'no' forcefully.

Generally speaking, in times of triggered fear, the developmental need will be about 'feeling safe'. That's when the first couple of rows of the table—the earliest stages of childhood development—are likely to display the relevant needs and offer clues as to the most helpful nutrients.

Let's look at some more illustrative examples:

Forgotten Trauma

Imagine a mother who is almost breathless with fear when her child is undergoing a routine and simple surgical procedure. Who knows? Perhaps some childhood trauma involving a distressing medical intervention has been triggered for her, but right now, she cannot remember anything of the kind. Nonetheless, her fear is real and deserves respectful validation, whether or not she can tell the story that justifies it. She needs—and deserves—some sensitively delivered reassurance from the practitioners; she needs to feel *held*.

The Hungry Heart

A man has an eating disorder, specifically, overeating. If he delays a meal or tries to reduce its size, he is afflicted with unbearable despair. Even without any recall of how his hunger drive first came to be so out of balance, you could say that his unfulfilled developmental need revolves around the themes of orality and nourishment.

The needs that characterise the baby stage of development, as seen in the second row of our table, might be a helpful metaphor—if nothing else—for this man's battles with nourishment and satiation.

This man could say 'yes' to nourishment in many different ways, so that his need does not remain so orally fixated. He could consciously broaden his life's pleasures by, for instance, listening to specially selected music, dancing, singing, visiting art galleries or taking Nature walks.

He could deepen the quality of his dialogue with his friends and family, reaching out for more fulfilling and *emotionally authentic* interpersonal contact. He could try eating more slowly, closing his eyes and inhaling while he chews his food, paying attention to every texture and flavour and allowing himself to be permeated with delicious sensations. With proper attention, food can nourish the heart and soul, not only the stomach.

In all, he could learn to receive a broader range of life's pleasures more deeply. People who are emotionally fulfilled rarely overeat.

To Win or to Love

A father drives his son exceptionally hard at sport, yelling critiques from the sidelines and occasionally backslapping him, but only after his son's most audacious plays. His son is starting to show signs of cracking emotionally under the strain of trying to please his dad, and he barely remembers how to enjoy his sport for its own sake.

As part of his treatment for alarmingly high blood pressure, the father's doctor recommends that he enrol in a series of mindfulness classes. There he is encouraged to probe for the roots of his stress. In one of the group sharing sessions, the father concedes that since as long as he can remember, he has been obsessed with achievement. He knows what it is to feel admired, but he scarcely has a sense of what it is to feel loved. He resolutely avoids showing his softer emotions or admitting his failures and insecurities. Friends and family barely get a glimpse of his realness.

Childhood stories are a no-go zone for this father—too 'touchy-feely'. Nonetheless, he understands how seriously his psychological armouring has impacted his health. He gets the message that somehow, he needs to learn to contact his emotional vulnerability, to allow himself to feel loved; for which pride had been a poor substitute.

In the absence of any backstory, we could say (figuratively) that this father's issues hover around the third and fifth rows of the Table of Developmental Needs. Accordingly, his developmental nutrient would involve learning how to open up about his softer feelings and daring to allow others to love the more vulnerable aspects of his nature.

If he is to truly relent on pushing his son so hard, this man firstly needs to ease up on himself; to loosen his shell and let others know him more closely. He needs to lighten-up; so he can free his son to have fun, to make mistakes and to play his sport for the love—and not merely the glory or the triumph—of the game.

Shrugging-off the Burden

A woman carries a lot of bottled up frustration and broiling resentment. At work, she has been typecast as 'the capable one'. She thinks she carries more than her share of responsibilities—while her co-workers tend to passively over-rely on her. She feels guilty when she wants to say, 'No, that's enough!' Not surprisingly, her children's daily demands trigger glowing embers of animosity. Mostly she manages by grumbling to herself, or bearing it all in silence.

Though she struggles to remember anything about her life as a toddler, this woman is aware of a general sense of having felt squashed, held back. Looking at the toddler stage of development in our Table of Developmental Needs, she strongly identifies with the toddler's need (see the fourth row) to be vociferously defiant towards authority figures. Her heels want to dig into the ground, and her hands want to push back against the pressures of Life. She feels this natural impulse may have been crushed in her as a small child; despite her sketchy-at-best narrative recall of early childhood. Nonetheless, she chooses to trust what her body tells her, and her strong gut-felt connection with the toddler's need to self-assert and to protest. Consulting the table has confirmed her intuition, and has helped her define her needs. She decides to enrol in a psychodrama class where she can practise new skills of assertiveness and boundary setting, while having fun in the process.

Follow your Bliss

A father will think up any excuse to avoid helping his school-aged son with his homework. He finds it hard to be genuinely encouraging. When his son approaches him for support, he responds dismissively, and when the boy tries to share his passion for science the dad appears disinterested. His wife asks him why he is standoffish in the face of his son's love of learning, but at first he is as puzzled by his own reactions as everyone around him.

This father had always described his own time at school as unremarkable, 'just fine', he liked to say. At his wife's urging to examine his personal experiences relating to education, he'd sincerely reply that nothing was worthy of note. But when—subject to his wife's insistence— he finally browses through the Table of Developmental Needs, specifically the row involving the 'competency' stage, it occurs to him for the first time that his school life had mostly been a drudgery. Until now he'd not seen reason to give this a second thought, having no framework for validating how he'd often felt as a schoolchild. Passing his experience off as simply 'normal'—how things are 'supposed to be'—he had not given any credit to the boredom he'd suffered at school. It had never occurred to him that things could have been different, let alone better.

Reading through the section that speaks of the 'Right to Playful Learning', it dawns on him that no one had ever asked him what he truly loved to do. For his entire school life he had not been allowed to pursue his passions, to become absorbed or develop competency in the activities that naturally attracted him. Awakening to this loss brought up much sadness. Especially as, since as far back as he could remember, he had harboured a deep desire to learn about sophisticated woodworking techniques, such as inlay, wood-turning, French polishing and advanced joinery. He had trivialised this longing as 'just a hobby'—something to put off until retirement.

Now seeing his long-held desire elevated to the status of a 'developmental need' stirred something in this father. He resolved to stop downplaying his vocational longings. Before long, he signed up for a series of woodworking courses—committed to fulfilling his ambition. And who knows, perhaps one day to move from 'enthusiast' to 'professional'. Little by little, as he restored his own connection to playful learning, he found himself increasingly able to share in and celebrate his son's delight in the sciences.

Of course, we won't always need to consult the table to prompt realisations about our core, developmental needs. At times all we'll need is to tune-in to how we are feeling, and immediately that clarifies what our needs are and how we can move forward. And that's when playful creativity comes in handy. Adult-appropriate ways to satisfy our Inner Child's needs are not always immediately apparent. Sometimes this bears a little thinking, a little inventiveness—perhaps even a little mischief and derring-do. In Chapter 13 we will look at many diverse and imaginative examples of how we can translate our inner-child's need into a nutrient that applies to our life as it is right now.

So, even when you are unable to remember a relevant childhood experience, or when you don't understand the significance of the experiences you do remember, your feelings hold vital information. The developmental map can help you name the needs associated with how you are feeling and set your course towards the experiences that would satisfy these needs.

The Body as a Bridge to Empathy

I have often worked with people who prefer not to revisit childhood, and I respect their reluctance to do so. When our own childhood story must remain veiled, it does not necessarily block all avenues for understanding our children's feelings and needs. If we know how, our own bodies can be portals to another person's universe. No time travel necessary.

By simply emulating our child's body posture—imitating his movements, her way of breathing—we begin to resonate with their emotional reality. Inhabit another person's physical bearing and you begin to see the world through their eyes. Enter another's bodily attitude and you know a little more about their pain, their joy, their longing and their struggle. You have made contact.

Exercise 11: Embodying Despair

Try walking around the room for a minute or so with your shoulders hunched, your arms dangling, and your eyes downcast, and you will understand someone who has experienced a lot of defeat in their lives. You will be able to sense their despair, from the inside.

Exercise 12: Embodying Startle

Open your eyes as wide as you can, and with a sharp gasp breathe high in your chest while lifting your shoulders up towards your ears. Here you are embodying the inner experience of someone who has experienced great shock.

Exercise 13: Being a Baby

How might we fathom the vulnerability of a baby, when for most of us, this memory seems a million miles away? If you lie on your back and reach your arms upward, you might feel a twinge of the longing and the helplessness that only a baby can know.

You can also capture some of the bliss that can flood a baby if you ask someone to rock you gently and rhythmically in a hammock; be sure to let your head and shoulders go completely, and gently close your eyes.

Having your scalp gently stroked can also deliver you into that transcendently delicious zone.

Exercise 14: Being a Toddler

The next time you are alone at home and you happen to be feeling some anger or frustration, throw yourself onto a bed and beat your fists and feet repeatedly on the mattress. You can do this on your back, slamming your arms and legs down over and over while tossing your head from side to side. Scream—as loud as your concern about your neighbours will allow. Welcome to the world of your toddler. You might glimpse a little of what her rage feels like or what his despair feels like, as well as how powerful and enlivening it can feel to fully let go emotionally.

Have you ever tried sitting in a child's chair at a table with friends? What changes do you begin to notice in your emotions and your thoughts as you look upward at everyone around you?

Exercise 15: Being a Teenager

Want to feel like a teenager for a few moments? What if you already do, without knowing it? Think about some of the things you do to secure the acceptance of your peers. Which is the tribe you dress for with that tie, that hairstyle, that beard, those shoes? Think about the accent or the slang you use; does it serve to gain your membership of a particular peer group or social class?

There are many additional, playful ways to explore and re-experience some of the flavour of the adolescent existence. Try jutting your jaw forward to feel defiant.

See how satisfying it feels to slam a door.

Practise rolling your eyes, and say, 'Whatever!'

Slouch in your chair, with one leg draped over the armrest.

It's most important, when doing exercises such as these, to move quite slowly and mindfully into the positions, paying very close attention to what happens internally.

✳ What feelings come up as you adopt these postures?

✳ Notice even the subtle, fleeting emotions—the deeper layers of feeling that usually move too fast for us to sense in our normal, busy states.

✳ What thoughts pass through your mind?

✳ What impulses arise within?

✳ Last, but not least, what do you feel you need when you are embodying these child-like states?

These exercises can help bring valuable insights into what your children need from you and from the world around them. *Be* your child, and then you'll *understand* your child.

The exercises I gave as examples here barely scratch the surface of possibility. Actors, directors and body-oriented psychotherapists have devised a vast repertoire of embodiment exercises that grant us a momentary, tentative immersion into each other's feeling-states. This powerful method enables us to see the world from another person's point of feeling and to gain profound insights into their motivations.

Posture is attitude; movement is emotion. Knowing this allows us to walk a mile in someone else's moccasins. If you are willing to be observant, creative and a little daring, you can adapt this basic principle of empathic embodiment to bring you closer to understanding anyone in your life. Suspending our adult composure for a few moments, and adopting a child-like physicality, is an immediate version of our Inner Child Journey that puts us in direct, intimate contact with a deep aspect of ourselves, while also creating an empathic bridge to our children. Don't be too surprised to discover this Process can be a lot of fun.

Curiosity Is the Therapy

And now, let's take some pressure off. The Inner Child Process should not be thought of as arduous—a riddle to be worked out or a lifetime of problems to be resolved. We can carry this Process more lightly than that.

Sometimes all we need to feel happier, renewed and uplifted, is a witness to our pain. Even if we do nothing else, simply connecting with childhood feelings can be transformative. That little question, 'How do you feel?' is an open hand extended in support—an acknowledgement of your existence and your value. A child who has waited a long time for attention cries with relief when he is finally heard. It is the same with our Inner Child. Listening to his voice can be intrinsically fulfilling—to the point that nothing further is needed.

Perhaps this is among the most fundamental of human needs; to share our feelings with someone who is interested in us. Connection is what satisfies the heart; it is our simplest but greatest longing. An emotionally authentic connection can produce profound shifts in just moments. Empathic listening is sometimes the very nutrient that makes the difference—without even a peep at our developmental map. In fact, when empathic listening is enough, we can skip the Fourth Movement in the Journey altogether since its goals have already been met.

As a facilitator of another person's Inner Child Journey, your prime responsibility is to be an empathic *witness*. Please don't think it is your burden to help them work everything out. But if you've ever experienced what it feels like to be listened to with genuine interest and an open heart, you'll know that this humble act does not leave people unchanged. Open curiosity—towards ourselves and towards each other—is one of our greatest gifts. Perhaps it is the most important child-like faculty that we retain.

CHAPTER 13

Your Developmental Nutrient

You've arrived at the point of your Inner Child Journey where it turns into a real-world adventure. You now enter uncharted territory. A little risk is involved. Dare you accept some fresh and new experiences? Your Inner Child has called to you, asking for your deliverance. Magic can now enter your unfolding story as you begin to script a very new itinerary for yourself, discontinuous from the old.

This chapter helps you find appropriate, life-changing developmental nutrients, to answer the developmental needs brought to light in your Journey.

To Heal Is to Grow Is to Heal

The 'Ah, no wonder!' experience brings a sigh, and relief floods us when we finally understand the 'why' behind our children's reactions and ours. True validation is a turning point in our relationships and that's why we don't always have to take the further step of finding a developmental nutrient. Sometimes simple validation is all it takes to resolve a crisis. There is no rule in psychology saying that we absolutely *have to* meet every rising developmental need to feel complete. Even when our environment does not grant us our wishes, self-validation can bring us an inner peace that surpasses the turmoils and insufficiencies of our daily lives. Self-empathy enables us to say, 'When the world is not okay *for* me, I am okay *with* me.'

> *Self-empathy enables us to say, "When the world is not okay for me, I am okay with me."*

On the other hand, sometimes our only way forward is to fulfil a key developmental need. Meeting this need—even in a small way—has two powerful advantages.

Firstly, we experience personal growth. We mature as individuals, stepping into a more expanded state of being. In human psychology, healing is less about *repair*, and more about sequential development. Every repetition of a new behaviour (as we will see later) sparks a rewiring in our brain's networks—subtly deepening our capacity for relationship and broadening our self-expression.

The second advantage gained from personal development is that when we are well nourished we can, with far greater ease and joy, nourish and liberate our children. Any parent knows, through bitter experience, what a strain it is to give our children the kinds of emotional sustenance that we have not received ourselves. We try (Lord knows!), valiantly and doggedly at times, and get drained and resentful in the process. Real giving comes from fullness, not from depletion. When we feed ourselves, we have more to give to others.

So, you decide when self-validation is enough, or when you should risk new behaviours beyond the familiar. Your bodymind will inform your decision—if you pay attention.

Your children will often trigger emotions in you that are linked to long-buried needs. Don't be too surprised if, upon completing your Inner Child Journeys, you find yourself feeling grateful to your child for helping to shine a light on your Inner Child's suffering. Only when we awaken to those needs that lie in waiting, deep in our subconscious, can we hope to finally have them met. Answering the call of our Inner Child brings us happiness, inner peace and self-empowerment. It makes us better parents, better carers, better teachers. The Table of Developmental Needs will help you find nutrients corresponding to the needs that have been triggered for you, according to the emotional age (developmental stage) that these needs arise from. So how do we find an adult-appropriate nutrient to address our Inner Child's need?

Finding your Nutrient: The Fourth Movement

As we saw earlier, you don't need to go all the way back to being a baby or a child to heal old wounds and to grow those parts of yourself that yearn for expansion. We don't have to dress up as primary school kids or crawl back into our bassinettes to resume the developmental trajectories that were interrupted for us.

Having said that, a number of psychotherapy modalities do evoke trance-like states involving childhood regression as a way to rewrite the most painful aspects our personal histories. In an emotionally safe and confidential environment, clients are supported to enter a simulated bodily experience that is powerfully evocative of childhood, babyhood and even in-utero states of consciousness. The therapist then provides a nourishing and restorative new experience of life's early passages that can be profoundly transformative, with benefits felt for the long term (examples include somatic psychotherapy, psychodrama and family constellations). There is much validity to this somatic re-experiencing approach, when life permits it. But it's not the right way to go for everyone, nor is it easy to set up. Moreover, regression therapies are only safe when facilitated by a qualified and experienced therapist.

Time and again, experience has shown me that regressive trances are not the only way to find healing and release. In fact, some of the most life-changing moments I have experienced, or witnessed in my clients, happen while firmly rooted in the here and now. The Fourth Movement in our Journey involves finding the adult version of our Inner Child's unmet wish and discovering ways to give ourselves the corresponding developmental nutrient.

Devising an appropriate nutrient to meet your emotional need can be a playful and creative exercise. It goes something like this: firstly, consider the *theme* of the emotional need that has come up for you. Looking at your need and the wishful imagery that accompanies it, let's say it bears a general theme of 'nourishment'.

How might you be able to nourish yourself in a new way, as an adult? Would you dare to reach out, allow yourself to receive and enjoy some nourishing experiences that stretch beyond your usual? What is the most beautifully nourishing experience you could give yourself right now? Tomorrow? Very soon? To really make a difference, you might need to commit to giving yourself this nourishing experience—or a mix of them—on a regular basis. So, what kind of nourishment speaks best to your heart?

Let's forage through a whole caboodle of possibilities, to see what jumps out at you. More hugs? A quiet space to relax with a novel? A walk by the ocean, through a forest, in a park? A regular massage? Joining a local a cappella singing group? Having richer, more honest and self-exposing conversations? What do you find most nourishing?

What if 'protection' is your theme, in other words, *your* need for protection? Let's say that your Inner Child Journey has shown you a time when you were left alone, in paralysing fear, to face an overpowering threat. Thinking about your life today, has a certain task been dogging you for a while? Do you have an albatross around your neck that has kept you nailed down, frozen, irresolute? Have you been needing to confront a cantankerous neighbour about their barking dog? Or submit a complaint to an oppressive authority, or apply for a complex permit from an overbearing bureaucrat? Thinking about that awkward branch that needs trimming, way up high in a tree overhanging your roof? Or baulking at removing a large, hairy spider that has made its home in your wardrobe?

Can you, as an adult, nudge yourself to ask a friend or professional to stand in for you? Or perhaps ask a buddy to accompany you to a frightening situation as your emotional support? Most importantly, can you allow yourself to receive— to let your Inner Child bask in the warmth of another's protection? Pay attention to your inner voices; notice if you feel shame or embarrassment at the thought of leaning, for a moment, on another's strength. Remember the prototypal steps by which we all move from unskilled helplessness to skilled self-empowerment—the first step involving someone else doing the difficult thing *for* us. (See page 218 for more.)

If you can let a trusted person take over for a spell and allow yourself to fully enjoy that experience, it can dynamise your growth towards becoming a better self-protector. And the best part is that you never benefit alone. When you have allowed yourself the warmth of another's protection, it changes how you respond to your children's need for protection.

What if instead, your theme is about boundaries? If you take a few moments to think about significant people in your life—besides your child—you are highly likely to discover that you need to assert stronger boundaries with someone. It is no accident that boundary-related issues have been triggered for you via your interactions with your child. Our trigger-points are, after all, signposts for underlying emotional wounds.

What support do you need to learn to say 'no' or 'enough' more clearly— more powerfully and without guilt? Besides your child, who are the people you need to draw a line in the sand with? What steps can you take to learn boundary-setting skills, or perhaps to boost your existing skills? Who could help you fortify your limit-setting abilities?

Most of us could use a little help in this area. There is always room for us to become more effective communicators; better attuned to our rights for space, separateness and rest. Build and repair your personal edges, and you will find yourself less triggered by your child's budding—and often less than elegant!— attempts to declare independence.

Perhaps your theme involves the 'right to be playful'. How might you be more playful in your work? More whimsical in your leisure time? How daringly can you push your own envelope and step out of comfortable conformity? Rediscover your own playfulness, and notice how this changes your connection with your children— with *all* children, in fact.

Our developmental needs are as varied thematically as the many stages we grow through as youngsters. Our buttons are pressed, and our emotional age elevator plunges us down through the levels, each with its own unique needs. The doors of the elevator open and we are shown the incomplete need; the unfinished business that for years and years had been clamouring for our attention, while we looked the other way.

Sometimes our baby needs are activated—yes, even when we're adults, when we're old as well. Sometimes it's the frustrated needs from our toddler years, sometimes our school-age arrests and sometimes the incompletions of adolescence.

Every loose end in our founding story finds a way to nag us, to chaff at us until we listen. When an *outside need* has been activated, the nutrient involves receiving, while an *inside need* pushes us to act or self-express in a new way.

Either way, our willingness to respond to our Inner Child is never without reward. Every consciously-taken nutrient helps free us a little more, to access the emotional intelligences that each stage offers, to grow in spirit. Bring your Inner Child the nutrient he or she asks for, and your adult-self gains in wisdom, confidence and compassion.

Shall we take a brief look at a few more examples of nutrients to match the developmental need?

About Self-expression

When your children's ruckus dredges up uncomfortable feelings about how your own voice was once suppressed, you could say that the theme being highlighted for you relates to self-expression. Were you shut down as a toddler? Silenced as an adolescent?

What steps can you take today to re-learn how to speak your heart? Your developmental nutrient might involve practising voicing your feelings and opinions to others a little more often, a little more bluntly. It might involve practising saying 'no' more readily, when you need to, or daring yourself to protest against social injustices a little more vehemently.

About Sexuality

In every home, the theme of 'sexuality' looms large sooner or later. If you feel disturbed by your children's physicality, that might be a signal for you to attend to your own issues surrounding the themes of passion, pleasure and preferences.

Depending on the kinds of emotions triggered in you by your child's sexual development, perhaps your developmental nutrient involves speaking more candidly to your partner or trusted friends about your fears, your shame and your desires. Or perhaps the issue is quite different and you've been alerted to an urgent need to set better boundaries, to learn to say 'no' to unwanted touch, hugs or physical closeness.

About Vocation

Often parents and teachers tangle with children's motivation—or lack of it—in relation to learning and study. Unsurprisingly, the Inner Child Journeys that ensue tend to uncover the adults' life-long struggles with 'vocation' or 'competence' themes. What if, along the way, you were saddled with shame, did battle with authoritarianism or missed out on good mentorship?

What might your nutrient be then? What can you change today about the way you work, so that you enjoy it more? Can you change your work environment? What if you need to alter the nature of your work altogether, to align more closely with your heart? The more we enjoy our own work, the more effective we become at helping our children find their own fire.

For each developmental theme we can find a corresponding developmental nutrient, and a safe-enough way to reach out and award it to ourselves. Giving ourselves the nutrient is a transformational commitment to our own healing and unfoldment. First we heal ourselves, then we can heal our children.

The unhealed wounds of childhood continue to resurface throughout our lives. If we were abandoned, we re-encounter abandonment in one form or another; if we were bullied or repressed, we continue to battle with issues of power or authority, and so on, until we begin our path of healing. That these themes persist throughout our lives is precisely why we are so easily triggered by our children.

Yet as soon as we consciously begin to meet our Inner Child's needs, we become less susceptible to having our buttons pressed. Every effort to nourish our Inner Child frees us to parent with more ease and enjoyment. If parenting rubs salt in our wounds, it's so we can discover them, and apply the much-needed salve.

If parenting rubs salt in our wounds, it's so we can discover them, and apply the much-needed salve.

How Developmental Nutrients change Us

At times the power of imagination alone can generate substantive shifts. This is especially true under trance-like conditions, such as with creative visualisation in meditation, or under hypnosis. Focused attention is one of the four conditions that intensifies our ability to create new states powerful enough to stimulate changes in the brain (more about this on page 252). Try it out. Creative visualisation can be one of the more effortless approaches to personal growth and healing.

Just take a few moments to imagine yourself enacting your newfound nutrient. This works especially well if you imbue your visualisation with as much detail as possible. Pay particular attention to how you feel as you imagine yourself experiencing your nutrient. In your visualisation, what are you saying? What do you hear? What do you see around you? What do you smell? How does your body feel? What happens for you emotionally?

If your visualisation involves an *outside* need, ask, 'How do I feel as I imagine myself *receiving* this?'

If it involves an *inside* need, ask, 'How do I feel as I imagine myself *doing* this?'

Your imaging will sometimes be enough to trigger a deep emotional release, delivering you into a new—and more expanded—sense of self. This vision quest might suffice to transform how you understand your child and the behaviour that had triggered you in the first place. If you find, through the artistry of your imagination, a balm that fulfils your heart's need, you have also found clues on how to respond more helpfully to your child.

More often than not, however, you'll need to add a behavioural challenge. The greatest and most enduring shifts occur when we *behave into* a new state, many times over. Repeat an action until it is etched into your neuro-muscular memory and it promotes the growth of new wiring in your brain to accommodate the new ability. Once encoded in your neural tapestry, a new strength remains available, more readily accessed for future use.

Whether it is about receiving, enjoying, declaring or giving, we know our nutrient takes us into new territory because it feels somewhat risky. At first it feels uncomfortable to receive more than we usually permit ourselves—to voice our feelings more forthrightly, to make uncharacteristic demands or to set new limits in our relationships. As when entering cool water, we might flinch at first. The joy comes as we give in to our new reality, and swim. We venture and we gain.

Remember, when you devise the adult version of a developmental nutrient, let yourself be imaginative about what it might look like and how it should be delivered. Be playful and a little daring as you generate ideas. How will you give this nutrient to yourself? How can you safely say what you need? What is an edgy—but safe enough—way to express what you usually refrain from? What is a fun way to step out of your comfort zone?

Here are some examples of developmental nutrients that people have chosen at this point in Inner Child Journeys.

To Nurture the Nurturer

There was a mother who became highly fretful and over-vigilant when her baby cried. She was an avid adherent of the attachment parenting approach, but her anxiety left little room for pleasure in mothering. To better understand her fearful responses, she decided to undergo an Inner Child Journey. On her Journey she connected with the terror she'd experienced as an infant when her own rather detached mother would leave her to cry alone for long periods. The unmet developmental need that was triggered by her baby's cries involved the theme of nurturance. A deep and wordless grief welled up as she contemplated the bewilderment and aloneness she had known in the most fragile time of her life.

As her tears passed, she began to think about how she might create for herself a safe, bodily experience of nurturance—a way to feel babied most tenderly and sensitively, to know the feeling of being truly held. After much deliberation, she decided to buy a hammock, and to ask her partner to rock her in it gently while she lay back and closed her eyes. She found this experience so delicious that it left her in a profoundly relaxed state for quite some time. As she became more accustomed to feeling nurtured, she began to more actively seek out nurturing experiences, taking aromatic warm baths when she was exhausted, and accepting affectionate embraces from her friends as she had never done before. As her bodymind began to settle into what now seemed to be a more nourishing world, she began to find herself less fearful for her baby, and more able to mother her child pleasurably, with greater ease.

To Nourish the Nourisher

Another mother, despite her best intentions, found breastfeeding to be draining and laborious. When her friends talked about breastfeeding as relaxing, at times entrancing and even sensually pleasurable, she had no idea what they meant. It hurt her to hear about an experience seemingly beyond her reach.

She had heard enough about her own infancy to know that she had been weaned after only a few weeks at her mother's breast. Often busy and somewhat standoffish, her mother had struggled to be maternal. As an adult, this mother had tended to bury herself in work, almost never sitting back to enjoy a moment of self-indulgence.

Her Inner Child Journeys put her in touch with an inner emptiness, an emotional starvation that bordered on despair. For good reason, her hunger had been on hold, waiting to be re-awakened in more sustaining times.

Reflecting on how she might redress this theme of nourishment in her present-day life, she resolved to embark on a daily program of sensory reclamation. Perhaps Mother Nature might feed her senses in ways she had barely known as a child—that is, if she could open herself up to receiving. She vowed to remember daily to fill her senses with all the earthly offerings that surrounded her. She would eat her meals more slowly, devoting her attention to every flavour, every texture, every bite. Closing her eyes, she would inhale the perfume of flowers or sea breezes. She would allow birdsong and beautiful music to penetrate and resonate through every fibre of her body. When time permitted she would feast her eyes on splendour, promenading through gardens or strolling through galleries. Her baby would, of course, usually accompany her so they could both share in these delectations. Breastfeeding itself became an act devised to please mother as well as baby; whenever possible reclined in the rhythmic comfort of a rocking chair, humming a well loved tune, breathing gently.

As taking in nourishment—mindfully, deliberately—moved from novelty to routine, this mother found herself increasingly at ease giving nourishment. She also discovered that, curiously, receiving and giving were sometimes one and the same.

To Support the Supporter

A father found himself compulsively mocking his young son at any display of emotional sensitivity. He could not bear to allow his boy, God forbid, to be seen in a jumble of 'girly' emotions. Unsurprisingly, this father had been met with the very same admonitions from the men and boys he'd been surrounded by as a child. But he could see that this intergenerational pattern had to be arrested, because his son was becoming more distant from him and more aloof with each passing year.

Before this man could embrace his son's affectability, he'd first have to reconcile the shame burden he'd carried his whole life. He'd have to learn to accept and express the softer underbelly of his own nature. He might also need to stoke a fire in his belly, to push back against the taunts and jibes that were commonly meted in his subculture—to stand up for his right to feel. His theme: the right to vulnerability and support.

As part of his campaign to restore closeness with his son, he began challenging himself to speak more openly about his fears, his embarrassments, his failures and his grief. Though at first this made him squirm with discomfort, he began to reveal his feelings through life stories he shared with his son. For help to ease into this newfound candour, he joined a men's group where he found both the support and role modelling for courageous, heart-centred dialogue. Additionally, he dared himself to speak up and demand respect from his friends should they ever make light of his newly emerging softer side. Brick by brick, the wall that once separated him from his own father was dismantled, making room for his son to come close to him again.

To Liberate the Teacher

A university tutor became resentful every time his students began joking around in his class. He found himself judging them as frivolous and recalcitrant. If he didn't bite his lip, he feared he would snap at them about 'frittering away their time'. Nevertheless, he suspected his rigidity was interfering with his effectiveness as a tutor, and it puzzled him why some harmless classroom antics would trigger him to this extent. His own passage through youth held vital clues. A junior version of himself was calling out for his attention.

In keeping with his parent's ambitions, he had been educated in a strict, authoritarian-style school. He had shelved so many of his burgeoning passions and dreams to fulfil expectations that were not his, to remain 'serious' and to disregard his yearnings. Revisiting this period of his life brought the tutor an unexpected pang of sorrow. The resentment that he felt towards his students had masked his grief and rage. His wings had been clipped. A key developmental need—the right to pursue his own interests in his own way—had been betrayed. Would he still have become an academic had he been allowed to chart his own course? He could not even answer his own question. This showed him, quite starkly, how far he had strayed from his own north.

His students, in their own roguish way, were modelling what he might have sounded like, had he been free to be himself. The theme of following his bliss had now come sharply into focus. So, how to begin? What developmental nutrient might oil his wheels of whimsy, rekindle his *joie-de-vivre*? If he risked uncovering his passion, where might this take him?

As he mused about this, he was thunderstruck by the sudden recall of two activities he had been besotted with in a past that seemed so far away now. Surfing and amateur theatre; twin loves that had once magnetised him almost to the point of obsession. He almost winced as he realised how completely he'd forgotten these passions, and how rapt he had once been in both. Without knowing where this would take him, his next steps were now clear. His developmental nutrient would be to buy a new board, return to the surf whenever he could, and to make himself known to his local amateur theatre company. Almost immediately, as he committed himself to reviving his passion, he felt a zest for living returning to him and his irritation with his students beginning to lift.

To Protect the Protector

Thrilled and mystified by the transformations her body was undergoing, a teenaged girl had begun to experiment with makeup, acting coquettishly and playfully admiring herself in the mirror. When her mother first discovered her, engrossed in her new womanly play, she was surprised by the ferocity of her immediate reaction. Before she could think about it, she heard herself lobbing a scalding rebuke at her dumbstruck daughter, warning her of unspecified but dire consequences if she continued exploring her newfound femininity. The daughter was speechless with shock and humiliation.

Some time later as she reflected on the way she'd snapped at her daughter, the mother contemplated what had happened to her at a similar age. At 12, she'd been sexually molested by a relative—a nightmare she had (wrongly) attributed to the first appearance of her breasts. Through the eyes of a frightened, pubescent girl, she'd always felt that her maturation was to blame for bringing her this new and very perilous kind of attention. For many years she had harboured a confusing whorl of rage, betrayal and shame—that haunting, sickly sense of having been begrimed at the core—volcanic emotions she'd believed were now behind her, strewn on the floors of her many therapists' rooms. And since she'd thought she was 'over it', she was unprepared for that day her daughter's self-adornment exposed a deeper layer of her anxiety. The feeling of endangerment was not gone; it had lain dormant and was now flashing redly at the sight of her daughter's nascent sensuality.

The mother had lost sight of how unsafe the world still felt to her; her boundary felt flimsy, violable and under threat. Her daughter's triggering had brought home to her what she had not wanted to face; that sometimes she still felt paranoid, as if cornered. At times, when she needed to say 'no' to an unfair demand at work, she would inexplicably flush with fear and her throat would feel dry. Her flare-up at her daughter was a reminder. It was time to take the next step in her growth.

The mother's Inner Child Journeying had put her in touch with how alone and imperilled she had felt as a young girl. Her deepest, hitherto unspoken wish was for an ally, someone to be on her side and to protect her if needed. As her first developmental nutrient, she reached out to her most trusted friend, asking for her witness and her emotional support. Her friend, a bolshy woman who understood her struggles quite well, gladly offered to be her cheer-squad, as well as a shoulder to cry on when she felt overwhelmed.

Once she felt less alone and that someone had her back, the mother was ready for her next developmental nutrient to address her theme: 'boundaries'. She started strengthening her interpersonal boundaries. Since she tended to feel particularly queasy when needing to say 'no' to her male co-workers, she committed to practising this as often as possible. Remembering the past advice of therapists, she knew she'd have to begin with smaller challenges—the smaller, easier 'no's'—and build-up gradually as she gained confidence. The mother had signed up for 'boundary gym'.

With time, her regular self-assertion practice helped calm her nerves for those times that still lay ahead, when she would be called upon to guide her daughter through the maze of adolescent sexuality and relationships. Her prize: the ability to teach her daughter about self-protection, without overly alarming her or shutting down her joyful entry into sensual aliveness.

To Reclaim Playfulness

He was 5 years old, and he'd found a new love. Not for a person, but for an activity. It happened almost overnight, and such was the thrill brought by his new pastime that it would be a long time before he finally gave it up. Almost every day—or at least, when no-one was watching— this boy would gleefully empty the entire contents of his mother's refrigerator and one by one arrange it all over the kitchen floor. Being a thorough operator, his job was not done until every last jar of mayonnaise, wilted lettuce and clove of garlic was out, re-purposed as signposts on his quirky floor-map. There he would stand, admiring his freshly re-designed landscape, adorned with foodstuffs of all colours, in varying states of freshness or decay.

Cut to the moment his mother arrives on the scene for the umpteenth time, shoulders sagging, surveying the familiar disaster before her in bedraggled resignation. She would have muttered, 'Here we go again', if only she could muster the energy to speak. It felt like this ritual had been going on forever. He would disgorge every perishable from the fridge and, satisfied with his work, would leave her to put it all back in.

She had tried everything to persuade him to stop doing this, or at least to stick around and help her re-stock. She'd pleaded with him, threatened him, bellowed at him and even tried to buy him off with sweets and extra screen time. It was like talking to a bollard. He remained proud as punch of his installation art. In fact, the mother had a growing sense that the more scandalised and coercive she became, the more obstinate he became. What at first had begun as a whimsical experiment had now deteriorated into a spite-filled stalemate.

At the end of her wits, the mother embarked on her first-ever Inner Child Journey with the help of a counsellor. Duress has a way of softening our resistance to untried approaches. What they discovered was truly tragic. It could almost be said that this mother had never been allowed to be a child. She could barely relate to the concept of play. Her austere and orderly life, ruled by strict authoritarian parents, had scarcely contained a modicum of glee, a free moment to create and imagine, to climb and to giggle, to roll down a grassy hill. Perhaps as an adult, she was content with her lot, but she was entirely joyless. Her right to be playful had been taken from her. She could not possibly understand the delight her son derived from his mischief. He felt this and it rankled him. In the only way he knew how, he was trying to shake his mother alive.

The mother was stumped as to what might help her through this predicament. Her Inner Child had no reference for what to wish for. But since the theme of playfulness stood out, her counsellor came up with a wicked idea. He offered her ... a food fight! An offer she, of course, began by refusing. To her credit however, although she couldn't in a million years imagine how this might help her with her intractable problem at home, she agreed. The deal was, they had to start with relatively non-staining food. And the battle had to take place at the counsellor's office, with the counsellor.

The results were delightful. Within a few volleys of grapes, the counsellor saw the very first smile dawning across his client's face. A mixture of fun and embarrassment, her sheepish grin had cracked a granite demeanour, making her look many years younger. They persisted. It was messy. She laughed. Not-so-secretly, it felt devilishly sweet to her to see someone else's room succumb to a hail of food. And there it was; the pure elation of unbridled naughtiness had found her at last. Like it or not, she really *got* her son's shenanigans—from the inside. To understand a child, one first needs to *be* a child.

Refreshed from this most unconventional tangle with psychotherapy, the mother returned home to speak with her son. His face lit up like a supernova when, for the first time, she sat with him and asked him why he liked emptying the fridge so much. Though he had no deep insight to give her—saying simply, 'it's fun!'—he clearly loved being asked. Her genuine interest was worth gold to him.

After validating the pleasure he drew from his game, and confessing that as a food-war veteran she had known a similar pleasure, she then shared how hard she had struggled to clean up after him. She told him how very tired she was, and that she sorely needed his help. Feeling warmly connected with his mother again, help was something he was more than glad to give. At the next fridge-emptying event, they laughingly took out all items together. Afterwards, they both tidied up together until every last carrot and pickle jar was back in place. It was to be the last of these episodes. They had both moved on.

With few exceptions, as with most important things, our developmental nutrients tend to be free of charge. Much as we might like *stuff*—and for some, lots of *stuff*—connection is the real stuff of life. Above all we crave a more heartful connection with ourselves, with each other, and with the non-human world—though we seem curiously good at denying this longing. All health—physical and psychological—flows from connectedness and from our striving to enrich our capacity for connection. Developmental nutrients are infinite in variety but they boil down to the simplest of yearnings: to express something from a deeper place in ourselves or to connect with others more authentically. Absorb the nutrient and we feel ourselves expanding; this experience of growth is intrinsically exhilarating. And since we all are so interconnected, growth is, inescapably, shared.

Towards Realistic Expectations

Since the 1970s we've been bombarded by hype telling us to 'unleash' this or that inner fabulousness. Thumb through the most rousing section of a New Age, self-help bookshelf for a while … and soon you're thinking your destiny is to be super-human. Liberate your Inner Giant, visualise your perfect body, think and grow rich!

Overreach alert! I don't believe we can fashion and refashion ourselves in any old direction that takes our fancy. We cannot always dictate the terms of our growth.

Designer-self pop-psychology has been a somewhat heroic trend—thrilling but ultimately shallow. Tempting as it is to imagine ourselves scaling the heights, our inner beings are so much more than this. Moreover, our vain attempts at self-design can be a barrier against intimacy. Running after an idealised self side-steps human vulnerability.

Our deepest developmental impulses may have little to do with what our culture accepts. Becoming more self-assured does not always win us more friends. Pursuing our true vocation does not necessarily attract more admiration or wealth. Learning to be more honest does not promise to keep us from conflict. And self-nurturing is often frowned upon. Our inner success does not guarantee the trappings of material or social success. Most importantly, it's not our 'greatness' but our willingness to be emotionally vulnerable that enables us to truly connect with one another.

Growth has a natural flow and direction according to what is encoded inside us. A eucalypt can never, no matter how it tries, grow to be a pine. Growth progresses along the lines of *who we are*; the Inner Child holds many clues about the direction wherein our bliss awaits. Ecstasy comes from inhabiting the fullness of ourselves; unfurling the fullest possibilities of our DNA.

Let me offer this example of what I mean. If you believe yourself to be an introvert, for instance, it's pointless to invest your life force in trying to become an extravert. For sure, the extravert enjoys some advantages, but have you tried to understand the magic of your contemplative nature? Have you delved into the reason why you began to bark up the wrong tree, telling yourself you'd be happier as an extravert? What do you really need instead? By all means, growing your capacity for outgoingness when this is needed might serve you, but have you fully appreciated your intrinsic strengths? Learning to be more fully and enjoyably yourself will feel far more magnificent than battling to adopt a way of being that is not organically yours.

Although personal growth expands our capacities, it doesn't erase our fragility. We're all subject to being triggered; we all regress. We continue to ride the emotional age elevator up and down, as we saw earlier. We will always be vulnerable to feeling small when life triggers us forcefully enough. If we can understand this principle, we are saved from feeling like failures if we are not irreversibly altered by our most powerful moments of growth.

Don't get me wrong. Profound evolutionary leaps can and do happen. But personal evolution means you listen inwardly and align more faithfully with your deepest Self. Are you striving to grow—to be a truer version of yourself—or trying to be more like someone else?

My vision of healing is about evolution rather than change. The more we practise Inner Child Journeying, the better we become at recognising when we are in the midst of a body-flashback and the more gracefully we find our way through. As we become better parents to our Inner Child, we return to the present moment renewed; with more self-assurance, vitality and compassion for others. Nourish the Inner Child and the adult can progress to higher stages of maturation and wisdom.

If the Nutrient Seems Unattainable

Even a developmental step as small as a grain of sand can be valid and empowering. Even a baby step begins to lay down new neural pathways. These new synapses ensure that the new skills are more easily accessed next time we need them. In fact, smaller steps are better for developing new habits and strengths because overwhelming fear or discomfort freezes the brain's capacity to absorb and retain new learning. If your steps are too big, you might be setting yourself up for failures that seem to confirm a negative self-belief.

So if your developmental nutrient feels too big, downsize it until it feels just safe enough to try out, yet just big enough to feel challenged.

Let's suppose that your Journey shows you a need to set stronger interpersonal boundaries—something you have struggled with your whole life. If it feels far too daunting, for example, to flatly refuse a bothersome request from your employer the very next day, begin with a lighter challenge. Practise declining to assist a co-worker when you are too busy, or begin by saying 'no thanks' to an invitation to a social gathering you don't want to go to. Simply taking a breath outside your comfort zone, beyond your usual behavioural repertoire, begins a powerful reorganising process in your bodymind.

Suppose instead that your Journey reveals that you haven't nurtured yourself enough; since childhood you have been driving yourself too hard, feeling guilty when you are 'idle'. If you begin your new commitment to leisure with a week of perfectly unscheduled vacation time, you might feel so shocked by the lack of planned activities that you'd find the experience entirely unpleasant. And since pleasure is the object of the game, this would defeat your purpose entirely. In this case, taking the unusual step of reading a novel for two hours might hit the spot. There is a Goldilocks level for each challenge—not too hot, not too cold—and it is different for every individual. Does that make sense?

Never berate yourself for taking small steps. You would not do that to a child who is learning a new skill, and so you should not treat your Inner Child that way. Learning is by definition awkward, even a little clumsy, and it always evidences courage. If you hear a shaming voice inside you, telling you that you should know better at your age—or something similar—remind yourself that absolutely everyone on earth revisits childhood to heal wounds, to complete what remains incomplete.

As you become more at ease with the unfamiliar states that your nutrients bring you—the new levels of empowerment, affection, joy or relaxation—you can increase the size of your challenges by small increments at your own pace.

More than One Developmental Need?

Your Journey might put you in touch with more than one unfulfilled developmental need. That's fine. There is no rule about which of your emotional needs you should address first, nor how often you need to address them. Prioritising your needs is up to you.

Be creative about addressing your needs and willing to diversify the kinds of nutrients that you choose. There is usually more than one way to address the needs that come up in Inner Child work.

Let's look at four principles of neuroplasticity—your brain's amazing ability to heal and grow—that will greatly assist you at this point in the Journey.

Four Healing and Growth Accelerators

'Under the right conditions,' says neuropsychiatrist Daniel Siegel, 'neural firing can lead to the strengthening of synaptic connections. These conditions include repetition, emotional arousal, novelty and the careful focus of attention.'[43]

1. Repetition: 'Behaving into' your new state

To a large extent, we are behavioural beings living in a behavioural world. In order for change to take place—for us to develop new relationship skills, to alter our mood-scape and to satisfy our emotional needs—we need to move our bodies and use our voices. To grow, we need to *act*.

We are behavioural beings living in a behavioural world .... To grow, we need to act.

Bruce Perry explains how neuroplasticity, the brain's capacity to heal and grow, depends on behaviour. New behaviours and bodymind states, when repeated often enough, embed themselves in new arrays of neural webs that render those new behaviours more accessible and automatic—in other words, part of our character. New habits and responses are formed when, through the impact of regular practice, new brain fibres are established to support them. This means that if we want our brains to expand the structures that govern emotional intelligence, we need to deploy our desired behaviours not just once, but repeatedly. Perry explains, 'Patterned, repetitive activity is, in fact, necessary to all kinds of learning—whether building the neural systems needed to manage stress or trying to build stronger muscles.'[44] We only begin to settle into a new sense of ourselves by behaving in desired but unfamiliar ways, many times over.

Without regular practice, fresh neural shoots of wellness too easily whither and are lost, and so we return to older habits and states. When our elders used to admonish us with 'practice makes perfect', it might have sounded dull and burdensome. Turns out there's more than a kernel of truth to it. Perhaps we resisted the advice because repetition can become intolerably boring. The answer lies in awarding yourself the right to have fun. A playful attitude to growth and healing is very important. Vary your practice and play with your new behaviours, taking small but daring steps. In all mammals, play is how learning and growth happen.

A playful attitude to growth and healing is very important. Play with your new behaviours, taking small but daring steps. In all mammals, play is how learning and growth happen.

Repetition of behaviours embeds them in neurons and thus new behaviours become incorporated; new *traits* become new *states*. As new neural pathways multiply, a new behaviour that at first feels awkward or uncomfortable begins to feel more natural and enjoyable. I like to call this phenomenon *behaving into* a new state. When we want to feel different, the most powerful way to achieve this is to *behave into it*.

Let's say for example that you want to feel more nurtured and thereby better able to nurture others. You would need to behave into that state by actively giving more nurturance to yourself, regularly, repetitively and perhaps also by reaching out for nurturance from others. In other words, it won't do to have that massage, that warm bath or curling up with a good book just once.

Similarly, if you want to be more creative, you'll need to behave into it— perhaps by pushing the boundaries of your 'normalcy' a little each day, or challenging yourself to do something a little uncharacteristic each day. Same story if you want to become more assertive: you'll need to take graduated behavioural steps in that direction. Dare yourself to say a little more about yourself each day. Take small but significant risks in self-expression each day. With repetition, your new experiences nourish and expand the corresponding part of your brain until new behaviours and states become a natural part of who you are.

2. Focused attention

The second facilitator of neural growth is our focused attention. The more closely we pay attention to our bodies—our sensations, our feelings and our movement—as we take up our developmental nutrients, the more we stimulate neural growth. As much as you can, really take notice of how your feelings change as you move through your chosen growth experiences. This will accelerate your expansion into new states of being.

3. Feeling

Intense emotion is another accelerator of brain changes. If you take some deeper breaths as you engage with your developmental nutrient, it will help put you more deeply in touch with your feelings. Allow yourself to feel how this nutrient is affecting you by paying attention to sensations around your heart, your solar plexus, your lower belly. You might notice some trepidation in the pit of your belly as you step out of your comfort zone. Perhaps a gnawing sense of guilt grips you around the shoulders as you receive what you thought you were not good enough for. A tingle of excitement might pass through your upper chest as you take the risk of speaking out beyond your usual reserve. A hum might appear in your solar plexus, perhaps a sweet pleasure enveloping your heart as you accept a kind of nurturance that you secretly longed for. All of the above could sweep through you, or who knows, your experience might be of an entirely different flavour.

In the bodymind, sensation and emotion are one. If you can allow your emotions, if you can surrender to their natural flows, they hasten the expansion of new neural webs. Since energy follows attention, when you attend to your emotions they become clearer, more powerful. Rich emotional experiences intensify the effect of personal growth practices. Emotion can be an accelerator of development.

4. Novelty

As much as possible, be playful in your quest for growth and healing. Keep finding new and diverse manifestations of your developmental nutrient. What if you can have fun as you reach for what you need? Be cheeky as you set new interpersonal boundaries. If your life has become too serious, run as fast as you can to your local store and buy your favourite ice cream. Learn to dance salsa. Speak with your hands more, as Italians famously do. Eat with your fingers. Scream into a pillow. Dare yourself to tell people what you admire about them. Ask for help when it embarrasses you, and confess to the person you ask how embarrassed you are.

Make fun of your guilt by singing a song about it, drawing a picture of it. Write someone a love letter. Help a stranger. Ad infinitum!

Novelty is miraculous; it fires up our senses, protects us from stagnation and it defeats inertia. The stimulation of the new and the unexpected sharpens our attention and supercharges the growth of new tendrils in the neural webs that sustain learning.

How Do We Absorb a New Experience until it Becomes Part of Us?
1. Do it a lot.
2. Pay close attention when you're doing it.
3. Do it with feeling.
4. Find novel and diverse ways to do it. Have fun!

The Journey as a casual conversation

Sometimes our Journeying is a walk in the park, a conversation with ourselves or sharing our feelings with good friends.

The short and thrifty versions of the Process (Appendices 3 and 4) can be almost casually woven into conversation when our environment is conducive enough.

The connections created in emotionally open dialogue are often healing and transformative in themselves, without necessarily following up with a behavioural program. So, we can safely dip into Inner-Child-aware dialogue between trusted friends when we're in an accommodating space, armed with an agreement of confidentiality if necessary.

When Is Professional Help Advisable?

Safety

The Journey can also be a trek through a jungle, over an ice floe, perhaps across a desert. For that we need a guide; one who is trained, experienced and qualified to lead us safely through.

When delving into childhood story and body-memory, we can be surprised by powerful rushes of emotion. We don't always know what we will find when we plumb the depths of consciousness. Very early experiences are generally hidden from ordinary, narrative memory, but they can be accessed in deep states of contemplation. Recapturing our time *in utero*, or birth or perinatal body-memories can be sublimely pleasurable, but they can equally be terrifying or enraging, depending on what we have lived. It can also feel quite overwhelming and distressing when a traumatic experience that had been veiled by amnesia rises unexpectedly to the surface. The more advanced, contemplative, 'deep-sea dive' kind of Journeying can also bring up strong reactions such as nausea, vomiting, cold or hot flushes, trembling or shaking. When such potent emotional discharges loom, that is a time to seek the supportive guidance of a trained and qualified professional.

Sometimes the key to growth involves having the right support, feeling held as we pass through a moment of anguish or distress. Your emotional safety should come first; always respect your own limits if you encounter an experience that feels too scary to handle alone. That is the foremost reason why sometimes the help of a professional psychotherapist or counsellor is essential. Am I harping on too much about safety? Well, your Inner Child is, after all … a child! He or she is worth every precaution.

Overreach

And then there are those times when we seem hell-bent on choosing altogether the wrong developmental nutrient; that is another occasion when without the intervention of a counsellor, we'll simply be treading water. The nutrient we first clutch at might sometimes be a cover, designed to avoid a deeper emotional vulnerability.

A common example occurs when we overreach the needs of our Inner Child— expecting of ourselves to respond too soon in an adult capacity. This is putting the cart before the horse. As, for example, when we push ourselves to be accommodating towards others while inside we are feeling fragile or unsupported. Or when we try to be generous while inside we are feeling empty. Or when we tell ourselves to be forgiving while inside we are feeling threatened.

The child matures through validation, not demands and expectations. When we push and shove our Inner Child to grow up too fast and too soon, we do so to avoid feeling the vulnerability of our emotional need. Left to our own devices, we don't always choose what's best for us—and at the very least there's no harm in seeking a second opinion.

Addictions

Sometimes our minds seem to keep choosing the same kind of answer for our problems, over and over, even when this answer lands us in the same hot water time and again. The madness of humanity seems to be our penchant for recycling old solutions that have already miserably failed our old problems. And what tenacity we bring to this merry-go-round!

The classic example: we buy a mountain of stuff and when that does not fill the cavernous hole inside, we buy more stuff, shinier stuff and bigger stuff. Rarely does this give us what our hearts yearn for, nor does it resemble what children (both inner and actual) need. Despair, emptiness and depression just keep mounting in lockstep with our hoarding.

Choosing a nutrient that conceals our need, instead of feeding it, is the essence of addictive behaviour.

The Nutrient or the 'Drug'?

A stock market trader and speculator once came to see me for psychotherapy sessions, complaining of depression. He told me how his mood would darken to the point of emotional collapse during those cyclic times when his share values were tumbling.

When I asked how he envisaged my help for him, it became clear that he wanted me to boost him back up on the same old horse. He had no interest in how his self-value had come to be tied to his portfolio value. He merely wanted a psychological formula for being a more consistent winner. Disappointingly, this man had all the hallmarks of an addict, and wanted my help to score.

I felt that if I agreed to help on his terms, I would be enabling his perpetual emotional boom and bust. I declined, explaining to him that my work, should he want it, had very different objectives. He thanked me, but I never heard from him again.

A Dubious Nutrient

The trader reminded me of a failing trial lawyer with whom I had worked early in my psychotherapy practice. He had hoped I would somehow toughen him up so he could impress his father—also a lawyer but far more hard-nosed—with more forceful performances in court. It troubled me that I could not see any sign that this man loved his work, nor that he had chosen his career for reasons other than trying to live up to his dad. I did, back then, do my best to oblige my client in the way he had asked. It is no surprise to me today that my therapy failed.

I would not agree to help a workaholic to endure more hard work, or a mistreated spouse to remain loyal and forgiving. And because the voice of addiction is cunningly able to supersede the voice of the Inner Child, a counsellor or therapist's input is sometimes necessary.

It's not uncommon to hit a wall in the middle of Inner Child work when we simply cannot imagine what would help us to move through. That's when we're most likely to reach for the same old, familiar answers.

Wish-paralysis

We have trouble visualising what we need until we have received it, witnessed someone receiving it or until someone shows us, for the first time, the object of our need. Until then, our need is like a formless hunger. In Chapter 8, I called this phenomenon 'wish-paralysis' (page 172).

Table 5 (page 206) is there to help orient us when we get stuck. But it can be most helpful to hash it out with a therapist who is well versed in developmental psychology. It's not that therapists know what is right for us; all they can do is make informed suggestions. But a therapist can also help you to dig deep and listen to what your body tells you, to differentiate the pattern-like, habitual voices of addiction from the voice of your Inner Child. Your Inner Child is always trying to speak to you about your true developmental needs, and it takes a little practise to differentiate this signal through all the muck and static. A therapist who understands how to work with the body can show you how to trust your gut, to navigate by your own developmental template.

Though it is fine to take Inner Child Journeys alone, ultimately it may not be optimal to work alone too often. We gain so much more when we work with a group, with a friend or a counsellor. The support of others is irreplaceable, and we can learn so much from the great diversity of experiences that other people share with us. In Chapter 15 we will look at the benefits of setting up Inner Child Journey support groups. Being part of an Inner-Child-aware community is a wonderful, uplifting and transformative experience.

And Meanwhile, Our Children ...

Let's take a moment to re-orient our gaze outwards, away from our inner worlds and towards our children. Invariably, some situations need a *right now* response. I don't imagine that a reply such as this 'Son, let me take a Journey on that issue. I'll get back to you in an hour', would get you very far as a parent.

But with regard to ongoing, pattern-like parenting dilemmas, once you've done the first four movements of your Journey, you will return better resourced for supporting and connecting with your child. Over time, the healing and growth that happens, as you continue to follow through with your nutrients, will ripple outward to affect your children and everyone around you, beyond what can be measured.

CHAPTER 14

From Resistance to Healing

'Mañana!' 'I'm too busy!' 'It's not the done thing!' 'What would people think?' 'I'm just not that type of person!'

Resistance—our regular companion along the path of healing. If there's a growth impulse, there's surely an equal and opposite anti-growth inertia. We try to give ourselves a developmental nutrient, and we feel blocked. More usually we block our own progress. We sabotage our practice. We forget. We collapse. Or we bury ourselves in frenetic routines.

This chapter offers you helpful tools to ease your way through roadblocks that commonly appear along the course of a Journey.

When Resistance comes up

Resistance is a shape-shifter; it comes in many guises and gives many reasons. Not that the rationale is always duplicitous; sometimes it's necessary to ease up, take a break. Sometimes our foot dragging is quite conscious; it is eminently possible to suffer from growth exhaustion. But most often our resistance is unconscious and we give it another name.

Resistance is as certain as the next rainy day. Growth is confronting. It takes us into alien, uncharted waters, we feel momentarily as if we don't know ourselves, and we face the real possibility that some people in our lives will not like our changes. As we venture into untried relationship dynamics, we may be stumped by shame or guilt or embarrassment. Step well out of our familiarity zone and a bolt of fear charges up our spine. We recoil, and scurry back to the comfort of the devil we know. It's commonplace for us to be like the proverbial freed bird that, gripped with uncertainty, flies back to its cage.

Why Does Resistance Happen?

If we are ever to gracefully move through our own resistance, first and foremost we need to understand it. Let's take a brief look at why growth-inertia happens.

Our personal reactions to stress and conflict tend to follow a recurring pattern, and this pattern was, for the most part, learned. Our most predictable behavioural patterns took years to build, painstakingly, into the complex matrix of our nervous systems. They were not genetically pre-determined. These reflex-like responses are animated by extensive nets of neural pathways that were woven to drive our unique reactions to the world around us, based on how this world treated us in childhood.[45]

Our temper, our shyness, our clinging, our aloofness, our charm, our intellectualising, our impulsivity, our domineeringness, our endearingness, all these and many more character traits can be reactive adaptations to early life. The brain networks that constitute the engine room for these defensive traits were purpose-built, and at the time that we learned these strategies, they were critically helpful for us. Our unique psychological defences are our best guess at how to get through life's threats and challenges. Not uncommonly, they began as our means for surviving psychologically intact through some intensely traumatic experiences. Our recoiling in shame preserved us from conflict. Our dominating behaviours preserved us from oppression. Our dissociative states cushioned us from some intolerable horror. Our clinging preserved us from unbearable aloneness. The list goes on. And although our automatic defences are often troublesome to our relationships—they limit us and they alienate our children—once upon a time, they may have saved our sanity. At times, we might feel imprisoned by our defensive tendencies, helpless to overcome them. But we have much to thank these tactical strengths and abilities for, and we should never take them lightly.

Our idiosyncratic defence styles succeeded only by virtue of their being set to 'automatic'. When we feel threatened, our reactions do not wait for our instruction or permission, they just happen, and that is precisely why they work so well. Fight, flight or freeze must engage with hair-trigger immediacy, when the perceived threat is great enough. Only a long time after the real threat has passed do these responses become problematic, if they persist. In the meantime, the neurological architecture of our patterned defences is very resistant to change. Deep inside, we are not really so sure that we want to give these defences up.

We now understand that some of our deepest layers of defensive reactivity are the result of thousands of years of human struggle that has been passed down to us via epigenetic changes. The kinds of behavioural impulses that create a harmonious family and society do not emerge overnight, since our forebears have endured millennia of incessant war and dominator-style societies. The kind of trust that allows us to fully open our hearts arrives tentatively, in steps. And it's usually three steps forward, two steps back.

Still, growth and change are possible. Our ability to evolve, helped by the marvellous plasticity of our brains, is a natural endowment. But change doesn't happen casually, at the click of our fingers. We need to be deeply respectful of the reasons why we so often sabotage the learning of new ways, why we keep finding ways to apply the brakes. There is a frightened, nay, terrified child inside who does not too readily want to let go of something that once helped him or her feel safe.

For over a century it was commonplace among psychoanalysts and throughout the human-potential movement to chastise the all-too human resistance to growth, and to try to override the anxiety that drove it. The resistor would be cajoled, manipulated, tricked or browbeaten, rebuked with instructions to 'let go', 'just trust', 'get over it' or 'get off it'. Not too dissimilar to shoving a scared kid into the deep end of a cold swimming pool.

Of course, it can certainly feel disheartening when we find ourselves bogged down in our own quagmire. And it can feel frustrating to be faced by another's wall, or their covert foot-dragging, when we are trying to help them. But it simply doesn't work to blame ourselves or each other for resistance. We need to understand it deeply, and address the fear and shame that lies beneath it, before we can gracefully and courageously move forward in healing.

When Others Resist Our Changes

Don't be too surprised if some people in your life become displeased by your attempts to grow and expand your relationship strengths and skills. Strange as that might sound at first, growth is quite commonly met by at least a little resistance from outside, as well as from inside.

For instance, let's say you decide to practise being more assertive. You might be exercising a new way to say 'no', perhaps also asking more clearly for what you need. Conceivably, someone near you might feel threatened or challenged by your changing behaviour. You are no longer quite the person that they had become used to, and by amplifying your self-assurance, you are forcing them to adapt to a new you. You might initially hear some protest and you might experience some pushback against your expanding personal territory.

Since we are first and foremost social creatures, growth and healing are a shared experience. It's a good idea to let people in your life know—at least the people who are close to you—when you're considering practising a new relationship skill. Give them a chance to accommodate your new ways of being, and to understand the new skills that you are trying to deploy. If the people you care about are not caught by surprise, they are more likely to get behind you in your efforts, or at the very least, they are less likely to oppose you.

Don't be too quick to dismiss the objections and grumblings of friends and family as their 'resistance to my growth'. Learning new relating skills can be a clumsy process, full of mistakes and overreach. I recall a woman whose rookie efforts to be more assertive took the form of yelling at her husband. I also recall a man whose first venture into better self-nurturance involved abandoning his young family for entire weekends at a time.

Sometimes, the feedback we receive might be fair and helpful, and it's important that we listen. This ensures that in our quest for growth we remain respectful to others, and that we don't sabotage our own growth by treading on others' toes. Here are some simple tips for smoothing the way for your growth, in collaboration with your people.

> **Smoothing the Way for Growth**
> Include others in your growth plan.
> Tell them about the new skill you're intending to practise.
> Ask for their support.
> Be prepared to at least consider their feedback.

How to Work with Resistance

The 'grain of sand' approach is the best way to learn and then fortify a new ability. Some people call it 'baby steps'. (Revisit the discussion of how repeated, small steps encourage the growth of new, supportive neural pathways on page 249.)

When your nutrient—and the behaviour that would bring it to you—feels so scary or overwhelming that you cannot mobilise, then consider taking smaller steps. In fact, keep making your steps smaller until you reach a level of difficulty that does not remove your ability to remain present. There is an optimal, Goldilocks degree of challenge that fires learning in the best possible way. If we stay entirely safe, we barely grow at all. Learning requires us to be a tad uncomfortable, to take some risks. But if our steps are too ambitious, one of three things can happen. We may freeze on the spot, we may make dramatic changes only to undermine them later, or we may disconnect from our emotions while trialling new skills so the new abilities are not sustained.

How to Melt Resistance

To melt our resistance gently and compassionately, the approach might go something like this:

As you move your first grain of sand, you might feel awkward, embarrassed, perhaps a little guilty or even scared. Pay attention to those feelings closely, be kind to yourself, and acknowledge that you have taken your first step.

Move another grain of sand, still paying attention to how this feels. You are likely to find that a little enjoyment starts to creep in and the new relating skill you are working on starts to feel more natural. When this happens, move to the next step.

Increase your challenge by another small increment. Perhaps two grains of sand at a time, or more if that feels okay. Repeat until you start to find some pleasure in it; the intrinsic satisfaction and thrill of gaining a new potency.

After some time, your grain of sand can become a stone. Down the track, with the same attitude you might find yourself moving boulders with surprising ease. You now have a 'new normal'; the borders of your comfort zone have expanded markedly. Your new abilities are sustainable, as they are supplied by fresh neural networks that you've generated with your practice and time. How far will you go? That is entirely up to you. Make sure you give yourself hearty appreciation for your accomplishment. No matter how little you feel you have done, the enterprise of learning new relating skills takes a certain boldness of spirit.

A grain of sand can pass through a small crack in an initial wall of resistance, in a way that a large stone cannot.

A hard-working man finds it impossible to relax when he takes time out. Every time he allows himself some unproductive downtime, he is consumed with guilt. His efforts to unwind are fruitless until he accepts the need to begin with small, incremental changes. He starts meditating every day, for just five minutes at each sitting, no more. Over time, little-by-little, he begins to settle into longer and more enjoyable breaks.

A woman who has been besieged by agoraphobia as a result of a traumatic episode in her life, has baulked at all efforts to overcome her disability. But one small challenge feels conceivable. She begins by walking to a café 20 metres from her home, but there is a clincher—she will only go there to order her very favourite dessert, and on the proviso that her best friend, a woman that she feels entirely safe with, is there to greet her with a warm hug. It's a good start, and the recurring pleasure of this humble ritual begins to encourage her to extend her forays.

There is a serious man who is so emotionally repressed that he cannot bring himself to play on the floor with his 4-year-old son. Merely lounging on the floor feels awkward for him, and he is mortified at the thought that playing childish games might make him look silly. When his son plays imaginary games with his toys, his high-pitched squeals and made-up voices make the man cringe with embarrassment. If he is to forge a connection with his boy, he needs to find an entry level into whimsy. He finds his stride by beginning with a relatively quiet, focused game that involves building things with blocks.

When we progress slowly enough that we can stay present with every step—fully aware of our emotions as they arise—we are less likely to trigger a reactive recoil. Most importantly, if our steps are small enough that we can feel some pleasure in the process, it embeds our new abilities in new neural pathways all the more successfully.

Trust in Pleasure, Believe in Fun

Intentional growth should feel a little daring, a little exciting. When you take a step beyond what is usual for you, it should feel at least a little bit exhilarating. In the world of human motivation, joy is the high-octane fuel. As far as is possible, choose healing steps that can bring you pleasure, behaviours that can feel satisfying and fun.

As a younger psychologist I was sometimes called upon to deliver public talks related to stress management and conflict resolution. Public speaking—that dreaded monster. It was torture, every time. My vision would blur, and my command of language would turn to dust. On two occasions, I completely froze before my baffled audience. It was humiliating. I resolved to never speak publicly again. I was quite content to carry on for the rest of my professional life working in private practice.

One problem, though. In 2005 my first book was published. Quite abruptly, a realisation dawned on me that made my heart sink. If I never spoke publicly, the book I had worked so hard to produce would quickly whither on the vine. Unwittingly, I had outed myself from my hiding place. I had set myself a trap.

The moment I'd been dreading as I lay unsleeping at night, staring at my ceiling, arrived on the night of my book launch. My smiles and handshakes were forced. My stomach was convinced I'd come to attend my own execution. The initial milling, perfunctory chit-chat and customary canapés soon gave way to that heart-stopping bit when everyone sits down, falls silent, and all eyes turn to the lectern (or was it a guillotine?) When my publisher began to roll out his formal introduction, all I could hear was a whoosh-whoosh in my ears, and the inside of my mouth had turned to sand.

I have a confession to make. I caved in to my excruciating jitters that night, and did what I never do—self-medicate. My secret weapons: two glasses of sparkling wine and a natural herbal remedy that a friend assured me was good for calming the nerves. Despair is the mother of invention, right? Who knows, perhaps that's what got me over the line as I finally stood on legs that had lost all feeling. And haltingly, I began to speak.

But as my unpolished and poorly rehearsed address began to stutter forth, I discovered something unexpected. When I spoke of those things that I most cared about—the subject matter that had been my passion for many years—the terror subsided. It was my first distinctly visceral experience of fear being dismantled by passion.

Since that first return to face an old foe, years of speaking engagements enabled me to gain, quite gradually, some confidence and ease—a process that is by no means done yet. I still feel a fluttering of anxiety as I approach a microphone, but it is nothing like the incapacitating woe of the past. I love my topic and pleasure is a great healer. I believe a program for overcoming fear should be fun to apply. When I approach my presentations as a conversation, rather than a performance, the message becomes more important than me. In all endeavours, enjoyment melts fear and resistance.

You're more likely to retain newly acquired strengths when you experience enjoyment in the learning process. Enjoyment brings ease and focus; both conducive to the formation of new neural pathways. Enjoyment helps to relax resistance, and it helps us to look forward to our practise of new skills.

Stuck in Resistance?

When you encounter so much fear or shame that it makes your progress impossible, don't push yourself too hard. Give yourself a break, have a rest first.

Afterwards, it might be important to go deeper into your Inner Child's world. Let the fear that holds you back be the starting point of your next Journey. How did you learn to become so afraid, or so ashamed, of the need you are currently working with?

What kind of support might you need from others? Do you need an ally, a mentor, a friend to rally with you as you move towards fulfilling your Inner Child's need? This is why working in pairs or even in groups can be so advantageous. The final chapter is all about the many advantages of forming small and intimate support groups for shared Inner Child work.

The 'Light' and 'Super-Light' Processes

One thing certain to trigger white-knuckled resistance is the idea that all Inner Child Processes must resemble a psychotherapy session, complete with therapeutic regression and a dramatic emotional release. In fact, we are better off saving the deep-dive version of the Journey for occasions when we have a safe enough space for it, enough time to sit with strong emotions and perhaps also the support of a colleague, a therapist, or a group.

Some illuminating 'aha's' can come from a brief check in with our Inner Child, in the ease and naturalness of a conversation with a trusted friend. For this purpose I have provided the 'Inner Child Process—Light', and the 'Inner Child Process—Super-Light'.

You can find the 'Light' version in Appendix 3. It is comprised of just five questions, each pertaining to one of the movements in the Journey, set out so you can read them directly from the page. You can do this alone, or work with a partner. You can do the Process with eyes open or closed; you decide the depth of contemplation you're ready for.

The 'Super-Light' version—which you will find in Appendix 4—is so simple it can be done in a minute or less. In this approach, you are merely naming your triggered emotions and checking for any body-memory that might be involved. You follow up by asking your Inner Child how he or she is feeling, and what he or she might need to feel okay.

I'm often surprised by the enlightening realisations and the new sense of direction that such a simple and brief internal dialogue can bring. I have done the Super-Light version for myself while riding on a train, or sitting in my lounge room with a cup of tea. It has the feel of musing—an easy reverie.

This version can also be woven gracefully in and out of dialogue, much like having a conversation with a friend in which you spontaneously share tales from your childhoods. When friends open up to one another about the parenting challenges they encounter, I encourage them to ask each other: 'How was that for you when you were the same age your child is now?', or 'How were you treated when you behaved like your child does now?', and perhaps also 'What do you feel you needed as a child when you behaved as your child does now?' Inner Child exploration is often no more than a simple and caring act of curiosity.

Growth and healing can sometimes entail a painful transition. As far as possible, I wish for your growth processes to be easy, enjoyable and exciting. Since sharing is a key to ease and enjoyment, let's look now at creating Inner Child-aware friendships, support groups and communities.

CHAPTER 15

Building the Heart-connected Tribe

Have you ever found yourself feeling closer to someone just after they've shared with you one of their childhood stories? Have you noticed yourself feeling moved by someone as they allow some emotion to show? Have you noticed how others might feel closer to you because you've momentarily surrendered your composure, and let your own Inner Child show? How is it that our Inner Children bring us all so much closer to each other?

Talking about our childhood stories, our dreams, hurts and fears is a natural way to deepen interpersonal contact. This seems to be true around the world; the language of emotion transcends ethnicity and culture. We tend to be drawn intuitively to more poignant self-disclosure, sensing that mutual vulnerability is the path to intimacy. That special moment—a rite of passage—arrives between friends when we decide to take the plunge and begin—tentatively at first—to share some of our secrets. It is the gateway between acquaintance and friendship. The quintessential bonding ritual.

Fundamentally, when the time feels right for it, we want to be known and we want to know one another. The Inner Child offers a window to the soul. See another person as the child they once were, and it is hard not to be moved by them. In many ways, the Inner Child Process merely formalises a conversation that would otherwise happen naturally, and has done since time immemorial.

In this chapter we look at the wondrous benefits of Inner Child work when it is shared in a group, and the transformative potential of an Inner-Child-aware community and society.

A Meeting of Inner Children

Some of the most rewarding experiences I have had took place in workshops or encounter groups in which we took turns sharing our most significant childhood experiences with each other. As we lay aside our superficial composure and our social cloaking, we would feel the immense relief of being known.

It is hard to convey the blissful release that happens when our unadorned, authentic but fiercely guarded self is seen and heard. A transcendent connection happens when we take that daring and risky step into emotional vulnerability in the presence of others—the reciprocal shining of two suns.

> *A transcendent connection happens when we take that daring and risky step into emotional vulnerability in the presence of others—the reciprocal shining of two suns.*

Meeting the child that breathes beneath the scripted, adult veneer feels like a privilege to me. It moves me. The Inner Child is splendid; her innocence, his struggle, her dreams, his courage. The raw humanity present in shared moments of realness leaves an indelible mark on the heart.

It reminds me just how little we really know each other, how veiled we are ordinarily, and what a universe of mysteries is inside each human being.

I know that I am, in ways I cannot measure, a better person for having been touched in this way. I feel enriched, more human somehow, and these moments of true contact give purpose to my life.

Inner Children do not stay long, they are visible but for a minute, but the contact is healing, enlivening and restorative. An intentional group for Inner Child Journeying makes a safe home for this kind of sharing to happen. We descend slowly, one step at a time, into deeper truths. Shared emotional honesty is alchemical; it has a tendency to transmute pain into love.

Group work might just be my favourite setting for Inner Child Journeying, whether as a participant or as a facilitator. I love how we all spark each other's growth as we work together. The shared dialogue enables each person's unique experience to inspire, touch and inform everyone else. Each individual's Journey becomes, in a sense, a Journey for the rest of the group.

In a group setting, participants gain a palpable sense that the shame, the pain or the fear they'd borne in private is in fact part of a shared human story. Few things are more uplifting than the discovery that we are not alone, and that we never were.

It is not unusual for people whose Inner Children meet, to become friends for life. Emotionally authentic communication generates loyalty in droves.

Openness is viral; it ignites an empathic contagion. It is stirring to see how, when one person sheds a tear, others become quiet and attentive, and soon they too get a little misty. One person's laughter ripples around the room until all the bellies are shaking. When feelings of outrage or injustice emerge, these are also quickly shared. We are joined at the heart, and this comforts the spirit. Connection is the thing that we hunger for, though most don't seem to know it.

As a specialist in preventive medicine who started the first wellness centre in the US, and spent most of his professional life researching all aspects of human wellness and how to maximise it, my friend, John (Jack) Travis, MD, knows a thing or two about the conditions that optimise our health. Decades of research and experience led him to conclude that the principal key to human wellness involves making heart-to-heart contact with one another. As Jack says: 'The currency of wellness is connection.' From his own experience, and that of many others, he now addresses the hidden epidemic of partnerships failing shortly after a child is born, which he named Postpartum Abandonment Syndrome. He enthusiastically endorses the tools in this book to overcome the alienation that so frequently overwhelms new parents in nuclear families.[46] When we allow ourselves to enter moments of heart-opening contact with another, this has flow-on effects that radiate to all corners of our bodymind. The heart-to-heart connection permeates our being with direct, protective effects on physiological systems including the cardiac, digestive and immunological. Psychology is physiology.

 The heart-to-heart connection permeates our being with direct, protective effects on physiological systems, including the cardiac, digestive and immunological. Psychology is physiology.

When a group provides a safe space for shared, intentional emotional vulnerability, it acts as a pump, generating loving and healing energies that radiate to the families and wider community in its field. Of course, the connective rituals do not necessarily have to be about Inner Child work; people come together for a huge range of wonderfully enriching practices that include spirituality, music, dance and more. There are also countless personal growth and psychological healing approaches that do not involve the Inner Child. But when the Inner Child perspective is included in the dialogue, it is one of the most enriching forms of connection. You can fill a room with heart-melting empathy when the Inner Children are invited to meet.

If you prefer working alone, or in private with a counsellor, it's absolutely fine; these can provide a more intensive and sustained focus on you. For some people—and perhaps for all people at least sometimes—the emotions brought up by Inner Child work can be too overwhelming, even too threatening to bring into a group setting. Journey in the setting that feels safest and most appropriate for you.

But if the idea of group Journeying appeals to you, consider seeking out other Inner-Child-aware (or perhaps, Inner-Child-curious?) individuals, to gather as a tribe or support group. You might reach out to others, or perhaps join an existing group. If you already belong in a parent support group or similar, consider asking them if they'd be interested in sharing some Inner Child Journeying together. Even in those odd occasions when the Process does not immediately help with answers for parents or teachers, the connection it creates among the participants is life changing and uplifting.

Beneath the adult veneer

Healing: A New Perspective

We don't always have to repair something 'broken' in us to expand our ability to love and be loved. Neither is healing necessarily about 'thinking positive', nor about being 'happy'. When two or more people become intentionally vulnerable and share their inner truths across a space, it forges a kind of connection that is deeply fulfilling to the human heart. Psychological healing is not always about taking a wound and making it better.

Healing is about softening our interpersonal barriers at will, on our own terms, until we no longer feel alone with our pain, our rage, our fear and our shame.

Healing is about softening our interpersonal barriers at will, on our own terms, until we no longer feel alone with our pain, our rage, our fear and our shame.

Emotionally real interpersonal contact is of itself healing and transformative. *Connection heals.* The magic is in our willingness to be emotionally honest, with ourselves and with each other.

One moment of interpersonal contact can move us profoundly, altering our perspective and strengthening our relationships. But it won't always be enough; we still need to take personal steps towards growth. Although sometimes we heal in the crucible of relationship, at times healing requires a very personal undertaking. A program of personal unfoldment involves behavioural risk, the right developmental nutrients, with a clear orientation towards a future goal. We are sometimes called to work alone, or in private with a counsellor or coach.

But the healing effect of emotionally authentic dialogue is a different matter; it is not like the outcomes-focused quest to learn new skills, new behaviours. The healing that we experience in a moment of heart-to-heart connection is indefinable and happens in the present moment. When we dare to be emotionally open and vulnerable with each other, the contact itself is the healing spark, the richness of interpersonal connection is itself the nutrient. Mutual intentional vulnerability allows us to feel that we are part of a web of human interconnectivity. Immersion in this web fills us with new strengths, resilience and compassion. These unique benefits come from sharing the Journey in a group.

Forgiveness and the Process

I am not a fan of forgiveness; I have never recommended it. People have for ages meted out the expectation to forgive like there's a forgiveness-lever somewhere and all we need to do is pull it.

Somewhere along the line, psychotherapy got tangled up with religion and the assumption that forgiveness is a panacea crept in, unscrutinised.

Is forgiveness a healthy goal in all cases of hurt and grievance? I have my doubts, and I find the injunction to forgive to be a supreme blocker of empathy. It's not difficult, with a little contrived 'good will', to paper-over our pain and our rage. This merely delays the need to process the hurt and anger that naturally result from a violation. It's not that I am not interested in forgiveness, I just won't uncritically accept an imperative that seems tainted with moralisation. I prefer to keep the cultural separate from the therapeutic, the contrived separate from the authentic. And so, my understanding of forgiveness remains a work in progress.

Nonetheless, I have on many occasions become flooded with what I can only describe as a feeling of forgiveness—as if a breeze blows through me, lifting off my judgements and displeasure like dead leaves. Is this what forgiveness feels like, or is it just a strong nudge in its direction?

In any case, it's not an experience that arrives at my beck and call, rather, it's a change that happens to me; I am its passenger. I might be sitting with someone that I thoroughly dislike. I might even find them repugnant. A drastic clash of values, shall we say? Perhaps I am even appalled at things they have done to hurt other people, other beings, the natural environment.

But if I chance to hear a little about this person's childhood story; if I can for a moment see them as a child, my vision is altered. Inside, I hear the words 'Ah, no wonder!' Suddenly I understand—not intellectually but in my heart and gut— even the other's most foul behaviour.

Perhaps I still won't like this person. But somehow, I now find myself caring about them. We were all children once, utterly vulnerable, bursting with longing and dreams, yet abjectly at the mercy of the people around us. The horror, pain or loneliness of a child has no parallel. The reality of a child arrests all judgement, making equals of us all. If forgiveness speaks, I think it is saying, 'We *are* each other'. I suppose you could call that a moment of grace.

Forgiveness is not, in my opinion, a function of the will. I believe it to be an experience that permeates like the warmth of the sun. We cannot will ourselves to warm up. But if we know where to find the sun, we can walk towards a clearing and, very simply, stand under it. The warmth will surely come and our trembling will be gone.

I once had a client whose presence, I hate to admit, made me shudder from the moment I saw him coming. He was obese, oafish and unkempt, chewing with his mouth wide open as he gorged on the most unhealthy junk imaginable. To my dismay, he would bring his grub along to our sessions. The smell of rank cooking oil preceded him. To boot, he seemed permanently stuck in a morass; negative about everything. I did not look forward to his weekly visits. But as he began to tell me some of his childhood stories and I learned how badly neglected he had been, my compassion grew. His presentation and manner became less of a surprise or an offence to me, as I began to see the intolerable despair, the wretchedness and the shame that lay beneath.

Another one of my clients was often the target of my anger when I heard how punishing and verbally abusive she could be toward her children. That is, until she told me what had happened to her as a child. Her story chilled me to the bone. This woman had known horrors that no child should ever even hear. Sometimes when she spoke I found it hard to breathe. Ah, no wonder she was explosive when triggered by her children. Her body-memory was mostly a hell, with barely a trace of affection to refer to. My desire to be blaming lost its puff as I got to know this woman more closely. This did not stop me trying to restrain her acting-out against her children, but it removed the sharp edges from my voice as I spoke on their behalf. Forgiveness helped me to hold her so that she could hold her children. If forgiveness teaches us, it must be saying: 'Behaviour is biography; it does not reveal the person, but what the person has lived.'

Behaviour is biography; it does not reveal the person, but what the person has lived.

Forgiving ourselves

Self-forgiveness—perhaps that is the most difficult of all. But it works in the same way as it does with other people. A mile in another's shoes will help you understand them, so what does it take to walk a mile in your own?

Take an aspect of yourself that you have great trouble accepting. It might even be a part of yourself that you loathe. Let your feelings about this part of yourself be the starting point for an Inner Child Journey. Another worthwhile launchpad might be the feelings you get when you've acted in a way that displeases you.

Take as many Journeys as you need until you connect with the *you* that first behaved in the way you don't like. When you have your 'Ah, no wonder!' experience, you will feel a little less inclined to punish yourself. You will see yourself as wounded rather than objectionable, and instead you will want to find an appropriate developmental nutrient.

Forgiving humanity

And what about the great monsters of history? Infamous dictators like Joseph Stalin, Adolf Hitler or Nicolae Ceaușescu, atrocious creatures all. When I contemplate what they have done, I hate them. I feel a rising impulse to punish, to avenge the people—my parents included—whose lives they made so infernal. And yet, when I read detailed, historical accounts of their childhoods, I find myself moved to compassion. It can be unsettling to feel these two things simultaneously, side by side; to loathe and yet to have pity.

Nothing changes the fact that sociopaths should be apprehended, removed from power and quarantined from society. But when you realise that each of these tormentors was once a horribly tormented child, when you see that they could have, in a different environment, grown up leaving no stain on history, it becomes both impossible and irrelevant to condemn them.[47]

I'm not sure that I have truly forgiven history's oppressors, nor am I particularly invested in forgiving contemporary abusers. However, I cannot avoid feeling something for the children that they once were. We need a world in which children's emotional needs—not just their material needs—are consistently met.

Societal Implications

The Inner Child perspective helps us comprehensively re-shuffle our priorities; prevention is in, punishment is out. Seeing the child inside the adult compels us to shout from the rooftops: 'No child should ever grow up in violence or neglect!' Not only is the children's wellbeing at stake; but the fate of entire societies. Forgive me for stating the obvious. We're just so far away from lifting this commitment to the level it deserves.

In *Parenting for a Peaceful World*, I argued that childrearing reform, and the policies that would underwrite it, is well within the means of any nation. The abuse and neglect of children subtracts far, far more from the national budget than the policies that would eliminate it. Child abuse and neglect is the greatest tax on a nation, and the most absurd, since we already have the know-how and the resources to make it virtually disappear.[48]

> **Exercise 16: A path to Forgiveness**
>
> A wiser person than I could surely school me on my shortcomings in understanding forgiveness. In the meantime, I remain enthusiastic about the powerful role that Inner Child awareness plays in making forgiveness possible.
>
> Try it. Think of someone you really don't like, and if circumstances permit, find out what you can about the key, formative experiences of their childhood. Their parents' socio-economic status will tell you very little worth knowing. Focus instead on their *subjective* experience of childhood, with particular attention to the way their emotional needs were responded to.
>
> Don't just look at the information or detail—go deeper. Get a sense of what it would have *felt* like to be them. Dare to imagine what you would have felt if their experiences happened to you. See their early years through their eyes, heart and gut, and watch what happens to the lens through which you view them, and to your emotional responses to that person.

Sharing our stories and allowing ourselves to be affected by the stories of others can be profoundly healing and can restore our faith in each other. In a group, as we are touched to the marrow by the raw humanity of others, we begin to trust again in the basic beauty of human beings. Through the eyes of others we get a clearer sense of our own worth.

In time, these deeper-than-usual connections help us start thinking about violence and narcissism as scabs on a wound, rather than as intrinsic human failures.

Our bad behaviour is the smoke from a fire that was lit in childhood and has been painfully burning ever since.

Uncloaking the Inner Child leads to the inescapable conclusion that even the most distasteful individuals are our family. We share so much more than what makes us different. I feel uplifted and comforted by this vision.

Restorative justice is a highly effective conflict resolution practice done increasingly around the world. It is really a forgiveness generator that operates through mutual, intentional vulnerability. The perpetrator of a crime or infraction is compelled to listen to the feelings of the people he or she has hurt. Very often this leads to the crumbling of bravados, with the perpetrator in tears of shame and remorse. He or she might then be asked to explore what drove their malignant behaviour, with a view to learning healthier ways to get their needs met. Often once the victims see the offender's regret and accountability, their need for retribution abates. The softening of attitudes brought about by this intervention has often led to greater leniency in sentencing, and a policy of reparation rather than retribution.

Intentional vulnerability is key. This leads to the kind of connection that makes peace, generates loyalty and heals wounds. As we open to this kind of interchange, our projections about each other begin to dissolve, triggers are disengaged and the balm of empathy seeps in to the space between us. I think of this as the forgiveness factor.

Magic resides in the heart-to-heart connection. It bonds us and yet it frees us.

It affects more than the present moment; it also changes our future. When shared in a group, Inner Child work feeds the soul and creates a vibrant and life-giving community. These intentional tribes provide for us a lasting and strong web of support.

Forming Your Own Journey Circle

Of course, my version of the Inner Child Journey is by no means the only exercise that helps create that ineffable, uplifting sensation of connecting to something larger than ourselves. There is a formidable array of therapeutic methods and connective rituals to suit every type of person. Some involve dialogue, some body movement, others involve music or song, and innumerable ritual practices put us in touch with a larger sense of shared humanity. And of course, an Inner Child Journey support group can use whatever combination of connective dialogue and ritual that its members resonate with.

You might join an existing group that already incorporates this type of practice, and offer to share the Journey method in this book. If you are comfortable with the idea, and if it's acceptable to others, you might introduce the Journey to your parent support group, or to your staff room at school.

Inner Child work is not everyone's cup of tea—different practices suit different people. And for some people, the Inner Child Journey would not feel safe. As long as you respect boundaries and don't impose this idea, your invitation to share this adventure will attract the like-minded people most compatible for you to share group work with.

If you are feeling bold and resourceful, and have access to a safe and conducive venue (a comfy lounge room will do if you can secure its privacy during meetings) you could send out a message for like-minded people to join with you in starting a group. Social media is a powerful platform that helps you locate likely allies across a large catchment area.

It isn't necessary to convince others to try this Journey. Nobody likes being preached to. If you gather people who have an affinity or enthusiasm for this kind of process, your group energy will flow far more smoothly and warmly. And they are out there in droves.

Journey Circles for Teachers

Are you a schoolteacher or otherwise a member of a group that works with children? Remember the example I gave earlier about an Australian school in which staff meetings are inclusive of Inner-Child-aware dialogue? If your colleagues and management are amenable and if the culture of your team permits it, then you already have your group.

I believe the Inner Child perspective can offer revolutionary approaches to problem solving in education settings, add a whole new dimension of team building and take your staff body to a new level of mutual support and professional development.

I realise that many educational communities would consider Inner Child-aware dialogue superfluous, perhaps uncomfortably intimate. However, as the world continues its inexorable march towards increased psychological awareness, I believe some form of Inner Child work is likely to become an integral element of ongoing staff development. Until then, the teachers' and principals' Inner School-kid will remain, as the elephant in the room; awaiting acknowledgement.

Suggestions for conducting Groups

Once you have your group, use this book as a guide. If all members of your group have read it, that ensures the group will be solidified by a clarity of common purpose—not unlike a book club in which the participants discuss their responses to a book they've all agreed to read. The easiest way to step into the Inner-Child-aware space is to use the 'Light' or 'Super-Light' versions of the Process (Appendices 3 and 4) as a basis for sharing and dialogue. As much as possible, let the conversation be natural, allowing yourselves to be driven by your curiosity and caring for each other. The drawcard is your interest in meeting each other's Inner Children. You don't necessarily have to take the full Journey in your meetings, that's up to you.

If you want to adopt a more formal and contemplative approach, make a copy of the full version of the Process (Appendix 2). You can take turns leading group members through their own, private, closed-eye Journey by reading out each of the steps slowly, leaving a little space for feeling and reflection between each step. I have done this for groups of all sizes, at times up to a hundred participants.

At the conclusion of the Journey, people will want to share their personal experiences, listen to each other's discoveries and connect with each other. Make sure you leave enough time for group sharing after the Journey. Quite often the sharing that comes after the Journey is the best part of the whole process. Since each person is working through a different personal challenge, the range and diversity of learning can be immensely enriching. Your group is truly a meeting of Inner Children, of all ages and temperaments. The connections generated will be a powerful force for healing.

If ever you or someone in your group feels uncertain about the meaning or purpose of one of the steps, revisit the relevant explanatory sources together. Recall that Chapters 6–10 provide the most in-depth coverage of every step, and Appendix 1 offers a quick and easy review of each step. The more familiar you become with the steps, and the more clearly you understand the building-block concepts (page 125) the more smoothly your Process will flow and the deeper your Journey can take you. It will be advantageous for everyone in your group to have carefully studied those explanatory sections.

Remember that every step and question in the Journey is a suggestion. You certainly don't have to laboriously ask every question; with a little experience you will soon intuit the ones you can sometimes skip, depending on the nature of your Journey.

Use your time together to share your struggles and joys as parents or teachers and include relevant stories from your childhood. Open-up to each other about how your children trigger you. Most essential is to maintain a focus on taking ownership of your projections and your emotional reactions, acknowledging your body-flashbacks. Explore together what you want to learn about human relations and how you want to heal and grow, based on the lessons that your children bring to you.

Finally, a Journey-group can be a formidable boon to each member's growth if you support each other in an ongoing way with pursuing your chosen developmental nutrients.

Safety Agreements

The safety of your group will be dependent on three crucial caveats: the first one being a solid agreement of confidentiality regarding the material brought up in the context of the Journey. You can decide together exactly where to draw the line of confidentiality. Some groups agree to restrict confidentiality to those instances when a member especially requests it in reference to a delicate personal issue. Other groups prefer a more general agreement.

The second caveat involves the need to understand the limitations of your group so that it does not face an unfair and impossible load. If issues come up for a member that are beyond the capacity of your group to support them with, be ready to suggest follow-up consultations with a qualified therapist or counsellor.

Thirdly, I would strongly suggest that you make an agreement in your group not to abandon people to their pain if strong emotions are coming up for them. When someone's share leaves them feeling fragile emotionally, be sure to check in with them and ask if they would like any additional support, or holding, a hug or some other kind of physical touch. Needs will vary widely, some individuals will want the warmth of physical contact after a deep share, others will prefer to be left in their own space. The paramount concern is helping each member to feel emotionally safe, and recognising the diversity of needs each individual brings.

Should the Group Have a Leader?

Unless you engage a designated, trained and experienced group facilitator, I would suggest that your Journey-group would be better served without a leader—in other words, with a commonly shared and fluid sense of leadership. Let the book be your reference and guide, and make sure everyone is thoroughly versed with the safety-first instructions (see 'Create a safe experience', page 145). Resist any temptation to slip into the role of being each other's therapists; the greatest healing and tribe-building potential of a Journey-group rests on each member's willingness to let go and expose their Inner Child's voice. If a different member takes a turn at guiding the group through the steps of the Journey at each gathering, this will help maintain a sense of equality and mutuality in your group.

Ongoing Support with Nutrient-taking

You may or may not choose to devote group time to following up how individuals are faring with the steps of the Fourth Movement, choosing a developmental nutrient. If you do elect to support each other around the Fourth Movement, this exercise can introduce a little more complexity, including the occasional need to consult the Table of Developmental Needs when someone encounters wish-paralysis. Remember to offer suggestions rather than prescriptions, preferably in the form of questions.

Participants can help each other come up with creative ideas for developmental nutrients, and check in with each other's progress over successive meetings. Having a support group behind us makes a huge difference when we are trying-on new relating skills. If your group decides to venture into this realm, please make sure you are well versed in the relevant sections—the instructions and cautions—from Step 13 in the Journey and onwards. Otherwise, it's fine if you simply make your meetings about the richness of interpersonal contact, and the improved understanding of your children that comes from sharing Inner Child stories.

Of course, how you conduct your meetings is entirely up to you and your group. Make sure you remain flexible and open to change. Groups have a way of evolving quite naturally, developing their own idiosyncratic character. I don't imagine you would need to take a full Inner Child Journey at each and every gathering.

The 'Super-Light' version is often enough to open up whole new vistas and understandings as a response to the issues that participants bring in. But as you get to know one another more intimately, and gain an appreciation for each member's personal strivings, you will probably want to spend more time checking in with how each member is going with their family relationships and unique growth-paths. Let your curiosity and your caring for each other lead the direction that your group takes.

connection: The currency of wellness

Remember the mantra: 'Connection rather than fixing'. I would urge you to do all you can to make sure your group does not give in to the temptation to 'fix' anyone.

First of all the 'repair' focus tends to get in the way of the contact between you, presupposing that one person is the therapist and the other is the wounded client. Support groups work well because all members maintain an equal role. The willingness to be intentionally vulnerable needs to be mutual and shared. (A notable exception exists in the case of a group being led by a qualified facilitator who remains in that role for the duration of the workshop.)

Secondly, trying to 'fix' or repair ourselves misses the mark; we are not broken. Psychological healing is an eternal process of growth, a sense of stepping to a *next* level. Our issues are visited and revisited in new and more subtle forms, as each new life-challenge presses the same old buttons in our emotional age elevator. The deep nourishment of our spirit comes from the contact we make with each other as our Journeys intersect. Healing is not so much about mending cracks, as about finding a deeper connection with yourself, your tribe, your family and your children.

A final word. Remember to be cheeky; have fun with your group! Break-up the depth-dives with some levity. Sing together. Someone, bring a guitar. Why not a ukulele? A tuba perhaps? Share a meal. Above all, be playful, often. Vary the rhythm and tone of your meetings. Your Inner Child group should be a place that your Inner Child really wants to come along to. If you do engage in group Inner Child work one day, may it be a joyful enrichment to your life.

Creating the Inner-Child-Aware Society

When we remember the Inner Child perspective and weave it in to our conversations and daily endeavours, we free others from our projections; we become more responsible for our emotions and perceptions and our hearts become more available for connection. Life decisions that are informed by self-knowledge and the voice of the heart are invariably much better decisions.

Imagine a world—or if that seems too ambitious for now, a culture—where a commitment to insight and intentional vulnerability is the norm. What would life be like in a world in which adults understood that the way we see our children is clouded by our past? What would it be like to live among adults who regularly screen their impulses and commit to their own growth alongside their children? Imagine a world whose inhabitants accept that growing up is mutual; that our children grow us up just as we grow them up. What kind of world would we create if social policies were informed with a sharp awareness of a child's point of view?

Though outwardly we might speak with the voice of an adult, and make declarations with a tone of authority, so much of what we say and do comes directly from our Inner Child.

How often we are babies in uniform, toddlers in three-piece suits, juveniles with credit cards and big plans. With our Inner Child's needs and fears buried in the unconscious, we skilfully project a grown-up's persona, convincing ourselves and most—but not all—of those surrounding us, of our faux maturity.

How adroitly we rationalise our Inner Child's needs. We say we want justice when we hunger for revenge. We speak of loyalty when want to cling. We become directorial when we feel afraid. We boast when we feel ashamed. We control our children when we feel helpless. Out of fear of abandonment, we make promises we cannot keep. For the approval of elders long departed, we accept drudgery at the workplace and relegate playtime to the weekend—if that.

What would our lives be like if we awakened to our Inner Child's need, instead of making blind choices based on triggered body-flashbacks? How might our lives change with our Inner Child as our beloved passenger, instead of our haphazard driver?

Imagine our societal choices driven by a clear memory of how it feels to be a baby or child, rather than by intellectualisations, abstractions, economic formulas or commercial agendas. Would we still use industrial-scale childcare at a ratio of five babies per carer, if we actually remembered how it felt to be a baby? Would we still cynically convince healthy mothers to abandon breastfeeding in favour of artificial formulas for the pleasure of Big Business? Would we expect babies to 'self-soothe' and sleep alone? Would we still destroy natural childbirth in a hail of defensive and unwarranted obstetric interventions? Would we continue to deprive parents of appropriately paid maternity and paternity leave? Would we still allow children to be corporally punished if we truly remembered how this felt? Would we still lock kids in their rooms? Would we leave our youth alone to figure out the enigmas of sexuality and relationships if we remembered how scared and lonely we once felt? Would we let our young go through 12 years of school without being connected to their true vocational passions? Would we continue to treat full-time parents as second-rate citizens and school teaching as a second-rate profession?

If our modern societies are so disconnected and full of sadness, so exploitative and discordant with Nature, it is because we adults have by and large shut ourselves off from the child's reality. Despite all the doting and the indulgence of their material needs, we minimise and downplay children's emotional needs. This is the inevitable result of having denied our own Inner Child. Bring that Inner Child home, listen intently, and immediately we begin to connect to the world around us in a whole new way. If enough of us, a critical mass of people, become Inner-Child-aware, a beautiful socio-political fallout is assured.

I believe that our recent, more psychologically awakened generations offer great potential for societal transformation. Though it might seem hard to believe, given the daily portrayals of the world's atrocities, statisticians assure us that globally, *average* rates violence—domestic, criminal, civil and international—have been in sharp decline for several decades now.

But our woes are not over yet; we face a new crisis brought on by our pathological indifference to the ecological systems on which we depend. Dissociation and desensitisation can be as catastrophic for us as chronic violence. That still, small voice inside each of us wants our attention. If we listen and respond, we not only make our own lives better, we also make the world a better place for others, for our children and for our descendants.

Towards a New Image of Ourselves

This is truly a new era. Science has shown us that body-memory is a powerful driver of human behaviour and perception. This has helped us understand that our emotional problems are doorways to learning and development, should we choose to enter through. Simply by being themselves, our children trigger us. They push us to free ourselves from our illusions and projections—the recurring nightmares from our past.

Healing is not so much about repair—it isn't that dreary. Most of all, healing is an adventure. Inner Child work is not merely about finishing the business of our childhoods, it also reclaims faculties that might have been lost along the way. I don't believe we need to grow out of being childlike. In fact, we thrive and live well to the degree that we maintain a direct line of communication with our Inner Child, in order to access his or her invaluable gifts.

What are some of the faculties of child-likeness that we can benefit from throughout our lives? Let's see … what about the ability to be awed, to wonder at the many miracles of the natural world that surrounds us? Without wonder, life stagnates. What about playfulness? Without it, we cannot think laterally, step outside the box, invent or create; we shrivel up and become humourless and bland. Much worse, without the free-mindedness to be playful and innovative, we lose our viability as a species. What about cheekiness, mischief and devilishness? Without it we become stuffy, stuck in behavioural habits that stifle our aliveness. And what about the child's bottomless hunger for learning? Without this, we lose vitality and rapidly decline in health and happiness. Without the innocence of a child, the acceptance of mystery and the unknown, we remain armoured against transformative experiences, unable to surrender to falling in love, to ecstatic or numinous experiences, or to deeper states of connectedness.

Children are role models for me when they ask for the simple things they need without shame or guile. They ask to be held, they ask for companionship, a song, a game, a hug. And sometimes, they even ask to be left alone. Sublime directness, unbothered by culture. We would sound more like them, fresh and uncomplicated, had we not been so shamed, so manipulated, so punished and so abandoned. Each successive stage of childhood, from before birth to adolescence, is designed to grant us a new layer of emotional intelligence with unique tools and abilities that are meant to stay with us for life. Fortunately, we have ways to retrieve and reclaim any of the childlike strengths that we may have abandoned along the way. Our wellbeing and survival, as individuals and as communities, depends on our free access to all these developmental assets.

The most physically healthy and vibrantly happy old folks whom I have met have one thing in common. They can belly laugh, out loud. They find magic in the world around them. They take few things seriously, but they are passionate and dogged about the things that really matter to them. They enjoy learning new things well into ripe old age.

My mother began taking piano lessons at 83 years of age. A talented pianist as a young woman, she forewent her dreams of a career in music to study medicine. Both her aspirations—music and medicine—were abruptly cut short when she was forced to escape from communist Romania. For 60 years, my mother had not touched a keyboard, but her love of classical and jazz piano burned as incandescently as ever. For Christmas one year, my sister and I came up with the wild idea of surprising her with an electronic keyboard. No expectations. What did we have to lose? When we unveiled our gift, her hands cradled her face as she wept, wordlessly.

Perhaps this is the greatest inspiration my mother has left me—what she taught me at odd moments, when she wasn't trying to teach me anything. Her boundless playfulness; the eternal gift of her Inner Child. That she had lost all of her ability to carry a tune, and at first could only tinker unmusically on the keys, she did not care a jot. She was going to dabble on those blacks and whites no matter how it sounded, and she knew of no good reason to hold back.

Glorious freedom from plan or outcome. Before we knew it, our mother had booked weekly lessons and took to it like a duck to water. In a matter of weeks, with daily practise, the body-memory in her hands had begun to re-emerge and she was making rudimentary chord changes. It was almost a shock to find her one evening, gleefully swinging her shoulders, her fingers deftly dancing on the keys. Fifteen years old again. Mum had remained guileless, unapologetically child-like and open to joy. She revelled in her life, playing at her work and working at her play until she closed her eyes for the last time, most unexpectedly, at 86. She remains a role model for me. I miss her a lot. Never stop playing, Mum. I certainly won't.

All around the world, the family of humanity is conjoined in a shared pilgrimage towards recovery. Wounded, cut-off from each other and divorced from ecology, we seek to re-connect. Every day, our relationships provoke us—if we listen—to remember our lost innocence, to refresh our spirit, to re-open our hearts and to reinvigorate our personal growth.

In bringing the Inner Child home, we feel complete, forgiven, internally reintegrated. When we re-embrace those parts of our being that once felt unloved, we cease to fight against ourselves. And as this inner conflict and internal rupture eases, we are less prone to being triggered by what others do. We more readily see the pain, emptiness and terror that hide beneath the mantle of human 'misbehaviour'.

Make peace with ourselves and we make peace in the world. None of our Inner Child Journeys are taken alone. Even when we don't know it, recovery is a shared journey. Our children, our partners, friends and all those we touch are affected by each step we take towards self-love, in more ways than can be seen. We may never know all the ripples; we may never discover how far our own healing is passed forward. Love has no horizon.

Blessings for your Journeys, may they be abundant and fruitful.

APPENDICES

The Appendices are available in printable, PDF format here:
robingrille.com/inner-child-journeys/

APPENDIX 1

Summary of Inner Child Journey Steps

This Appendix contains the questions that comprise each step—within each of the five movements—of the Inner Child Journey. The explanatory notes have been abbreviated.

This Appendix is intended for review purposes, so you will not find it suitable to read from when conducting a Journey. The much simpler Appendix 2, and its lighter versions, 3 and Appendix 4, are intended for you to read from when you are undertaking your own Journey or guiding someone else though theirs.

Please feel free to modify the questions so they feel more natural to your personal speaking style. I recommend using the first person ('I') when you are taking your own Journey, and using the second person ('you') when you are being a guide for someone else. But that's entirely up to you.

Remember, you don't need to do all the suggested steps; many simply offer alternative routes to the goal of each movement. If you get no results from a question, try the next one. You can skip questions once you achieve the aim of each movement in the Journey.

First Movement: Looking Inwards

Step 1

Find a quiet, private space to sit or lie comfortably.
Close your eyes gently and allow two or three longer breaths.
With each exhalation, let go any bodily tensions …
and then gently draw your attention inwards.

Step 2

Now allow yourself to think about the *current situation* you are having with your child.

- ❀ What is a simple, straightforward way to describe your current *situation*? What is a simple way to define it?

Take your time and listen to your thoughts without judgement, letting them arise naturally.

If your thoughts sound blaming, accept them as they come, without censorship.

Step 3

Repeating your description of your *current situation* a few times in your mind, pay attention to how you feel as you do.

- ❀ How does your belly feel?
- ❀ How does your chest feel?
- ❀ Your throat?
- ❀ Your jaw?
- ❀ What do your arms and your hands want to do?
- ❀ Your legs?
- ❀ Do you notice any other bodily sensations or urges?

For now, simply observe each of these sensations and impulses without interpreting, acting out or seeking a resolution.

Welcome each of these sensations as they arise, and take careful note of each one.

Step 4

Now bring your attention to your self-talk; the 'voices' you hear inside.

- ❀ Are there any words inside you that want to be spoken? Or perhaps shouted out?
- ❀ What do you hear yourself saying to yourself, inside, about your child?
- ❀ What do you hear yourself saying to yourself about yourself as a parent (or carer, or teacher, or grandparent, etc)?

Do your best not to censor or modify these internal voices.

Second Movement: Tracing Back

Remaining with your eyes closed, proceed to the following steps.

You don't need to do all the steps from 5–10; each is an alternative doorway to reconnecting with relevant past experience. You don't have to ask every question within each step either. Think of each question as an alternative key to open a door.

Use the steps and questions in this movement that best put you in touch with a *source event* or *source situation*.

Step 5

- ❀ Are the feelings that come up for you in your *current situation* in any way familiar to you?
- ❀ Do you have any sense that you have experienced similar feelings before—perhaps even long before you became a parent?

Pay attention to any images that come to you now.

- ❀ When did you feel this way?
- ❀ How old were you at the time?
- ❀ Who was with you?
- ❀ What was going on around you?
- ❀ In this original situation (*source event*), were things happening to you, or were you witnessing things happening to somebody else?
- ❀ How were you reacting at the time?

Step 6

- ❀ If you are unable to remember a specific *source event* or original situation, what do you fantasise might have been happening around you as a child (or younger person) to make you feel these feelings?
- ❀ What is the *theme* of your fantasy?

Step 7

Thinking about your self-talk, the voices you hear inside in relation to your situation:

- Where did you first hear these kinds of things being said?
- Who first said these kinds of things in your life?
- How did you first learn this way of describing a person?
- What kinds of emotions or bodily sensations do you feel when you recall these voices now?

Step 8

- When you behaved as your child does today, or showed similar emotions, how were you treated?
- How did that make you feel at the time?

Step 9

- When you were about the same age as your child is today, what do you recall about your life then?
- How were significant others responding to you at the time?
- How did this make you feel, at the time?

Step 10

Consider the part of you that is most like your child. The part of you that thinks, feels or behaves most similarly to the way your child does, in your *current situation*.

- How well acquainted are you with the part of you that *is* your child?
- How do you feel about that part of yourself that is most like your child?
- What has the world said to you about that part of yourself?
- How has the world treated that part of you?

Third Movement: The Wishing Question

As before, you don't need to do all the following steps; each is an alternative route to help you connect with your deepest developmental needs.

Just use the questions in this movement that most effectively help you connect with your innermost wishes relating to your *source event*.

Step 11

- ✤ When the original *source event*—as you recall it, or as you imagine it—was going on around you, what do you wish might have happened differently?
- ✤ Exactly what do wish might have happened instead?
- ✤ What do you imagine might have helped you to feel better?
- ✤ Is there anything you wish you could have said or done, that would have helped you feel better?
- ✤ Is there anything you wish someone else might have given you, which might have helped you feel better?
- ✤ Is there anything you wish someone else might have done for you so that you might feel better?

Step 12

- ✤ If we could wave a magic wand that would make it totally okay for you to have exactly what you would have wished for (with no retribution) in your *source event*, then what would this wish be?
- ✤ In your wildest dreams, what would have made it all feel okay?

(The next question is only necessary if Steps 11 and 12 do not help you to find your Inner Child's wish. If you feel stuck, you may need to refer to Table 5, page 206.)

Step 13

- ✤ Imagine if, when you were in the middle of your *source event*, you were offered <u>this</u> outcome, or <u>that</u> possibility? How do might you have felt then?
- ✤ How might you have felt, in your *source event*, if by some magic <u>this</u> had happened instead? Or if, by some magic, <u>that</u> different outcome was offered to you?
- ✤ Imagine if, at the time of this *source event*, you were somehow given the freedom (with a promise of no retribution of any kind) to express exactly what you were feeling inside? What would you have wanted to say? Perhaps, what would you have wanted to shout? How might it have felt to say those things out loud?
- ✤ Imagine if, at the time of this *source event*, you were somehow given the freedom (with a promise of no retribution of any kind) to allow your impulses to come through and to let your body do whatever it needed to do? What might you have done? How might it have felt to do those things?

Fourth Movement: Healing the Parent

Step 14

- ✤ Thinking about your Inner Child's dearest wish (relative to the *source event*), what does this wish tell you about the *theme* of your developmental need? (Refer to the Table of Developmental Needs if necessary.)
- ✤ Thinking about your life as it is now, in what other situations do you feel similarly to how you felt in your *source event*?
- ✤ Is there a situation in your life today, in which you *need* something similar—or of a similar *theme*—to what you needed back then, as a child?
- ✤ Thinking about significant people in your life today, with whom do you sometimes feel similarly to how you felt as a child, in your *source event*?
- ✤ To what aspect of your life today might the *theme* of this developmental need apply most closely?

Step 15

- ✤ Can you give to yourself the essence of your wish, simply by imagining it being fulfilled? If yes, then take all the time you need to imagine your need being fulfilled in as much detail as you can.
- ✤ Pay attention to how you feel as you imagine receiving your wish coming to fruition; your need being met. What happens to the way your body breathes? What new sensations arise in your body?

Perhaps instead you could give to yourself the *essence* or *theme* of what your Inner Child desires—in a real and practical sense.

- ✤ What changes would you like to experience in your life in relation to your Inner Child's developmental need? Would you like to learn to do something differently? Or do you need something new from the world around you? Something you need to ask for, from significant people in your life?

Consider a new course of action that you can practise and begin to give it some detail. Make sure that the new behaviours you are attempting remain consistent with the *theme* of your developmental need.

- Can you now make a commitment to yourself to take steps— even if these need to be baby steps—towards fulfilling your Inner Child's developmental need (giving yourself your developmental nutrient)?
- Can you make this promise to your Inner Child?

Pay close attention to how you feel when you commit to giving yourself your developmental nutrient. Notice in particular what happens in your body: how your breathing changes and the sensations that move through you.

Fifth Movement: Connecting with Your Actual Child

Step 16

Now think about your actual child and pay close attention to how you feel.

- Have your perceptions about your child changed in any way?
- How do you feel towards your child now?
- How do you feel about your child's behaviour?

Step 17

- What might your child be feeling inside when he cries that way, when she acts that way, when he looks that way, when she speaks that way, etc?
- What might your child be asking for when he cries that way, when she acts that way, when he looks that way, when she speaks that way, etc?
- When you once felt or behaved similarly to how your child does now, what would have helped you? What would have best connected with your heart?
- If you were in your child's shoes right now, what do you feel would meet your emotional needs?

Step 18

Next time you interact with your child, notice whether your Journey has affected the way you look, speak and behave towards your child.

- Does your child seem to notice the difference?

Step 19

Make a commitment.

⊛ Given what you've just learned on your Journey, what will you undertake to do or say differently to your child next time the same issue comes up?

Step 20

Thank your Inner Child for opening up to you. Let your Inner Child know that you will be there again in future to listen, and that his or her feelings and needs will always matter to you. Acknowledge yourself for the courage and self-love that enabled you to follow-through in your Journey to this point.

Chronicling your Journey (fill in the blanks):

'When my child does ____(behaviour)___, I feel ____(emotions)___, I feel like doing ____(impulses)___, I think ____(thoughts)___ about myself, and ___(thoughts)___ about my child, and much of this springs from a time when ___(source event)___ was going on for me"

'When this ____(source event)____ was going on for me, I wish I could have said _____, or done: _____. Or: I wish someone else would have given me _____ or done _____ for me.'

'But today, I can receive the *theme* of this wish, in the shape of an appropriate developmental nutrient. I can make a commitment to respond to the needs of my Inner Child. This will help me to heal and grow.

'My Inner Child Journey has helped me understand what my child needs when he or she does these things, _____, and it has given me these new insights, _____, about how I can respond most helpfully to my child.'

Note: Please remember that if you feel uncertain about any of the steps in the Inner Child Process, you can find all the help you need in the in-depth explanatory notes of Chapters 6–10. Refer back to those notes from time to time until you feel comfortable with the Process.

APPENDIX 2

The Inner Child Process
(full reference version)

First Movement: Looking Inwards

1. Sit quietly, relax, make yourself comfortable and close your eyes.

2. Find a simple way to describe the challenging, *current situation* with your child.

3. How do you feel when this happens between you and your child?

4. What do your inner voices say—about you, about your child—when this happens between you?

Second Movement: Tracing Back

5. Are the feelings that have come up for you familiar in any way? Have you felt this way before your child was born?

    If so: when?

    How old were you?

    What was going on around you?

    > Or

6. What do you *imagine* might have been going on around you when you felt these same feelings in the past?

    > Or

7. Where—and with whom—did you learn the self-talk that arises when your child triggers you in this way?

Or

8. When you behaved similarly to how your child does today, how were you treated?

   Or

9. What was life like for you when you were the same age your child is now?

   Or

10. How has the world treated that part of you that is most like your actual child?

Third Movement: The Wishing Question

11. When the *source event* was going on for you, what do you wish might have happened differently? Do you wish you could have said or done something differently? Or is there something you wish someone else could have done for you?

    Or

12. If you'd had a magic wand to wave, how would you have changed the outcome of your *source event*?

    If you find it hard to imagine a wish:

13. Browse Table 5 (page 206). Do you see a developmental nutrient that resonates for you, that would have felt most helpful in resolving your *source event*?

Fourth Movement: Healing the Parent

14. Think of a current-life situation (not involving your actual child) in which you feel similarly to the way you felt in your *source event*, and in which your needs (or the *theme* of your developmental needs) might be similar.

15. How might you be able to give yourself an adult-appropriate developmental nutrient that addresses your needs, in this current-life situation? Can you commit to a new course of self-nourishing or self-empowering action?

Fifth Movement: Connecting with Your Actual Child

16. How do you feel towards your child now?

17. What might your child be feeling and needing, when he or she behaves in the way that you find challenging?

18. Does your child seem to notice a difference in your tone and behaviour since you undertook your Inner Child Process?

19. Make an agreement with yourself: what can you commit to saying or doing differently for your child, when he or she behaves in this challenging manner, from now on?

20. Thank your Inner Child for sharing his or her feelings and wisdom with you, and acknowledge yourself for having the courage to undertake this Journey.

APPENDIX 3

Inner child Process—Light version

This brief version of the Process involves just one question for each of the five movements. It is ideal when you have only a few minutes available, and you don't have the space for a more deeply contemplative inquiry.

1. How am I feeling right now?

2. When have I felt this way before, earlier in my life?

3. What was my need then; what would have helped me feel better?

4. How might I have this need met today?

5. What does my child need from me when he/she behaves this way?

APPENDIX 4

Inner child Process—Super Light version

Sometimes it's enough to simply pause and ask yourself what was going on around you when you behaved similarly to your child, or when you were roughly his or her age. That fundamental shift in focus— 'What of this is about me, and not about my child?' —can be revolutionary, opening-up a potential treasure trove of new insights. You have gone deep enough when you touch upon the *feeling*—and not just the thought—of having been a child once. Simply ask yourself the dual questions:

⊛ How was this issue for me when I was a child?

⊛ What would I have needed then?

APPENDIX 5

Table of Developmental Needs

Age range	Developmental theme	Psycho-emotional developmental needs (for the child)	Restorative, healing developmental nutrients (for the adult)	Resulting emotional intelligences
In-utero, birth, the perinatal period until 3 months	The Right to Exist (Connectedness)	To feel wanted. To be held, *sensitively*. To feel safe. To feel *seen*. To feel affirmed.	Being warmly received. Making our presence known. Saying 'I am here'. Feeling safe with others. Comforting touch, holding and eye contact. Inhabiting our body. Connecting with the Earth.	Trusting in Life. Groundedness. A strong reality principle. A feeling of inter-connectedness with all Life. *I am here, I am worthy and I belong.*

Age range	Developmental theme	Psycho-emotional developmental needs (for the child)	Restorative, healing developmental nutrients (for the adult)	Resulting emotional intelligences
Birth to 18 months	The Right to Need (Inter-Dependence)	To trust others. To feel secure. To have bodily and emotional needs met promptly. To have needs met on our own terms. To be held and comforted. To have pleasurable nourishment.	Reaching out for help, support, connection. Allowing ourselves to receive. Allowing the expression of grief.	Emotional security. Self-assertion. Ability to tolerate alone-ness. A feeling of Life's abundance. Balance of giving and receiving. Healthy trust and healthy scepticism. Tolerance of delayed gratification. *It's okay to have needs.*

Age range	Developmental theme	Psycho-emotional developmental needs (for the child)	Restorative, healing developmental nutrients (for the adult)	Resulting emotional intelligences
18 months to 3 years	The Right to Have Support (Autonomy)	To receive support for vulnerability—without demand or expectation. To receive protection in times of fear. To be allowed to learn and grow without pressure—at our own rate, on our own terms. To be shown boundaries without shaming or manipulation. To be *heard*.	Receiving acceptance for vulnerability. Learning to reach out for—and to accept—support. Learning to accept limitation and embrace failure. Learning to enjoy instead of trying to impress.	Humility. Honesty and realness, authenticity (instead of seduction and manipulation). Loving and respecting vulnerability, in self and others. Freedom from toxic shame or pride. Trusting essence rather than investing in 'image'. *It's okay to be vulnerable.*

Age range	Developmental theme	Psycho-emotional developmental needs (for the child)	Restorative, healing developmental nutrients (for the adult)	Resulting emotional intelligences
3–5 years	The Right to Freedom (Spirit/ Creativity)	To explore the world. To freely express emotion. To express negativity. To say 'no!' To say 'I don't want.' To say 'go away!' To assert our boundaries. To have space. To be shown interpersonal boundaries without shaming or punishment. To be protected without smothering. To play. To be *enjoyed*.	To expand outward in creative self-expression. To voice feelings. To assert boundaries. To repel shame and guilt. To separate what is others' experience from what is our own (healthy differentiation).	Healthy self-containment (instead of suppression). Healthy boundaries: knowing when to say 'no'. Strong self-assertion without violence. Strong self-expression. Spirit, creativity: a balance between the practical and the aesthetic. True empathy instead of *enmeshment or obligation.* *I am free to be me. I am free to play and create.*

Age range	Developmental theme	Psycho-emotional developmental needs (for the child)	Restorative, healing developmental nutrients (for the adult)	Resulting emotional intelligences
5–7 years	The Right to Love (Passion)	To express passion and sensuality. To give and receive affection physically, without invasion, judgement or exploitation. To explore and discover the pleasure of the body. To be free from moralisation or shaming.	To give and receive tenderness. To accept the softer feelings. To honour the body. To honour the right to privacy. To respect and set limits against unwanted intimacy. To give flight to the imagination. To trust feelings, rather than rigid or abstract rules.	Sexuality as an expression of love. Open-heartedness. Open-mindedness. Flexibility of mind. Freedom from conformism. Embracing paradox, nuance and relativity. *Pleasure is healthy.* *Sex is not separate from love.*

Age range	Developmental theme	Psycho-emotional developmental needs (for the child)	Restorative, healing developmental nutrients (for the adult)	Resulting emotional intelligences
7–12 years	The Right to Playful Learning (Competence)	To receive instruction without shaming. To receive patient mentorship. Peer-group belonging. Playful learning. To be allowed bodily integrity, privacy.	To learn playfully, without coercion or shaming. Freedom to pursue our interests and affinities. Support to develop competencies without imposed expectations. Bonding with like-minded others.	Competence. The courage to try new things. The ability to focus attention on a task. Acceptance of failure. Persistence. *Learning is exciting.* *I can be good at some things, and not so good at other things. Both are okay.* *I am a valued friend.*

Age range	Developmental theme	Psycho-emotional developmental needs (for the child)	Restorative, healing developmental nutrients (for the adult)	Resulting emotional intelligences
12 to early 20s	The Right to an Opinion. The Right to a Vocation. The Right to Sexual Autonomy	To form and voice opinions. To enjoy social-group identity and belonging. To receive support for pursuing our passion(s). To receive vocational mentorship and opportunity. Freedom of sexual expression and discovery. Questioning authority. Questioning culture.	Joining a 'shared-values' tribe. Following our bliss. Vocational development and enhancement. Flow-state immersion. Expressing and sharing our unique gifts. Respectful exploration of our sexual identity and desire. Learning about love and ecstatic sexuality. Voicing our opinions, learning to listen to and respect those of others. Contributing to community. Connecting to something greater than ourselves.	Heart-centred sexuality. Vocational fulfilment. Self-motivation. Self-responsibility. A sense of our place in the world. A sense of our value. Social and political awareness, and a commitment to democratic engagement. Healthy scepticism and self-assurance. *My voice is important. I have unique gifts to share. I can take responsibility for my actions and for my destiny. I am connected to a larger world, and I have a role to play in it.*

About the author

Eventually, Robin Grille grew up and became a psychologist with a private practice in Sydney, Australia.

In his quiet times, he wrote two parenting books, *Parenting for a Peaceful World* and *Heart-to-Heart Parenting*. Also a host of articles about parenting, education and child development that you can easily find on the web. In his not-so-quiet times he still plays percussion, guitar and sings with bands in his beloved Sydney Northern Beaches area.

Robin is passionate about the idea that we can create a world of justice, peace and ecological harmony if we put children's emotional wellbeing at the top of the agenda. He loves to travel and to bring his popular workshops for parents and teachers to schools and communities around the world.

If you'd like to find out more about Robin's work, or invite him to speak to your organisation, please visit www.robingrille.com.

credits

Every idea has a history, a lineage and in its delivery, an architecture. Every creation is the manifestation of multiple minds and hearts collaborating, and many special souls have had a hand in the making of this book. I celebrate and thank the protagonists here.

Leon Grill, my father—who inspired dauntlessness in the pursuit of true vocation, who taught me that work should be an expression of passion.

Rodica Grill, my mother—who showed me there's a playful way to do everything.

Yaramin Grille, my daughter—who has brought me my most poignant lessons, as well as my greatest joys—and, in so doing, gave a personal resonance to this book.

Linda Haigh, my partner—who believes in and supports my work without pause, even when the work drives me batty and I'm difficult to live with. Without you, my Life Companion, this would not have been possible.

Jessica Perini—Chargé D'affaires of flow, Director of making sense, Czarina of orderly penmanship.

John Travis—weed control, removal of indiscretions, Chief Advisory Council, interlocutor with Big Authorities and Bureaucracies.

Eric Fletcher—set design and lighting. Making everything look good. Making everything look right.

Jon Cooper—all artworks and special effects. Administrator of Magic.

Eric Fletcher again—book cover assemblage, front and back. I hope all my readers judge this book by it.

Endnotes

1. J Bradshaw, *Homecoming: Reclaiming and championing your Inner Child,* Bantam Books, 1992.

2. J Mitchell, *The Circle Game,* Siquomb Publishing Company, 1970.

3. V Flory, *Your Child's Emotional Needs: What they are and how to meet them,* Finch Publishing, 2005.

4. V Flory, 'A novel clinical intervention for severe childhood depression and anxiety', *Clinical Child Psychology and Psychiatry,* 2004, Vol 9(1), pp 9–23.

5. VJ Felitti, RF Anda, D Nordenberg, DF Williamson, AM Spitz, V Edwards, MP Koss and JS Marks, 'Relationship of childhood abuse and household dysfunction to many of the leading causes of death in adults', *American Journal of Preventive Medicine,* May 1998, Vol 14(4), pp 245–58.

6. Much of this research is discussed in R Grille, *Parenting for a Peaceful World,* Vox Cordis Press, 2013, Ch 16–29.

7. *Parenting for a Peaceful World,* Ch 20; *Heart-to-Heart Parenting,* Vox Cordis Press, 2012, Chs 11–14.

8. K Dychtwald, *Bodymind,* Penguin, 1986.

9. T Lewis, A Farini, R Lannon, *A General Theory of Love,* Random House, 2000.

10. *Ibid,* p 33.

11. S Porges, *The Polyvagal Theory,* WW Norton & Co, 2011.

12. *Ibid,* p 194.

13. Sounds True, Inc, Louisville, CO, 2008.

14. R Grille, 'What children remember, and how this affects their development', in *Parenting for a Peaceful World,* Ch 23.

15. D Siegel, *Brainstorm: The power and purpose of the teenage brain,* Tarcher/Perigee, 2013, p 168.

16. 'Transforming trauma-related shame and self-loathing', November 2014.

[17] See 'What children remember—and how this affects their development', in *Parenting for a Peaceful World*, p 257.

[18] D Siegel, *The Developing Mind: How relationships and the brain interact to shape who we are*, The Guilford Press, 1999, p 29.

[19] *Mindsight: Change your brain and your life*, Scribe Publications, 2009, p 154.

[20] For a more in-depth discussion of body memory and how it works, see 'What children remember—and how this affects their development', in my *Parenting for a Peaceful World*, Ch 23.

[21] *Brainwashing: The science of thought control*, Oxford University Press, 2004, p 167.

[22] Songwriters: Pete Ham and Tom Evans; 'Without You' lyrics © Kobalt Music Publishing Ltd, Tunecore Inc, 1970.

[23] R Grille, *Heart-to-Heart Parenting*, Chs 9–10; *Parenting for a Peaceful World*, Chs 20 and 28; R Grille, 'After attachment … what then?', *Kindred Media*, 11/12/06, kindredmedia.org/2006/12/after-attachment-what-then/ (accessed 7/5/19).

[24] 'After attachment … what then?', *Kindred Media*, 11/12/06, kindredmedia.org/2006/12/after-attachment-what-then/ (accessed 7/5/19).

[25] Developmental variations for neuroatypical children, such as children with autism spectrum disorder (ASD), for example, are beyond the scope of this book.

[26] For a stage-by-stage summary of the core developmental needs of early childhood, the critical first seven years of life, see my *Parenting for a Peaceful World*, Chs 24–29. Developmental psychologist Erik Erikson's original vision about the psychosocial developmental stages of the entire human life span remains useful and relevant today. Modern advancements in developmental neuropsychology science have added validity to these Eriksonian stages, confirming their basis in biology. A simple summary of the Eriksonian stages of human psychosocial development—and the developmental needs that correspond to each stage—can be found here: S McLeod, 'Erik Erikson's stages of psychosocial development', *Simply Psychology*, 2018, simplypsychology.org/Erik-Erikson.html (accessed 7/5/19). For an insightful account of the developmental needs pertaining to adolescence, see D Siegel, *Brainstorm: The power and purpose of the teenage brain*, Tarcher/Perigee, 2013.

27 BD Perry, 'Incubated in terror: Neurodevelopmental factors in the "cycle of violence"', in J Osofsky (ed), *Children, Youth and Violence: The search for solutions*, Guilford Press, 1997, pp 124–48.

28 S Baron-Cohen, *The Science of Evil: On empathy and the origins of cruelty*, Basic Books, 2012.

29 D Siegel, *Parenting from the Inside Out: How a deeper self-understanding can help you raise children who thrive*, Scribe, 2014.

30 R. Grille, *Parenting for a Peaceful World*, Chs 16–20.

31 R Grille, 'The school of world peace', in D Wright, C Camden-Pratt and S Hill, *Social Ecology: Applying ecological understanding to our lives and our planet*, Hawthorne Press, 2011.

32 For a wonderful set of bioenergetics exercises that help you *manage your emotional charge*, see A Lowen, *The Way to Vibrant Health*, Bioenergetics Press, 2003.

33 G Gendlin, *Focusing*, Bantam Books, 2007, focusing.org.

34 For a list of bioenergetic emotional-release exercises, see A Lowen, *The Way to Vibrant Health*, Bioenergetics Press, 2003.

35 You can find additional information about core developmental needs and their implications for adult relationships in *Parenting for a Peaceful World*, Chs 24–29.

36 An 'I' statement is a way to voice our feelings, needs or limits by taking ownership and avoiding blame or judgement. It ensures the listener will not feel threatened by our communication, and will therefore be more likely to remain open to us. You can find an explanation of 'I' statements in *Heart-to-Heart Parenting*, Ch 14 and *Parenting for a Peaceful World*, Ch 20. Although the context there is about the parenting relationship, the structure of the 'I' statement is universal and can be generalised to any of our relationships.

37 For information on childhood psycho-emotional development refer to *Heart-to-Heart Parenting and Parenting for a Peaceful World*, Chs 24–29. For insights on adolescent psycho-emotional development see D Siegel, *Brainstorm: The power and purpose of the teenage brain*, Tarcher/Perigee, 2013.

38 SM Johnson, *Character Styles*, WW Norton & Co, 2011; R Kurtz, *Body-Centred Psychotherapy*, Life Rhythm, 1990.

39 VJ Felitti, RF Anda, D Nordenberg, DF Williamson, AM Spitz, V Edwards, MP Koss and JS Marks, 'Relationship of childhood abuse and household

dysfunction to many of the leading causes of death in adults, The Adverse Childhood Experiences (ACE) Study', *American Journal of Preventive Medicine*, May 1998, 14(4), pp 245–58.

[40] The map of developmental needs in this section represents a synthesis of contributions from diverse strands of psychology, neuropsychology and psychotherapy. The main lineage comes from the tradition of body-centred (somatic) psychotherapy, which I have tempered with knowledge streams arising from modern research sciences (prenatal and perinatal psychology, attachment research, developmental neuroscience and interpersonal neurobiology). For a comprehensive list of scientific references, and a more in-depth account of developmental rites of passage, refer to *Parenting for a Peaceful World*, Ch 24–29. Additional sources include: *Bioenergetics*; *Character Analysis*; *Character Styles*; *Body-Centred Psychotherapy*; 'Erik Erikson's stages of psychosocial development'; IF Baker, *Man in the Trap*, The American College of Orgonomy, NJ, 2000; and D Siegel, *Brainstorm: The power and purpose of the teenage brain*, Tarcher/Perigee, 2013.

[41] BA Van Der Kolk and J Saporta, 'The biological response to psychic trauma: Mechanisms and treatment of intrusion and numbing', *Anxiety Research (UK)*, 2007, Vol 4, pp 199–212.

[42] Ibid

[43] D Siegel, *Mindsight*, Bantam, 2010 p 40.

[44] B Perry and M Szalavitz, *Born for Love: Why empathy is essential—and endangered*, William Morrow, 2010.

[45] For a more in-depth discussion on the interplay between genes and environment and how this shapes us psychologically, see my *Parenting for a Peaceful World*, Ch 21.

[46] Connected Couples—Thriving Families, connectedandthriving.org and MG Callander, *Why Dads Leave*, 2012, WhyDadsLeave.com

[47] My first book, *Parenting for a Peaceful World* contains several psycho-historical accounts tracing the violence of leaders, and of entire societies, to their childhood roots. It draws on the findings of neuropsychology, epigenetics and developmental psychology to explain the childhood environmental causes of chronic human violence.

[48] R Grille, *Parenting for a Peaceful World*, Chs 30–31.

Made in the USA
Las Vegas, NV
07 March 2023

68624657R10187